Praise for *On the Chocolate Trail: A Delicious Adventure Connecting Jews, Religions, History, Travel, Rituals and Recipes to the Magic of Cacao*

"This engaging journey into the extraordinary past of a much-loved product is packed with fascinating stories and thrilling bits of information."

—**Claudia Roden**, food writer and author of almost twenty classic works on Middle Eastern and Mediterranean cookery; most recently, the award-winning *The Book of Jewish Food*

"Bravo! ... Takes us on a roller coaster roll through the history of chocolate, from the beginning when it was only used as a drink to the present day.... A great read."

—**Joan Nathan**, award-winning cookbook author, *Jewish Cooking in America; Quiches, Kugels, and Couscous: My Search for Jewish Cooking in France*; and other books

"Meticulously researched and whimsically presented. Fascinating facts, amusing anecdotes and mouth-watering recipes.... An instant classic for chocolate devotees of all faiths!"

—**Francine Segan**, food historian, chocolate expert and James Beard nominated cookbook author of *Dolci: Italy's Sweets*

"A joy for history and chocolate buffs.... Traces the exciting and curious aspects of the evolution of chocolate. The reader is rewarded with fascinating nuggets of chocolate lore, as well as several yummy chocolate recipes."

—**Carole Bloom**, CCP, author, *Intensely Chocolate* and *Truffles, Candies and Confections*

"A treat! Part history, part travelogue, part cookbook, [it] ... will tantalize all readers and delight chocoholic ones."

—**Jonathan D. Sarna**, Joseph H. & Belle R. Braun Professor of American Jewish History, Brandeis University

"A knowledgeable, surprising and, of course, delicious book. Chocolate lovers (and that includes just about everyone) and Jewish historians alike will be delighted."
—**Leah Koenig**, author, *The Hadassah Everyday Cookbook*

"Fascinating and entertaining ... if you're interested in Jews or chocolate, you're gonna like this book. If you're interested in both, you're gonna love it :-). Like chocolate itself—wonderful as a gift, or you could just get one for you yourself."
—**Nigel Savage**, founder,
Hazon: Jewish Inspiration, Sustainable Communities

"Yes, separate milk from meat. And wool from linen. But do not separate Jews from chocolate. They shall be yoked together for all time. And now we have the definitive book on the topic, an eloquent and astutely researched history."
—**A.J. Jacobs**, editor-at-large, *Esquire* magazine; author of the
New York Times bestseller, *The Year of Living Biblically:
One Man's Humble Quest to Follow the Bible as
Literally as Possible*, and other books

"A fascinating ramble through the history of chocolate and the roles—sometimes central, sometimes peripheral—that Jews have played in bringing it from the forests of Africa and Spanish America to your table. The recipes are a tasty bonus."
—**David M. Gitlitz and Linda Kay Davidson**, authors,
A Drizzle of Honey: The Lives and Recipes of Spain's Secret Jews

"Calling all chocoholics.... I devoured this book. Readers beware! Stash fine chocolate in your pack before setting off on this delicious journey across time and space."
—**Pamela S. Nadell**, Patrick Clendenen Chair in Women's and
Gender History, American University; author, *Women Who
Would be Rabbis: A History of Women's Ordination, 1889–1985*

"A delightful, fascinating read full of history, religion, ethics, anecdotes and recipes that will make you hungry."
—**Paula Shoyer**, author, *The Kosher Baker:
160 Dairy-Free Desserts from Traditional to Trendy*

ON THE
Chocolate
TRAIL
2nd Edition

A Delicious Adventure Connecting Jews, Religions, History, Travel, Rituals and Recipes to the Magic of Cacao

RABBI DEBORAH R. PRINZ

For People of All Faiths, All Backgrounds
JEWISH LIGHTS Publishing

Jewish Lights Publishing
an imprint of Turner Publishing Company
Nashville, Tennessee
New York, New York
www.jewishlights.com
www.turnerpublishing.com

On the Chocolate Trail, 2nd Edition:
A Delicious Adventure Connecting Jews, Religions, History, Travel, Rituals and Recipes to the Magic of Cacao

2017 Quality Paperback Edition, First Printing
© 2018, 2013 by Deborah Prinz

The Library of Congress has cataloged the earlier edition as follows:

Library of Congress Cataloging-in-Publication Data

Prinz, Deborah.
On the chocolate trail : a delicious adventure connecting Jews, religions, history, travel, rituals and recipes to the magic of cacao / by Deborah Prinz. — Quality paperback ed.
volume ; cm
Includes bibliographical references and index.
ISBN 978-1-58023-487-0 (pbk.)
1. Chocolate—History. 2. Cocoa—History. 3. Cacao—Religious aspects. 4. Cacao—Religious aspects—Judaism. 5. Cooking (Chocolate)
I. Title.
TX817.C4P75 2013
641.6'374—dc23

10 9 8 7 6 5 4 3 2 1

Manufactured in the United States of America

Cover Design: Barbara Leff and Heather Pelham
Interior Design: Heather Pelham
Cover images: © FreeSoulProduction/shutterstock; © Aaron Amat/fotolia; © photo25th/iStockphoto; © Richard Vandenberg/iStockphoto

For my sweet-toothed mother and father,
Helen (*z"l*) and Ray Prinz,
my partner in adventure and chocolate, Mark,
our food-savvy children, Avigail, Rachel & Noam,
and for Amiel, Pele, Ziv, and Lior as they learn
the delights of eating.

Contents

Part Two

Other Religious Chocolate Revelations

Choco-dar

"CONNECTIONS BETWEEN JEWS AND CHOCOLATE? That would be like looking for a needle in a haystack!" said a cultural historian and journalist when I mentioned this project, just hoping for some insights, for a few tips, or for some modest encouragement. I slumped back in my chair, realizing that she could be correct. There may be nothing to it. What had I been thinking? After all, I had not heard of this theme of chocolate and Jews in all of my years of Jewish studies from religious school through rabbinical seminary or since. It had been easy enough to design an *On the Chocolate Trail* business card and to create a website for the project; now it seemed as though that would be the end of it. To concoct a lecture or an article about my intrigue for chocolate and religion, much less an entire book, began to seem completely daunting.

At the same time, I could feel my inner Nancy Drew transforming me. I just knew in my gut that there had to be a story. My choco-dar—my internal, serendipitous radar for chocolate discoveries and experiences—would somehow feed this research to uncover the stories of Jews, religions, and chocolate. After all, choco-dar alerts had entered my life at fun and surprising moments, particularly when traveling. One such fortuitous experience occurred as my rabbi-husband, Mark, and I traveled in our VW van from Paris on a small road to Carpentras in southern France. Mark drove while my head sunk deep into my reading and my laptop. I randomly looked up just in time to notice a billboard boasting a bright orange checkmark against a black backdrop that I quickly recognized as the logo for Valrhona chocolate, which I happened to have seen for sale at a local San Diego market. I grabbed Mark's arm to urge him to pull over and park. Checking the map, we realized that we had chanced upon Tain-L'Hermitage, the small-town home of the international headquarters for Valrhona, reputed to be one of the best chocolate makers in the world. We traipsed into the company store where, to our delight and admittedly our gluttony, every item for purchase was also available for tasting, from curry-flavored chocolate, to chocolate-covered nuts, to bonbons, to hot chocolate. We sampled it all—or tried to. Then, as we paid for our selections, the cashier tossed in even more treats.

My choco-dar kicked in again later when we altered our route at the last minute to investigate Turin's chocolate by crossing the Alps from Sospel, France, into northern Italy. Mark calmly managed the van through the truly scary switchbacks in very mild weather on the French side. At the border tunnel's entrance, a red light stopped us—a very long red light, a light that remained red though there was no traffic. The light was equipped with a timer so we knew that, conscientious rabbi-travelers that we are, the wait would be a full twenty minutes. Finally, with the permission of the green light, we passed through to snow on the Italian side. As we marveled at the contrasting temperatures and the snow-whitened chalet roof-tops sprinkling the mountainside, we caught sight of "*Venchi: Spaccio del Cioccolato.*" This roadside *Venchi* chocolate factory, in business since 1878, offered a well-stocked bar as well

The sign at the Venchi chocolate factory welcomed us warmly just after crossing the Alps.

as specialty chocolate balls made with Cuban rum. Without hesitation, we celebrated our arrival in Italy along this dramatic drive through the Alps into the winter chill with chocolate!

Admittedly, chocolate was the reason for our stop in Turin, where I hoped to sample the local specialty chocolate drink known as *bicerin*. We found what we were looking for, and much more, as my choco-dar revved up once again. They say that the intimate, low-ceilinged, candlelit setting of Caffè al Bicerin, founded in 1763, boasts the best *bicerin* in Turin. Always run by women, the Caffè's location near the Santuario della Consolata meant that women often broke their Lenten and Communion fasts there. The name of the drink and the Caffè recall the handle-less glass in which the *bicerin* is customarily served. As Mark and I savored the much anticipated *bicerin* with its layers of hot chocolate, coffee, and cream, we unabashedly stared across the small room where a couple of men scooped a thick, chocolaty substance out of a large bowl. Checking with the waitress, we learned that they were downing warm chocolate soup poured over hazelnut cake. We could not resist that *torta di nocciole con cioccolata calda*. What a rich two-course chocolate lunch that turned out to be!

After a bit of shopping in the Al Bicerin retail store next door—and, yes, amazingly more tasting—our intention to leave Turin was undone by my irrepressible choco-dar. Looking for a map for the next leg of our trip, we luckily learned about the Turin Chocolate Festival taking place at that very moment just a square away. Without discussion, we delayed our departure from Turin to enjoy our first, but not our last, chocolate festival, this one featuring chocolate makers from all over Europe. While we could not stay for the entire multiday, annual festival, with its chocolate-related entertainment, tastings, and classes, we did wander around the booths, gobbled up treats, and stocked up on delicacies such as chocolate pasta and a most delicious chocolate liquor. We reluctantly left Turin. A few days later our daughter, a religious studies major, asked if we had seen the Shroud of Turin. We rabbis licked the chocolate off our fingers and confessed, with some embarrassment, that we had completely forgotten about the Shroud.

In Spain my choco-dar activated again. We had read a text panel at the Barcelona Chocolate Museum explaining that Spain had hosted a Cistercian chocolate tradition with special ecclesiastical chocolate rooms. The next day, as planned, we headed to Belchite in the northeast of Spain to pay homage to the ruins of the 1937 Spanish Civil War where Mark's (middle) namesake, Sam Levinger, was fatally injured. I barely caught a glimpse of the sign off to the side of the road to the monastery. The sign led us to a last-minute stop at the Royal Abbey of Santa Maria de Poblet, a Cistercian monastery founded in 1151 at the base of the Prades Mountains, and its medieval monks' chocolate room.

My choco-dar also works pretty well Stateside. Years ago a couple of my lovely congregants, knowing of my interest in chocolate, wanted to introduce me to their family friend, chocolate expert Carole Bloom, author of several chocolate and dessert books. Carole was on a book tour at that time so we could not connect, even though we then both lived in San Diego County. However, a few years after our move to the East Coast, Mark and I took some yoga classes in Carlsbad, California, while on vacation and overheard the names of other people in the class. After our fourth class, I saw Carole enter a car with the license plate "DESSERT." When Mark and I stopped a few moments later at the nearby Chuao Chocolate store, we saw one of Bloom's books displayed. Her photograph confirmed my suspicion. Finally, after all those years, I met her at the next yoga class.

When we moved into our cozy New York City studio apartment, where this book was written, the corner supermarket was in the midst of major renovations. It reopened six months later, with an entire room larger than the size of our apartment devoted only to chocolate. It now supplies our daily basic chocolate dosages.

Choco-dar also led me to *On the Chocolate Trail.* By happenstance I heard a story on National Public Radio about chocolate stores in Paris by chocolatier, foodie, and pastry chef David Lebovitz. Following up on his leads during a sabbatical trip to Europe, Mark and I came upon our first clues about chocolate and Jews. Thus began *On the Chocolate Trail.* Two rabbis—my adventuresome husband and I—on our chocolate exploration, tasting and unpacking connections of religions to chocolate production and commerce which furthered cacao's travels through the Western World. The fifteenth-century dispersion of Jews from Spain created a trail of Jewish business interests in chocolate that continues today. Choco-dar sometimes simply led me to chocolate eating; more significantly, it revealed heretofore unexplored links between religion and chocolate.

Where the Trail Has Led

The book found me.

Who knew that the first edition of *On the Chocolate Trail* would stir such a sweet spot. Initially I understood the chocolate trail to be about chocolate's spread from the New World to the Old World and then globally. My thinking about the trail then expanded to the far-reaching research and journeys we pursued while tracing the religious sagas of chocolate. Now I travel a different trail, on an extended book tour presenting about these many chocolate learnings.

It turns out that *On the Chocolate Trail* serves up something for everyone: those who like chocolate but not history, history but not travel, travel but not religion, religion but not food, or all of that. What's not to like? Audiences at congregations, food shows, historical associations, museums, and professional conferences worldwide hunger for its stories, keeping me on the road several times a month. Just after the book's publication one colleague stunned me with an invitation to be the scholar-in-residence at his synagogue. Since then, I have often been a weekend "chocolate scholar" or the "chocolate rabbi." I am introduced as the world's leading expert on religion and chocolate. Recently, I have been invited to co-curate a traveling museum exhibit about Jews on the chocolate trail for the Herbert and Eileen Bernard Museum at Temple Emanu-El of New York City. I field questions about my favorite chocolate, my weight (since I eat chocolate every day), religious traditions ("May it be eaten with a meat meal according to kosher food rules?"), and even breast milk chocolate ("Can breast milk be mixed into chocolate?"—it cannot). People reveal their chocolate stashes and secrets to me. As one colleague confessed:

> I have a drawer in my desk where I keep what I call my Clergy Chocolate. I eat the chocolate as a reward, or when I need a pick-me-up, and I do share it when the need arises.

> One of my congregants, knowing my love of chocolate,
> gave me a large candy bar that I keep on top of my desk.
> It is entitled "Emergency Chocolate." I have not needed to
> break the seal ... yet.[1]

A post about the Kwechansky family's chocolate factory in Montreal at my blog brought relatives together for the first time.

Since the first edition of the book was published, I have munched on bright blue and white chocolate–painted Passover matzah featured at a tasting event in Atlanta. I have admired bi-colored chocolate, white and dark, flowing in the fountain at a Valentine's Day gala in Houston. I have gobbled up regional treats: Maine's chocolate-covered potato known as needhams and chocolate-enrobed peanut butter buckeyes of Ohio. Hosts often serve up recipes from the book. Rabbi Shaul Osadchey and his caterer at Beth Tzedec in Calgary concocted a three-course dinner of black bean and chocolate soup, chocolate vinaigrette dressing for the salad, and chicken with chocolate mole (see the recipe section) for the entrée. Of course chocolate desserts abound. Inspired by *On the Chocolate Trail*, a rabbi in Pennsylvania accompanied his Rosh Hashanah sermon about spiritual growth with small chocolates and magnets imprinted with "Raising the (Chocolate) Bar for a Sweet New Year." At another synagogue, the spice box for the Saturday evening ceremony of havdalah (which marks the end of the Jewish Sabbath) contained cocoa nibs, along with cinnamon and cloves. To engage two hundred participants in conversation at an event in Portland, Oregon, organizers distributed conversation prompts about chocolate. Another reception served up only fair trade–certified tasting bars. Some colleagues have built on my chocolate-themed presentations in their welcomes or benedictions. For instance, Rabbi Amy Perlin in Virginia concluded the Sabbath service with these words:

> Our God and the God of all generations: The chocolate
> you created in nature 100 percent pure is bitter. It requires

us to add the sweetness. So often that is true of life. May we add sweetness to life this Shabbat.[2]

I am delighted that *On the Chocolate Trail* has generated such creativity. I savor audience appetites for the *On the Chocolate Trail*'s chronicles of nourishment, sweetness, and resilience that bypass the worn, tragedy-themed view of Jewish history. I also relish how chocolate bridges different faiths. Mayans/Aztecs, Jews, Catholics, Protestants, and Quakers converge on the chocolate trail. This universal comfort food has migrated with persecuted refugees and has fortified resourceful minorities.

My choco-dar still thrives. Not long ago I shopped for a chocolate-colored dress to wear when I present. Only when I tried it on at home did I notice that the pattern featured cocoa pods. Choco-dar also led me to a poignant personal story. In 2009 I attended an academic conference about colonial-period Jewish merchants. I raised my hand and asked if anyone knew about the chocolate trade. Silence. After the session a very kind scholar mentioned an archival collection related to Jews and chocolate in Dutch. I deferred tracking it down then, because the English material at American research institutions already inundated me. The thought of an archive in Jerusalem, in Dutch no less, almost pushed me beyond my chocolate limits. Translating it all would have been extremely expensive. I had to resign myself that *On the Chocolate Trail* would not capture every story. I reasoned that this Dutch material could be a later add-on to the trail, perhaps an article.

Finally, in the summer of 2012 *On the Chocolate Trail* edits and rewrites were nearly finished. My publisher, Stuart Matlins, and I were excited that *On the Chocolate Trail* would be the first-ever book about chocolate and religion. That August Mark and I were in Jerusalem with a couple of free days. We decided to investigate the Dutch chocolate materials. I scanned the online collection of the Central Archives for the History of the Jewish People and wondered if this would be worthwhile. As I glanced at the substantial list of the 141 boxes, I noticed the researcher's name: Izak Prins, a Dutch variant of my last name. Yet we had no knowledge of a family connection in Mark's carefully curated family tree. I randomly requested a few boxes from off-site storage for our appointment. Within a couple of days, Mark and I were trekking down a windy, hillside path to a barely marked trailer at an isolated corner of the Givat Ram campus of the Hebrew University to sort through the Prins collection of *Joden en chocola*, "Jews and chocolate."

We picked through Prins's chocolate wrappers, publications, photos, and spidery notes obsessively scratched on small scraps of paper. Even if I had known Dutch, I probably would not have been able to decipher the scrawls. Buried amidst all of that documentation we found an article by Prins from the *Jerusalem Post* (March 1, 1957) titled "Chocolate and Politics." I scanned through the details and then saw this last paragraph:

> The present writer has written a book on "Jews and Chocolate—Explorations in Cultural History in the Diaspora" and a history of Israel chocolate making is in preparation as the second part of the work.[3]

Oy! The flush I felt was a mix of surprise, disappointment, embarrassment, and jealousy. *On the Chocolate Trail* would not be the first volume about Jews and chocolate after all. How could I have missed such a crucial resource in my research? This was especially odd since Mark had thought that I had over-researched. I did not know what to do—quickly write to Stuart to hold the presses? Hide? Start over?

I decided to hunt for the Prins title. The archivists knew nothing about the book or a manuscript. I had noticed that Prins had written to Brill Publishers, an academic press in the Netherlands. I contacted them. No, an editor politely replied, they knew nothing of Prins or his book. I checked online. Nothing. I queried Jewish research libraries in America, Europe, and Israel. No book. In September 2013 I wrote a post at my blog about the Prins choco-dar coincidences and my search for his work. In the meantime I also e-mailed with Prins's grandsons, David and Daniel. They were completely unaware of their grandfather's research about Jews and chocolate, much less a book.

Then a distant cousin of Prins, Henry Joshua, posted a comment at my blog. He confided that when he and his mother had visited Prins at his home in the Jerusalem neighborhood of Bayit Vegan in 1958, Prins had mentioned that he was writing about chocolate. Joshua continued, "Prins died in 1968 without finishing his book."

I felt sad because I would have liked to have learned from Prins's research. He had intended to write a book and had been unable to complete it. At the same time, I was relieved that mine was still the first book connecting Jews, religion, and chocolate. Izak Prins and I share a surname plus a passion for chocolate and Jews. We also have the same birthday (not the same year). Choco-dar. Though we may not be biologically related, I am pleased to continue Prins's work in this mysterious way. From Prins to Prinz, the trail of Jews and chocolate widens.[4]

Introducing the Second Edition

Media attention, popular culture, audience questions, growing consumer awareness, and changes in the chocolate world have sparked the new material in this second edition of *On the Chocolate Trail*. I am happy to offer up a totally new chapter, "Gods in My Chocolate," which explores twenty-first-century controversies about deities formed from chocolate. While chocolate generally unifies, outrage and disgust plague these chocolate gods, despite the intentions of their artisans.

This edition also features approximately ten new sidebar stories, updated information about chocolate museums and factory tours around the world, and additional historical and contemporary recipes.

In these last few years we have seen an expanding array of chocolate choices for consumers, an increase of small bean-to-bar artisan chocolate makers, deeper conversations around worker justice, fear of chocolate shortages, and concerns about sustainability in the chocolate industry. Therefore this edition also includes a completely revised chapter about the ethics of chocolate and how to select the best (see chapter 11). The 2015 U.S. Department of Labor study makes the ethics discussion in this material even more critical. Chocolate economics, cacao tree sustainability, environmental issues, and honest business practices mix into these complexities. A sidebar about single-origin chocolate (from a specific country or region or farm), for instance, amplifies one option for our chocolate choices. The "Grenada's Green Chocolate" sidebar highlights a company driven by one man's vision for a chocolate enterprise protective of the natural world. The panic around predicted shortages of chocolate starting in 2020 is also addressed in a sidebar. Another sidebar discusses the downfall of a very popular hipster Brooklyn company, Mast Brothers, which publicly claimed to have been making chocolate by hand from the cocoa beans since its start, until a food blogger called that into question. The updated and revised list of chocolate companies evaluated by ethical criteria also provides an enhanced tool for consumer decisions.

Media headlines and popular culture drove other material. Fascination with the Broadway show *Hamilton* led me to explore chocolate usage by our founders in "What Did Alexander Hamilton Drink?" (see chapter 3). Less historical and perhaps a bit hysterical was the Jewish community's uproar over the secret Santas hidden in chocolate Maccabees (see chapter 11). Not hysterical at all is the sweet story of a centenarian chocolate maker, at one time the oldest man alive, living in Haifa, Israel, which accompanies the chapter about Israeli chocolate (see chapter 6). Since that famous episode of *Seinfeld*, everyone wants a chocolate babka. The sidebar "Chocolate Babkathons: New York City" feeds the ever-growing popularity of this delicious treat.

New information responds to audience questions as well, particularly about religious food laws and chocolate, and specifically for Passover. Certainly our times require clarity about halal certification for chocolate within a Muslim setting.

Sidebars also add poignant Holocaust stories to chapter 5. One features youngsters who had to give up the chocolate of their youth. Since the first edition, I learned more about the touching story of the Madelaine Chocolate Company, a family of Holocaust survivors who also suffered through Hurricane Sandy. A third sidebar relates my family story about valuables smuggled out of Nazi Europe in chocolate, which echoes a scene in the television series *Transparent*.

Of course there are a few more sweet recipes, and I have also included three savory options. The three-course chocolate meal could celebrate a religious holiday or a secular occasion. So reach for some good chocolate treats and enjoy!

Acknowledgments

My choco-dar instincts and sleuthing were also triggered in libraries and archives, where this research was generously supported by a Starkoff Fellowship and a Director's Fellowship from the American Jewish Archives, Cincinnati, Ohio, as well as a Gilder Lehrman Fellowship from the John D. Rockefeller Jr. Library, Williamsburg, Virginia. Deepest gratitude is extended to the many people who assisted me, including the staff of the American Jewish Archives, the American Jewish Historical Society, the Hebrew Union College–Jewish Institute of Religion, the New York Society Library, and the John D. Rockefeller Jr. Library, as well as Rabbi Josh Beraha, Rabbi Jillian Cameron, Rabbi Lisa Delson, Benjamin Fox-Rosen, Emily Geminder, Chana Kupetz, Brian Hughes, and Hilary Ramp.

I am very grateful to the leadership of the Central Conference of American Rabbis and to Temple Adat Shalom for time afforded for travel and study. Amazing graphic artist, Barbara Leff, enthusiastically helped create the book cover. The staff of Jewish Lights hankered for this book's release. Publisher Stuart M. Matlins took a chance on a book outside the usual scope of his publishing program. Editorial and production vice president Emily Wichland kindly guided me through the stages of publication and skillfully helped shape the final manuscript. Thanks go as well to Justine Earnest, assistant editor; Jennifer Rataj, publicity manager; and the staff at Jewish Lights. Copyeditor Debra Corman deserves special acknowledgment for making this book happen. I would also like to thank Turner Publishing for making this updated second edition that you now hold in your hands possible. The following scholars generously responded to my queries, shared feedback, and in some cases read chapters or sections: Dr. Robert Ferry, Megan Giller, Clay Gordon, Dr. Leo Hershkowitz (*z"l*), Dr. Stanley Hordes, Dr. Sara Malino, Rabbi Richard Marker, Dr. Carla Martin, Dr. Marcy Norton, Kevin Profitt, Dr. Marc Raphael, Rabbi David Sandmel, Dr. Jonathan Sarna, Ilana Schatz, Reverend Susan Sica, Dr. Michael Signer (*z"l*), Dr. Brigitte Sion, Dr. Susan Terrio, and Dr. Gary Zola.

Several others generously read the entire book, including Noam Gross-Prinz, Rabbi Alan Henkin, Agnes Herman, Avigail Hurvitz-Prinz, Chana Kupetz, Libbe Madsen, Dr. Jessica Prinz, Edwina Riblet, and Rabbi Sara Rich. Chocolate maven Dr. Judy Logback offered helpful suggestions. Pastry chef Hannah Gross read, interpreted, and implemented recipes, serving as a fun food consultant. There were many chocolate tasters as well. I remain responsible for any errors but not for any resulting weight gain.

Chocolate discoveries occurred in our travels within the United States and to several countries, including Belgium, England, France, Israel, Italy, Mexico, Spain, and Switzerland.

Many thanks to the kind people who gave us tips, clues, and directions along the trail.

I am most grateful for the sweet harvest of blessings I have enjoyed along the chocolate trail: for my fellow chocolate traveler, Mark—his questions, photos, navigation, share of the chocolate calories, and enduring love; for the many kind people who have delighted in these stories with enthusiasm and curiosity, amplified by their craving for this mixture of religion, food, and chocolate; for the learning that I have acquired, the chocolate I have sampled, and the chocolate trails yet to be revealed.

I hope that this first-ever book about Jews, religions, and chocolate will assist you in maximizing your choco-dar; I intend to continue to pay close attention to mine. As I bring this inquiry to a close, I am sated by the requisite chocolate snacking—whether traveling or at my computer, at food shows or in my neighborhood. There is now only one thing left to do: clean the chocolate smudges from my keyboard.

Introduction

PICK UP A PIECE OF CHOCOLATE AND PARTAKE IN AN expedition into Jewish and religious history. *On the Chocolate Trail* melds an enjoyment of chocolate with an exploration of chocolate's religious narratives and rituals, unwrapping tantalizing new themes in the first book on this topic. It highlights unique Jewish connections to chocolate against a historical backdrop of religious engagement with chocolate. Delight your mind and your taste buds as this book unscrambles the mysteries of Jews, religions, and chocolate along a trail of economic development spanning several cultures, countries, centuries, continents, and convictions. This chocolate journey layers curiosity, gratitude, pleasure, opportunity, and success onto an underside of disdain, critique, abuse, and persecution. It embraces marginalized groups such as Quakers and Jews and also notes individuals who came to be known as "chocolate uncles." As chocolate is malleable, so this story reflects the resourcefulness and resilience of the chocolate lovers featured in this book. Chocolate is an immigrant food. This ultimate comfort food brings people together.

This chocolate path parallels the highway of Jewish history, particularly that of Sephardi (Jews of Iberian descent) and other Jewish migrations (as in the case of chocolatiers Eliyahu Fromenchenko of Elite Chocolate from Eastern Europe to Israel,

Karina Chaplinsky from Argentina to Israel, Stephen Klein of Barton's from Vienna to New York, and Oded Brenner of Max Brenner from Tel Aviv to New York). It builds on deep pre-Columbian traditions and intersects with twists and turns of Catholic and Quaker chocolate encounters. Jews jump on that chocolate trail early in some places (New Spain, Oxford, Brabant); in significant Jewish centers (Amsterdam, New York, Newport); as great chocolate entrepreneurs (Chillon and others in New Spain, the Gomez family and Aaron Lopez in North America); and as experts (Amsterdam, Martinique, Bayonne). This New World product of chocolate blazed a new world of commerce, appetite, and opportunity for Jews as well as for others.

Jews and Christians meet on this chocolate trail. Faith traditions share chocolate consumption, ritual, and business interests. Today's commercial chocolate endeavors track back to a continuum of life-cycle and holiday use baked in pre-Columbian spiritual understandings. Jews and Christians displayed a fascination with the cacao trade, arriving at it from different perspectives and beliefs. Struggles around propriety, constraints, and enjoyment could be seen in both Judaism and Christianity. While there have been—and still are—abuses related to chocolate—from the Spanish Inquisition to the Holocaust, from Bayonne to West Africa—this path also nurtured and sustained. When we consider the visionary, ambitious, and versatile entrepreneurs who made a life of chocolate—the British Quaker companies and Milton Hershey, Camille Bloch and the Holocaust controversies in Switzerland, the unique business approach of Barton's—we also see that they contributed to the lives of others.

From chocolate use in religious settings, we learn food wisdoms about chocolate eating as a potentially sacred endeavor. Religious life has been enhanced by chocolate. Chocolate has been enhanced by religion. A challenge remains to develop a chocolate culture of ideals, expressing commitments grounded in faith values.

What Are Cacao, Cocoa, and Chocolate?

Let's start by understanding some of the basic terms related to chocolate, its cultivation, and its manufacture. The chocolate we love begins with trees. The terms used during the multistage process of deriving chocolate from those trees vary. Some use *cacao* and *cocoa* interchangeably, as in this book. Others define *cacao* and *cocoa* quite differently. In that view it helps to note the transition from wet plant to dry product. *Cacao* then refers to the tree, the fruit pod that grows on the tree, and the seeds that nest inside the pod. The term *cocoa* applies after the fermentation stage as a term for the bean, the resulting semi-finished powder, and the cocoa butter. In either usage, chocolate comes to mean the processed product, finished for eating, for drinking, or for further use in another product, likely with sugar added in.

The cacao tree is native to the Amazon rainforests of South America, probably Ecuador. Early domestication took place in Mexico and Guatemala. The tree is shaded by taller trees until it matures. Cacao trees need a climate found twenty degrees north and south of the equator. The plant's scientific name is *Theobroma cacao*, meaning the food of the gods. Cultivated since approximately 1500 BCE, it has been transplanted to many parts of the world such as Hawaii, Vietnam, and Indonesia. Today, West Africa's Ivory Coast and Ghana export the largest segment of the world's cocoa.

The thick rind of the pod encases white pulp and thirty to fifty seeds. Pods ripen throughout the year, with two main harvests about six months apart. There are primarily two types of seeds: criollo and forastero. Forastero is most widely available. Criollo, meaning "native," is the highest quality. Trinitario is a hybrid of these two, bred in Trinidad in the 1700s to be disease resistant. Dozens of genetic varieties exist.[1]

Once the pod is removed from the tree, usually with a machete, its husk is composted. The seeds and pulp are gathered for fermenting at the farm. This makes the sugars acidic and sometimes alters the color of the seeds from white to brown or light purple, with pre-cocoa flavors. At this point, they are the size of almonds or coffee beans.

The beans are spread over large surfaces for drying in the sun. Artificial heat dryers may be used in especially tropical and humid climates. Drying enables shipping in bulk in jute bags usually via container ships. With a few exceptions, cocoa beans are not processed into chocolate in the locale where they are grown. The required equipment is often too expensive, as is temperature control in the tropical heat.

Once at the chocolate factory, the beans are processed in several stages:

1. Beans are sorted, cleaned, and roasted.
2. Beans are then cracked and deshelled in a winnower. Shells are blown away from the broken pieces of cacao, which are called nibs.
3. Crushing the nibs creates a paste of the chocolate. This may be done by hand on a metate stone using a *mano* (roller), as in the colonial age of discovery in Spain, North America, Bayonne, and Amsterdam, and still today in Mexico, Central America, and South America. Prior to the 1800s chocolate was formed by hand into fist-sized balls. A ball would be grated into a special chocolate pot and mixed with hot water and sugar using a *molinillo* (stirrer), which generates a foam. This primarily yields a drinking chocolate, as does grinding with a *tiendas de chocolate* (electric mill), as is done in Mexico and other Central or South American countries today.

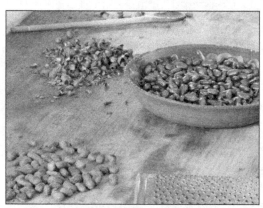
Shelling roasted cocoa beans by hand.

4. Industrial machines in first-world countries produce a smoother chocolate for eating. The resulting "cocoa liquor" contains no alcohol, has not yet been sweetened, and refers to the liquid nature of the chocolate at this point. Sometimes this is called cocoa mass.

5. Through the grinding stage, a hydraulic press separates the cocoa fat/butter from the liquor, creating a cocoa cake. These are then recombined in varying quantities, depending on the intended use of the chocolate—for baking, eating, or drinking. Compound chocolate, often used in candy, needs to be labeled as such and often has vegetable oils added in to lower costs.

6. The chocolate mixture is then conched—or massaged— to mix together the ingredients. Depending on the equipment used, longer conching may result in higher-quality chocolate. Sometimes an emulsifier or smoothing agent such as soy lecithin is added to reduce the processing time and make the chocolate less expensive.

7. The chocolate is then tempered. This is the heating and cooling process that gives the chocolate a desirable glossy look and a snap when broken. Nothing resembling pinholes should appear, and the coloring should be even.

8. The taste of chocolate depends on many factors, including the type of seed, length of fermentation, form of processing, ratio of cocoa liquor to cocoa butter, quality of the additional ingredients in the product, and more.[2]

Jews in Navigational Sciences Help Discover Cacao

The trailhead for this chocolate passion lies at the crossroads of the age of exploration and the discovery of the New World at the end of the fifteenth century. Jews of the time inherited the then radical concept of a round world from the fourth-century text "The earth is made as a ball" (Jerusalem Talmud,

Avodah Zarah 42c). Medieval Jewish scientists advanced many innovations related to navigation that furthered New World discoveries. Explorers Christopher Columbus and Vasco da Gama consulted with Abraham Ben Samuel Zacuto regarding westward travel to the Near East. Zacuto plotted Columbus's route. Just as Columbus's voyage began, Zacuto faced charges from the Spanish Inquisition, the crusade against heretics by the Roman Catholic Church, and fled to Portugal, where he devised an improved metal astrolabe.

Ten Facts about Religion and Chocolate

1. Some people think that Jews brought chocolate to France.
2. The 1602 victory of the citizens of Geneva, Switzerland, over the Duke of Savoy's attempt to destroy the Reformation is commemorated each December with soup pots made from chocolate.
3. The bishop of Chiapas, Mexico, was poisoned because he prohibited local women from drinking chocolate during Mass.
4. North American Jewish and Quaker colonial traders were involved in the chocolate trade.
5. Junipero Serra depended on chocolate for his work in building missions in California in the eighteenth century.
6. Cistercian monks in Poblet, Spain, designated a special chocolate room.
7. At age sixteen, Austrian-Jewish confectioner Franz Sacher created the now famous Sachertorte.
8. Chocolate was first introduced to the Spanish court of Prince Philip by Dominicans.
9. Inquisition jails in New Spain allowed the drinking of chocolate by prisoners.
10. Since Europeans first encountered chocolate, Jews and clerics have been on the chocolate trail.

This device, used to fix location in relation to the sun, stars, and moon, became the standard in subsequent exploits by colonialist adventurers. These and other advances by Iberian Jews set the backstory for the discovery of the New World's chocolate resources.[3]

Jews and Catholics First to Sight Cacao

Jews may have been among the first Europeans to see cacao in the New World, especially if Columbus was Jewish, as some believe.[4] Members of his first crew were born Jews or descended from Jews. Conversos—a term usually used for Jews converted to Christianity and/or descendants of converted Jews—such as Alonso de la Calle, a sailor; Rodrigo Sánchez of Segovia, a comptroller; and others crewed the first voyage of 1492. Luis de Torres was baptized just in time to act as Columbus's interpreter. Their journey was supported by the vastly wealthy converso Luis de Santangel, chancellor of King's household, comptroller-general of Aragon, who argued in favor of the proposed voyage to Ferdinand and Isabella. Santangel also used his own funds to help underwrite this and other expeditions.

All of these contributed to the European discovery of a cacao bean–laden canoe during Columbus's fourth voyage, in 1502, in the Bay of Honduras, as reported by Columbus's son, Ferdinand:

> Many of the almonds [cacao beans] which the Indians of New Spain use as currency; and these the Indians in the canoe valued greatly, for I noticed that when they were brought aboard with the other goods, and some fell to the floor, all the Indians stooped to pick them up as if they had lost something of great value.[5]

Follow the Chocolate Trail through the Chapters

The awareness of chocolate in the European world depended in no small measure on people of faith. It migrated from the New World to the Old World and back again, often through them.

The first part of this book, "Forging the Jewish Chocolate Trail," reveals how Mark and I chanced on clues to a very long Jewish and religious chocolate trail.

Chocolate migrated to France, specifically to Bayonne in southwestern France, which generally spouts the claim that Jews introduced chocolate making to France. Chapter 1 explores other chocolate locales with Jewish specialists and how Jews were perceived to possess chocolate-making expertise. Today's elegant and plentiful French chocolate culture may very well be indebted to Jews.

Chapter 2 unpacks the seepage of pre-Columbian chocolate customs into the ritual practices of Jews in New Spain. Seventeenth-century Inquisition records from New Spain document some of the earliest and abundant Jewish business involvement with chocolate. In this context, xenophobia injected suspicion and cruelty right into the chocolate and onto the Jews who drank it, sold it, and traded it. In some cases, chocolate outed Jews and in general confounded Christians.

In colonial North America, the chocolate interests of Sephardi refugees could be uncovered in the holds of their ships, in their shops, and in their homes. Chapter 3 traces how Jewish merchants such as Aaron Lopez, Daniel Gomez, and others dipped deeply

European Chocolate Processing

European countries pride themselves on distinct approaches to chocolate processing, measuring the microns to distinguish the chocolate in terms of texture:

- Belgian chocolate tends to be around twelve microns.
- British chocolate tends to be around twenty-four microns.
- French chocolate tends to be in the range of twelve to twenty microns.
- Swiss chocolate tends to be in the range of fifteen to twenty microns.

into cacao trading and the processing of chocolate. Rebecca Gomez was the only woman of her time to manufacture chocolate.

Despite distinct messages and rituals, Christmas and Chanukah connect through chocolate coin customs. Chapter 4 investigates how Chanukah and Christmas chocolate melt into gelt by unraveling some celebratory themes of these December holidays.

The fifth chapter looks into chocolate during and after World War II. It examines chocolate's use by the military, its role at the liberation of concentration camps, its succor and support for immigrants and refugees, and its contribution to survival and renewal. This contrasts sharply with the unbelievable deprivations of that time, making for an unusual period of chocolate experiences.

One could say that Israelis are *meshuga* (crazy) for chocolate. Chocolate permeates Israel, as observed in chapter 6. A chunk of Israel's growth as a state may be seen through its chocolate industry, which reflects both immigrant stories and the entrepreneurship of Israel.

The second part of this book, "Other Religious Chocolate Revelations," tracks the mysteries of chocolate's trek back and forth between the New World and the Old. Religious peoples—pre-Columbians, Catholics, Quakers, and others—stuck their fingers into the business of chocolate worldwide. They struggled, as did Jews, with permeability and boundaries for their chocolate.

When Jews and Catholics encountered chocolate, they did so in an environment full of Mesoamerican wonderment and awe, an earlier tradition that saw cacao as the divine food of the gods. Chapter 7 unveils the backdrop for the Jewish story as it details how the earliest chocolate drinkers in South and Central America, living before Columbus, idolized chocolate and saturated their cultic life with it.

Jews and Christians built upon this pre-Columbian chocolate dependency. Europeans' first contact with chocolate in the sixteenth century both excited and confused Catholics. Chapter 8 divulges how Catholics diffused chocolate into Europe, into South America, and along the El Camino Real (or the Royal Road) in California even though Catholics were also beset with quandaries and conflicts about chocolate.

Quakers mixed chocolate into their dreams for a better society and into very lucrative businesses in Britain. Chapter 9 shows how their utopian visions spread from the chocolate factory outward to the community and how they influenced other chocolate companies, including Hershey's and Israel's Elite. At the same time, this chapter exposes how some of these companies compromised their ideals.

This second edition includes a new chapter that investigates faithfulness and irreverence in chocolate, questions that surface in the molding of chocolate gods and Jesus (chapter 10). Authors, musicians, and artists, as well as chocolate vendors, contribute an array of views about the propriety of gods in our chocolate.

Many complexities surface when measuring our food values against our chocolate consumption and purchases. Chapter 11, "Shopping for the Best Chocolate: Values and Ethics," examines these issues through a discussion of fair labor and sustainability practices.

Your Chocolate Chronicle

If reading the stories within these chapters jogs your memory of a story of chocolate and religions, I invite you to hop onto the chocolate trail by posting your recollections at my blog. Please share them at www.onthechocolatetrail.org.

Recipes

If you are hankering to indulge in some chocolate as you meander along this chocolate trail, I invite you to try the recipes included with each chapter and also at the end of the book. They have been coded to indicate vegan (V) and gluten free

(GF). A few of these recipes connect to yummy goodies we discovered in our travels. I also found some in historical materials as I researched. Others were introduced to us by friends. Mark created the citrus salad with cocoa nibs. We have devoured the results of each recipe. Please feel free to send me your favorite historical, contemporary, or family chocolate recipes.

Supplementary Material at the *On the Chocolate Trail* Website

You will find a lot of helpful resources and educational material at the *On the Chocolate Trail* website including *A Haggadah for a Socially Responsible Chocolate Seder*, lesson plans for teaching about Jews and chocolate, a book club discussion guide, traditional Jewish texts related to chocolate, additional photos, and data related to colonial chocolate use in North America. See www.onthechocolatetrail.org.

Additional Resources

Several additional resources are included at the back of the book to enhance your exploration of Jews, religion, and chocolate, and possible travel experiences, including more recipes, "Timeline of Chocolate and Religion," "A Consumer's Guide to Buying Ethically Produced Chocolate," and "Chocolate Museums and Tours around the World."

I hope that you enjoy the journey as this book guides you into these stirrings of age-old passions for chocolate and religion.

PART ONE

Forging the Jewish Chocolate Trail

Basque Chocolate Cake

This unique combination of chocolate and cherries directs our taste buds to the flavors of the Basque area of Bayonne, France, where Jews are said to have initiated local chocolate making.

Ingredients:

¾ cup unsalted butter
5½ ounces bittersweet chocolate
3 large eggs
¾ cup sugar
⅓ cup all-purpose flour
¾ cup black cherry preserves, for serving
Crème fraîche, for serving

Instructions:

Preheat the oven to 375°F. Lightly butter and flour a 9-inch round cake pan. In a large heatproof bowl set over a pan of simmering water, combine the butter and chocolate. Melt over moderate heat, stirring frequently, until smooth, about 4 minutes. Remove from the heat and let cool slightly. In a medium bowl, using an electric mixer, beat the eggs with the sugar at high speed until thick and pale, about 3 minutes. Add the flour and beat at low speed just until combined. Fold in one-third of the melted chocolate, then gently fold in the remaining chocolate; do not overmix.

Pour the batter into the prepared pan and bake for 20–30 minutes, or until a toothpick inserted into the center comes out clean. Invert the cake onto a rack and let cool.

In a saucepan, warm the cherry preserves over moderate heat. Cut the cake into wedges and serve with the cherry preserves and crème fraîche.

Quantity: 6–8 servings

Chapter One

Did Jews Introduce Chocolate to France?

"JEWS BROUGHT CHOCOLATE MAKING TO FRANCE," I read in the brochure I happened to pick up in a chocolate store in the Montparnasse neighborhood of Paris. Jews were the first to bring chocolate to France? How could this be? I wondered, channeling the professor who had doubted the efficacy of this project. This amazing morsel of history had been omitted in my serious Jewish education and had not surfaced in over thirty years of study about Judaism as a rabbi. I knew plenty of Jews devoted to eating chocolate. But I had no clue until then of any history tying Jews and chocolate together, much less about Jews introducing chocolate to France. Not until Paris.

Only a month earlier, during my morning workout on Valentine's Day, I had chanced upon a National Public Radio interview with a well known Paris food writer reporting on chocolate shops in Paris. Perfect. What a great way to see Paris, I thought. My husband, Mark, and I were in the midst of planning a late-winter sabbatical journey through several European countries in a VW van. He had thought that we should skip Paris and push on to the warmer south. I had never been to Paris and wanted to stop there. When I mentioned the chocolate in Paris, Mark immediately rerouted the trip.

I took my map of Paris and plotted chocolate store locations so that chocolate visits would accompany our touring: chocolate shop / the Louvre, chocolate shop / Eiffel Tower, chocolate shop / Paris Opera. We savored as many *chocolateries* on the list as possible, plus those that we discovered as we wandered the *arrondissements* (districts). Often when we inquired about the attendant's favorite, we were rewarded with samples, which became so numerous they lasted for months. While browsing and tasting in L'Atelier du Chocolat de Bayonne, a chocolate boutique on the Left Bank, itself a find as it was not on our original list, I read this astonishing passage in the company's literature:

> À Bayonne l'origine de la fabrication et de la consomma-
> tion du chocolat semble remonter au début du VXIIème
> siècle, lorsque les Juifs pourchassés par l'Inquisition
> s'installèrent dans le bourg de Saint Esprit.

Then I reread this sentence, wondering if my high school French had accurately captured its meaning. The booklet indeed claimed:

> At Bayonne the origins of the manufacturing and the
> consumption of chocolate happened at the beginning of
> the seventeenth century, when the Jews exiled from the
> Inquisition settled in the suburb of Saint Esprit.

It took a few moments for me to absorb this link between chocolate and the Jewish people. The sophisticated and elegant chocolate of France connects with Jews in Bayonne. This factoid might have sweetened our Jewish educations. How could we have missed out on this scrumptious detail?

Admittedly, as I noticed in that pamphlet, several theories exist about chocolate's arrival in France. Some credit royal marriages with bringing chocolate to France, either through the marriage of Anne of Austria (the Infanta of Spain) to Louis XIII in 1615 or through the marriage of Maria Teresa of Spain to Louis XIV in 1659. Others claim that chocolate arrived in France with clerics and monastic orders, gifts from those in Spain to their French counterparts. And others suggest that chocolate entered France as a medicine.[1]

Jews Specialize in Chocolate

As I considered this connection between chocolate and Jews in France, however, I realized that it made sense. Jews exiled from Spain in 1492 and then from Portugal in 1496 engaged in international trade as they continued their linkages to each other through birth, business, or family bonds. Over the years since its discovery by Europeans in 1502 in the New World and its import to Spain in approximately 1520, chocolate developed into a colonial extract industry. Jews still living in Spain or with family contacts in Spain would have easily learned about chocolate, even as the Spanish throne sought to maintain a monopoly over it.

With more detective work it became clear that in their relocations from Spain and Portugal, these Jews played a critical, if not unique part in the cocoa business. In addition to Catholic clerics, Jews who converted to Christianity or were descendants of converted Jews (conversos) diffused Spanish methods of chocolate making across Europe with specialty workshops in Bayonne, Amsterdam, and other European cities. For instance, the first coffeehouse in England, The Angle, which served hot chocolate, as later coffeehouses did, was opened by a converso Jew named Jacob in Oxford in 1650 at the time of the readmission of Jews to

Jacob the Jew established the first coffeehouse in Oxford at this site. Along with coffee, the Angle served hot chocolate.

England. Some sources refer to him as "Cirques Jobson, a Jew."[2] The Grand Café on the High Street memorializes that site today.

In addition, chocolate making became a Dutch Jewish specialty, especially after the rise of the cocoa trade with Curaçao in the 1650s. Jews were considered excellent chocolate makers in what was called another typical Amsterdam Jewish industry. When appointed the Spanish ambassador to the Hague in 1655, Don Esteban Gammarra fretted that he would not be able to access his customary daily chocolate in this strange environment. To assuage his fear, his staff informed him that "the best chocolatiers—including a man named Pacheco, who flavored his chocolate with vanilla—were the Jews of Amsterdam."[3] Not only that, but in Belgium in 1663, Emanuel Soares de Rinero, a converso, received the first permit to fabricate chocolate in the province of Brabant.[4]

In the French Caribbean island of Martinique, Benjamin d'Acosta de Andrade, a Jew formerly of Bayonne but likely born in Portugal, cultivated cacao trees. Owner of the two largest sugar plantations, he also established the first cacao-processing plant in French territory. As a result, chocolate eventually became the most important export from Martinique. D'Acosta de Andrade may have also experimented with shaping cacao into pellet form.[5] Sadly, the growth of the profits from the Caribbean colonies prompted Jean-Baptiste Colbert, the chief minister of Louis XIV, to shift ownership of properties in the Caribbean settlements directly into the control of the French crown. When all Jews lost their property in 1664, D'Acosta de Andrade did, too. A 1681 petition circulated by Jesuit fathers accusing Jews of blaspheming Jesus and of killing babies born to their Christian slaves prompted the king's order expelling Jews from the French colonies in 1685, thus ending the Jewish chocolate business in Martinique of that period.[6]

To access and purchase cacao from Venezuela, ship it via Curacao and then to Amsterdam, Dutch and Dutch Jewish colonists established Tucacas on the Venezuelan coast around 1693. One of those Jewish merchants was Phelipe Henriquez of Curacao. Over a million pounds of cacao were traded there annually. In Amsterdam, Abraham Zuzarte ran a coffee and chocolate house; Isaac Monsanto, a chocolate maker on the welfare list of the community, supplied chocolate in 1752.[7]

The Rabbi's Chocolate Diaries

The first personal rabbinic testimony of chocolate consumption comes from the mid-eighteenth century, in the diaries of Rabbi Haim Yosef David Azulai (1724–1806). Commonly known as the Hida, he documented widespread chocolate drinking among the Jews of Europe of his day.

Of Sephardi descent, Hida was born and educated in Jerusalem. He published over sixty works of Jewish law and prayer, plus his travel diaries. Some consider him to be the greatest Sephardi scholar since Joseph Caro, the author of the authoritative sixteenth-century Jewish code known as the *Shulchan Aruch*. Due to this erudition, Hida was selected to be a messenger from Israel to the European Jewish communities. His diaries mention chocolate at least ten times between 1755 and 1778.[a] On his travels he drank chocolate, ate chocolate, and was gifted chocolate. His hosts entertained him with chocolate in Italy, France, and the Netherlands. During a very mountainous journey in a snowstorm from Cuneo, Italy, to Nice, France, he confessed that he resorted to eating "some raw chocolate, and I ate about a litre!"[b] In Amsterdam chocolate was served with sweets following a bris (circumcision) in 1777.[c] Following prayers in Montpellier, France, he drank chocolate with the synagogue's major benefactor and others.[d] All over Europe these Jewish communities were benefiting from chocolate, as was Rabbi Azulai.[e]

Rabbi Jonathan Eybeshutz of Metz berated his congregation for their resistance to the spiritual reform of Judaism, this even though they were early adopters of chocolate.[8] In the eighteenth century in Denmark, when guild restrictions prevented Jewish involvement, Jews instead pursued trade in tea, coffee, and chocolate. These became known as "Jew trades," a phrase abolished when Jews became citizens in 1814.[9] It was a Jew, Franz Sacher, who created the Sachertorte, a dense, dark chocolate cake made with apricot jam, at the age of sixteen in 1832. As a trainee at the home of the chancellor of Vienna,

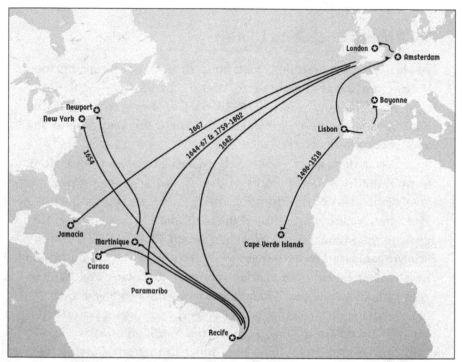

The dispersion of Jews after the Expulsion from Spain corresponds to the early diffusion of chocolate from the New World.

Prince Klemens Wenzel von Metternich, it fell to Sacher to create dessert for special guests when the head chef fell ill. Sacher's impromptu cake pleased the crowd. His son Eduard parlayed this into a great business, first at the Demel Bakery in Vienna and then at the Hotel Sacher. Today, Austrians debate the quality of the Demel and the Sacher versions of the pastry.[10]

Surprisingly, according to some chocolate mavens, it may have been Jews in France who first developed chocolate Easter eggs. These were passed around during church services to provide morsels of sustenance.[11] In the 1920s the Belgian Kwatta cocoa and chocolate factory, which was owned by the Jewish Stokvis brothers, was one of the largest factories of its kind.

Having learned about these striking early Jewish connections to chocolate in London, Amsterdam, Brabant, Martinique, and elsewhere, Mark and I hoped to tease out the Jewish chocolate story of Bayonne when we visited the southwestern region of France. Along with nearby St. Jean de Luz, the port of Bayonne offered both an accessible refuge and an easy transit point for Jews escaping the Inquisition on their way to freer destinations such as the Netherlands. Jews collecting or administering family estates in Spain or Portugal also found Bayonne convenient for such business.[12] As far as the Inquisition was concerned, any trip of an Iberian to Bayonne was certain indication of the "crime of Judaism."[13]

Jews Launch the French Chocolate Business

By the 1630s there were approximately sixty Jewish (probably converso) families living in Bayonne, France, which had formally admitted small numbers of conversos. Outwardly they lived as Christians. However, since the Inquisition was not strong in France, they slowly became more public about their Judaism. In 1654 the Jewish community sought assistance from the parish priest of the suburb of St. Esprit to purchase a cemetery plot, which was granted. He also allowed Jewish mortuary and funeral rituals there. Until 1668 Jewish deaths were recorded in the registers of the Christian burials. By the end of the century, the Jewish population of Bayonne had grown to eight hundred, with thirteen synagogues in St. Esprit.[14]

Bayonne Jews such as Emil Péreire, Isaac Péreire, Alvaro Luiz, Jacome Luiz, and Aaron Colace were crucial leaders in the contraband trade with Spain, including the business of exporting, re-exporting, and smuggling cacao.[15] Spain was the primary European market for chocolate at the beginning of the seventeenth century. Bayonne's extremely valuable port enabled traders to bypass the Spanish embargoes of 1621, creating lucrative economic traffic between Spain's Castile region and other Jewish communities, particularly Amsterdam. Aaron Colace opened a Bayonne office to

Complexities of Jewish Identity: The Sephardi Diaspora

The events leading up to the establishment of the Inquisition and the Expulsion from Spain combined to create intricate descriptions of the Sephardi community, externally and internally defined.

Inquisition: The Roman Catholic Church campaign against suspected heretics that began before the twelfth century; the Inquisition in Spain was formally established in 1480, in Portugal in 1536, and in New Spain in 1571. New Spain, a viceroyalty of the Spanish empire, included much of North America, present-day Mexico, Central America, the East and West Indies, Puerto Rico, Jamaica, Cayman Islands, Trinidad, and the Bay Islands.

Expulsion: From Spain in 1492 and from Portugal in 1496.

The complexity of the Sephardi experience when expelled from Spain in 1492 led some scholars to speak of "diasporas within diasporas." This developed into a uniquely commercial diaspora that connected to the then "seaborne empires" of seventeenth-century Spain, Portugal, Britain, France, the Dutch Republic, and Denmark. These Sephardi Jews did not have monolithic experiences, though success sometimes came from the uncertainties they experienced. Some moved a great deal, while others were more settled. They lived in and moved among varied settings: Catholic or Protestant; Western Hemisphere or on the European continent; agricultural, mercantile, or urban.

Several terms refer to the nuanced Jewish identity of Jews in this period:

Anusim: Hebrew term for Jews and their descendants who were forcibly converted, many of whom continued to observe Judaism in secret.

Converso: Jew converted to Christianity and/or descendant of converted Jews.

Crypto-Jew (*Judios*): Hidden Jew secretly practicing Judaism and outwardly observing Christianity, forced to convert to Catholicism to escape the Inquisition. Some of these Jews traveled between Spain and Portugal and may have escaped both countries.

Marrano: The Portuguese derogatory term, meaning "pig" or "swine," for a Jew converted to Christianity.

Meshumadim: Hebrew word for voluntary converts without a desire to return to Judaism or to practice it secretly, sincere in their conversion to Catholicism.

Nation: In the late sixteenth century, after Spain annexed Portugal, Portuguese conversos migrated to Spanish cities such as Madrid and Seville. Spaniards called these Portuguese immigrants *Portugueses de la naçion Hebrea*, or "Portuguese of the Hebrew Nation," because they were thought to be less sincere in their conversions. With time, they took the name upon themselves out of a sense of pride, calling themselves *homens da nação*, or "Men of the Nation."

New Christian / *Christãos Novos*: Jews and descendants of Jews who converted to Christianity, a term that developed in Portugal.

Portuguese: Sometimes refers to Jews from Portugal who fled the Inquisition.

Sephardi (plural, Sephardim): Jew descended from Iberian ancestry; to be distinguished from Ashkenazi, or Jew descended from Western Europe.[a]

In Spain the conversos were pretty rapidly integrated into society. After 1530, Portugal's crypto-Jews made up 3 percent of the population. Because of Portuguese hatred of Jews and therefore conversos, the category of *Christãos Novos*, or New Christian, developed, making it difficult to assimilate even when they returned to Spain after 1580.

A great advantage for Sephardi Jews in the development of the Atlantic trade of this period stemmed from the financial credit that could be extended based upon trust within the Jewish community. Whether Jews, conversos, or crypto-Jews, they collaborated to further their business interests. Kinship and mercantile ties remained strong, connecting these refugees in all areas of the world despite the thousands of miles separating them.[b] Travel and trade bound them along the shipping lanes as some of these Jews became active in the cacao trade.

monitor the market between Spain, Amsterdam, and Caracas, primarily shipping Caracas cacao between Amsterdam and Spain.[16] In just a six-month period from 1621 to 1622, at least thirty Dutch vessels unloaded goods in Bayonne's port for secret transport to Madrid by mule train through the mountain passes. Given this tremendously profitable trade through Bayonne, in which Jews played a key role, merchants of Amsterdam petitioned to open a Dutch consul office in Bayonne in 1624. These ties between the Bayonne Jewish merchants and the Amsterdam Jewish community furthered the commerce of cacao.

Because of this chocolate trade and because of the local Jewish chocolate makers, Bayonne became known as a chocolate center.[17] In September 1725 it was reported that Bayonne chocolate was sold in marble-sized balls prepared on a stone (*à la Pierre*), or as known in the New World, a metate. With time, the reputation of Bayonne chocolate was so well established that dealers in Carcassonne, a fortified town in the southwest region of France—a significant distance in those days—preferred chocolate primarily from the Bayonne area. Bayonne chocolate became identified with specialized preparation and ingredients known as *à la Bayonnaise*. By 1856 Bayonne had thirty-three chocolate facto-

The city of Bayonne, France, home to early chocolate making by Jews.

ries, several of them using steam-powered machinery.[18] This supremacy of Bayonne may be seen in a review published at the end of the eighteenth century about the chocolate made in a Paris shop:

He employs Spanish, Piedmontese and Italian methods as though Madrid, Florence, Genoa and Turin were teamed up in his boutique and were vying with Bayonne with the supreme honor.[19]

Indeed, the hot chocolate Mark and I tasted in Bayonne had a distinct flavor and, as in the old recipes, had been whipped by hand, its *mousseux* (foam) topped by whipped cream. It percolated us into earlier chocolate history. The unusual flavors (was it cinnamon?) evoked in our taste buds a chocolate trail reaching from Mexico, to Spain, to southwest France.

Chocolate Complications Bubble in Bayonne

Bayonne's chocolate bubbles with complications. On one hand, we found repeated statements that Jews first brought chocolate making to France. This idea reappeared in many reputable research sources and in tour books. As Mort Rosenblum wrote in his book *Chocolate: A Bittersweet Saga*, the Jews of Bayonne "made the first French chocolate early in the seventeenth century."[20] *The Encyclopaedia Judaica* reads, "Bayonne Jewry helped to introduce the chocolate industry to France."[21] Jewish cookbook author Joan Nathan shares this view, writing, "These refugee Jews ... brought the traditions of chocolate making to Bayonne."[22]

In Bayonne itself we observed that many chocolate stores, several museums, and the city's tourist literature reiterate the Jewish origins of French chocolate. At the local Basque Museum, the instructional labels taught that Jews fleeing the Inquisition initiated the French chocolate industry. A few blocks away, the company-owned Le Choco Musée Puyodebat text panels mentioned again that Jews brought chocolate making to Bayonne. At a second company-owned chocolate museum, the Planète Musée du Chocolat in the neighboring town of Biarritz, the owner's daughter confidently touted this same idea to me. The Ville Bayonne city website restated this claim to visitors, as did local postcards. The map produced and distributed widely by the City of Bayonne Office of Tourism highlighted this message. Several historians of the Bayonne area argued that chocolate arrived in France as a result of the royal grant of refuge in southwest France to Iberian Jews escaping the persecutions in the sixteenth and seventeenth centuries. Without question, this account of Jews introducing chocolate making to France became quite popular in Bayonne.

Despite the frequency of this Jewish chocolate tale of Bayonne, things there were not always so smooth. From the beginning the Jewish chocolate industry of seventeenth-century Bayonne encountered discrimination, jealousy, even anti-Semitism. Although in 1602 King Henry IV stipulated protection of the Jews by the local governors, Bayonne imposed restrictions on Jews. Jews could not own or rent commercial or residential property outside of the St. Esprit suburb, and they could not live in Bayonne proper. Jews had to leave the city of Bayonne each evening by sunset and were prohibited from selling chocolate on Sundays or Christian feast days. This meant that Jewish chocolate makers had to carry their grinding stones to and from the retail stores and homes of customers in Bayonne each day. In 1681 Bayonne leaders implemented an ordinance to limit Jews' wholesale chocolate trade outside of St. Esprit, forbidding Jewish sales in retail shops or directly to individuals in Bayonne. In violation of that decree, the Jewish merchant Abraham d'Andrade, probably related to the Andrade of Martinique, rented an apartment in Bayonne for chocolate manufacture. Several later attempts to enforce these ordinances suggest that they had been ignored.[23]

Competition between the Bayonnais and the Jewish chocolate makers grew. The Bayonnais founded their own exclusive guild of chocolatiers in 1761, imploring the mayor and municipal leaders of Bayonne to recognize them as the sole chocolatiers of Bayonne while seeking to secure prohibitions against chocolate making by Jews. The city leaders favored the guild request, granting its eleven petitioners exclusive rights to run shops and sell chocolate. After the city of Bayonne and the Bordeaux law court registered these statutes in 1761 and 1762, the Jews appealed to the Count of Gramont, who instituted an investigation that led to the intercession of the king.

The resulting defense of the Bayonne Guild of 1763 complained that chocolate had become part of the daily Bayonnais diet. Its letter argued that extreme caution needed to be applied to chocolate preparation, since Jews "habitually falsify what they sell and should be prevented from making [chocolate]." It reasoned that Jews should work and sell only in St. Esprit. Fortunately, in 1764 a legal brief on behalf of the St. Esprit Jews was presented to the Bordeaux court. It argued against the guild statutes on the grounds that the Jews had long practiced the chocolate craft in Bayonne.[24]

Two Bordeaux lawyers who had been invited to write an opinion for the guild were ambivalent. They agreed with the mean spirit of the guild's argument, claiming:

> We certainly believe that the production of chocolates by the master chocolatiers of Bayonne will be of higher quality than that of the Jews.

However, neither did they wish to intrude on the "natural liberty" of "Bayonnais bourgeois" to choose their chocolate suppliers, reasoning that

> If a bourgeois from Bayonne cared so little for his own self interest and is such an enemy of his own stomach as to prefer the chocolate of a Jew, why should one prevent him from having the Jew come to his home to make it?[25]

Finally, after three years of these legal arguments, the court annulled the special status of the Bayonne Guild, permitting Jews to continue their chocolate making in Bayonne. French monarchs had intervened repeatedly to reaffirm the original rights accorded Jews in the southwest, rights that had been registered with the Parliament of Paris in 1550 and reconfirmed by Henry III in 1574, Louis XIV in 1656, and Louis XV in 1723 and 1754. Following the French Revolution, Jews were granted full citizenship in 1791. Ironically, records from the Jewish Consistory of Bayonne reveal that St. Esprit Jews were moving away from chocolate making by that time. In 1807 Jews still making chocolate included Isaac Lopès, Jacob Torrès, Abraham Castro, Isaac Desaa, and Daniel Gommès Casseres.[26] By 1860 only two Jewish artisans practiced the craft, even as the chocolate industry of Bayonne employed 130 workers.[27]

Bayonne Features Jews in Its Chocolate Marketing Today

Despite this strained history, today's Bayonne chocolate makers and town leaders oddly have revived this notion about the link between Jews and French chocolate. In citing Bayonne as the original site of French chocolate preparation due to Jews, they have sought to reestablish Bayonne's authenticity and primacy in a revived French chocolate industry following World War II. Claiming Bayonne as the center of continuous chocolate manufacture in France in this contemporary marketing, they overlooked the discrimination against Jews by Bayonnais merchants and nobles, a historical fudge. This makes Bayonne essential to the French chocolate industry of today, though none of the chocolate companies functioning in Bayonne now traces its roots directly to the Jewish chocolate industry of the seventeenth century. The few Jews living in the Bayonne area no longer work in significant aspects of the local chocolate trade. Nevertheless, this story of Jews introducing chocolate to France pervades Bayonne. We may speculate whether the first creation of chocolate in France occurred in Bayonne or whether that chocolate was made by a Jew. Clearly, Jews played a very real part in the chocolate of France in Bayonne. Someday one of the other narratives of the transmission of chocolate to France, via royalty or cleric, may be proven to be more accurate. Nevertheless, in this complicated reassertion of its chocolate heritage, Bayonne privileges the idea that Sephardi Jews introduced chocolate fabrication to France. This launches Jews firmly onto the chocolate trail.

Mexican Hot Chocolate

This version of Mexican hot chocolate roots the Catholic and Jewish story of chocolate drinking in the Inquisition in New Spain or Mexico.

Ingredients:

4 ounces unsweetened chocolate
4 cups milk
2 cups heavy cream
¾ cup sugar
1 teaspoon ancho chile powder (or to taste)
1 teaspoon chipotle chile powder (or to taste)
1 tablespoon ground cinnamon
½ teaspoon ground cloves
1 tablespoon vanilla extract

Instructions:

Melt the chocolate in a large bowl over a simmering pan of water. In a separate heavy saucepan, heat the milk and cream on low until hot, but not boiling. Add 3 tablespoons of the hot milk to the chocolate in the double boiler and mix well. Stir the rest of the milk mixture, sugar, chile powders, cinnamon, cloves, and vanilla into the chocolate. Whisk chocolate briskly for 3 minutes, over the double boiler to thicken. (*Note:* To make it less spicy, use less chile.)

Quantity: 8 servings

Chapter Two

The Inquisition

Chocolate Outed Jews and Divided Christians

TO HUNT FOR FURTHER INFORMATION ABOUT THIS intersection of Jews and chocolate we uncovered in Bayonne, Mark and I traveled to Spain, the origin of Europe's age of chocolate discovery. While Spain identifies several tourist destination routes such as the Silver Route, the Route of the Caliphate, the El Cid Route, and the Way of St. James (*Camino de Santiago de Compostela*) Pilgrimage Route, we were disappointed that no route identified chocolate or Jews. We had no choice but to create our own *Camina Xocolata* (chocolate trail) of four chocolate museums, two chocolate factories, and countless chocolate stores ranging from the historical to the highly industrialized in Madrid, Barcelona, Valencia, and Astorga.

Our Spanish chocolate trail started with a café, Chocolateria San Ginés in Madrid, founded in 1894, with what some call the best hot chocolate in Spain—very warm, flavorful, chocolaty, and pudding-like. The typical Spanish chocolate thickening agent turns out not to be cream or chocolate but rice flour or, in some versions, cornstarch. No wonder this soothed my upset stomach. Spanish doughnuts, called churros, or ladyfingers, called *melindros*, customarily accompany hot chocolate in Spain, as in Mexico. Barcelona's Petrixol street

The many chocolate drinks and their accompaniments available in Spain.

hosts several chocolate drinking shops and numerous chocolate candy establishments. Granja Dulcinea Café offers a cold chocolate milk plus three hot chocolate options—a regular thick hot chocolate; a "French" hot chocolate, which is less thick; and the "Swiss" (with whipped cream, perhaps referring to white snow on top of mountains, though it is not customary to top hot chocolate with whipped cream in Switzerland). Our chocolate sampling definitely fortified us for our touring.

Spain: Many Chocolates, Few Jews

At the Barcelona Chocolate Museum we learned about Fray Aguilar, a Cistercian monk who shipped chocolate with the recipe to the Cistercian Monastery of Piedra (Monasterio de Piedra) and possibly also to the founding monastery at Poblet, shortly after chocolate's arrival in Spain in 1520. Since then, there has been a "Cistercian chocolate tradition."[1] Our spontaneous detour to see the still-functioning facility at Poblet, originally founded in the twelfth century, led us to the delightful medieval monks' "chocolate room" and the medieval kitchen display of chocolate-making accoutrements, including a copper

As seen near the chocolate room at the monastery at Poblet.

chocolate pot and a wooden chocolate stirrer. Imagine lounging in that chocolate room with a cup of nutritious, warming, energizing chocolate after arduous work in the fields and hours spent kneeling in prayer on cold stones. That's the life of a clergyman!

We gained a clearer understanding of earlier Hispanic chocolate preparation and its use by the monks at Poblet from the Comes Chocolate Museum, owned by the fourth-generation Comes family patriarch, Pedro Melero, in Sueca, located in eastern Spain. Their Spanish-only

The quaint, family-owned chocolate museum and factory in Sueca, Spain.

video shows the period-costumed family grinding beans on a stone (*à la piedra*). In live time, Pedro tossed the cigar-like chocolate rolls pizza-style while animatedly lauding natural ingredients, denouncing preservatives, and extolling his minimal equipment. His textured drinking chocolate contains unrefined sugar with 80 percent cacao, similar to that of Mexico and Guatemala.

In contrast to Comes, the fully mechanized Valor Chocolate Factory and Museum in Villajoyosa, about fifty miles south

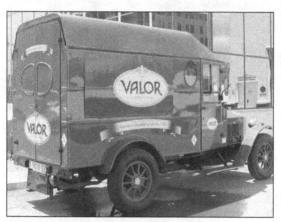

of Sueca, produces most of Spain's chocolate. Valor uses very sensual, almost soft-core "adult"-oriented advertisements to pitch their chocolate. Cocoa beans from Ghana line the storage area. The business was started in 1881 by D. Valerian López Lloret—Valor was his nickname—and his was

Spain's largest chocolate producer, Valor.

one of at least thirty families in the area making chocolate and selling it by cart around the countryside.

About five hundred miles northwest of Villajoyosa, in Astorga, another chocolate center, many chocolate stores peddle multiple brands of the very thick chocolate bars seen throughout Spain. Tourists and priests frequently visited this stop along the Way of St. James (*Camino de Santiago*), the Christian pilgrimage route to the Cathedral of Santiago de Compostela in northwestern Spain. Tradition has it that the remains of the apostle James are buried there. This historic city hosts yet another chocolate museum, where we learned that the clergy's fondness for chocolate created significant demand for it in Astorga. The exhibit highlights a chocolate "guillotine"

Thick chocolate bars are common throughout Spain; these are made in Astorga.

used for cutting through those local slabs of chocolate. Also, the *maragatos* (muleteers), who dominated the transportation system in this area in the seventeenth century, easily delivered the chocolate to other regions of Spain. Because Astorga's weather is cool and dry, chocolate could be ground quickly and stored appropriately.

Our DIY (do-it-yourself) delectable Spanish chocolate circuit, however, left an unappealing aftertaste because Spain provides minimal markers identifying the historic role of Jews. Former synagogues have become restaurants or gift shops. The Golden Age of Spain and the Inquisition are barely noted. Jews were not permitted to live in Spain from 1492 until 1950, and the current Jewish community is a small immigrant population composed primarily of North Africans, Israelis, Argentinians, and Americans. I wondered whether it could really be that Jews of Spain would have completely missed out on chocolate. After all, Jews were expelled from Spain at about the time Columbus discovered chocolate in the New World in 1502.

It took decades until the Spanish court even tasted chocolate, and then more time for chocolate recipes and skills to spread to the populace. Admittedly, the Spanish enjoyed the privilege of the exotic chocolate import in significant quantity only after Seville welcomed its first chocolate cargo in 1591, though there had been smaller, private imports prior to that.[2] These shipments ultimately achieved such renown that they voyaged with what was called the "chocolate wind," or *viento chocolatero*, the name given in Mexico for the favorable northern breezes.

As we poked further into that history, however, it became clear that Sephardi Jews were probably riding those chocolate winds as well, furthering the chocolate trail. When Spain annexed Portugal in 1580, some Jews of Portugal, fearing an even more virulent Inquisition, ironically sought safety back in Spain, where the Inquisition had become dormant and they were less well known.[3] As a result of the kinship and economic ties between Spanish and Portuguese Jews along commercial trade routes, Jews probably knew of chocolate as soon as most in Spain did and indeed played a significant role in chocolate's diffusion throughout the Western world to places such as Amsterdam, Bayonne, England, and New Spain (see chapter 1).

Surprisingly, it was New Spain's Inquisition records that revealed that Jews there actively traded chocolate and used chocolate in religious rituals. The New World offered freedoms unknown to Jewish communities of prior periods and knew nothing of earlier restrictions such as ghettos or requirements for wearing distinctive badges.[4] The Inquisition, however, hunted practicing Jews.

Judaism Persists Despite the Inquisition

The public Catholicism and private Judaism of these Jews varied. Crypto-Jews may have met secretly for prayer in New Spain in the homes of leaders such as Simón Váez Sevilla and Tomás Treviño de Sobremonte. Because they could not always

The Inquisition

Generally, the Spanish crown sought to keep Jewish riches in Spain, prohibiting Jews from taking money, gold, or silver with them when expelled and confiscating these precious materials from them.[a] The tribunals of the Holy Office of the Inquisition were royal institutions, and they worked independently of Rome, though sanctioned by the pope for theological purposes. The Holy Office eventually had branches throughout Spain and then, after 1571, in the New World as well. The Inquisition pursued these conversos all the way to New Spain, centering its work in Mexico City. In 1571 the Holy Office appointed an inquisitor for New Spain, Dr. Pedro Moya de Contreras, who arrived that same year.[b] Accused Judaizers were only 16 percent of the total number of people investigated or tried by the Inquisition in New Spain. Other offenses included fornication, bigamy, blasphemy, Lutheranism, and sexual misconduct. However, unconverted Jews in New Spain were required to leave or be deported, their property seized under the rules established by the Inquisition.[c] Jews, though not many of them, were the first of the Inquisition targets to receive the formal sentence of burning at the stake. Hundreds of people were tried for the crime of *Judaizante* (Judaizing or behaving as a Jew).[d] Had the Mexican Inquisition pursued *Judaizante* activities more intentionally, it might have benefited financially from the loot they could have stolen. Indeed, a number of local writers used Jews as leading characters.[e] While the Inquisition was inconsistent and slow moving, any rumor warranted investigation, with punishments in an auto-da-fé (public imposition of sentence) ranging from stripping of rank/honor, to confiscation of property, to imprisonment, to wearing of Inquisition clothing (*sambenito*), or in rare cases, to death by fire. Joseph de Olmo witnessed such an auto-da-fé in Madrid in 1680 where King Charles II presided over the daylong proceedings. Chocolate and other refreshments were provided for the high-ranking officials. At this same event, Marie de Villars, the wife of the French ambassador, decried the tortures and executions of Jews by the Spanish Holy Office. She later wrote to a friend commending the Spanish custom of chocolate for its health advantages.[f]

be sure about the Jewish calendar, the observance of holy days and festivals was a challenge. For some, avoiding pork and praying for the coming of the Messiah adequately expressed their secret Judaism. Others believed that only the knowledge of and intention to follow Mosaic laws were enough to keep Judaism alive. On Fridays they bathed, prepared special foods, and changed linens in preparation for the Sabbath. Almost all married other crypto-Jews. Generally children were raised as Catholics until the age of thirteen. Sometimes they circumcised themselves as adults. Bizarre circumcisions included cutting a piece of flesh off of a left shoulder, a custom observed by females as well. Many abstained from food and drink on the traditional Jewish fast days of Monday and Thursday as a form of penance for their outward observance of Catholicism.[5]

Chocolate Bewitches New Spain

Chocolate's desirability generated financial controversies and also concerns about propriety and mores. Several cases before the Inquisition in Guatemala and in New Spain argued that chocolate had been used in sorcery to seduce, craze, or control. In pursuing these suspicions, the Roman Catholic Church essentially swallowed pagan beliefs about the powers of chocolate. It apparently believed, along with the indigenous Indians, that the unfamiliar texture and unusual color of the popular drink could conceal witchcraft additives and the church therefore prosecuted several bizarre, non-Jewish cases. In Yucatán toward the end of the sixteenth century, Sánchez de Aquilar reported that Indian women put spells in chocolate to bewitch their husbands. Juana de Sossain Tlaxcala used chocolate to ensure carnal success as she plied at least a couple of men with doctored chocolate. The "famous" sorceress María de Rivera, a *mulata* (of mixed ancestry) in Puebla, Mexico, told her client to grind cacao and add certain powders to captivate the man she desired. Thirty-year-old

Cecilia de Arriola was charged with sorcery by her husband, Juan de Fuentes, in 1695. His bewitched behavior, he claimed, led him to rise early, allowing her to sleep in, and prepare her chocolate for her. In 1730 twenty-one-year-old Manuel Antonio Caldero accused his wife of causing his insanity. One night she, her mother, and her sister offered him a cup of hot chocolate. Noticing that it was heavier than usual, he asserted that when he looked more carefully, he found suspicious particles in the foam. Setting it aside, he later found it filled with white worms, the cup moving around on its own. Manuela Gutiérrez, a twenty-year-old *mulata* servant, was advised by a *mulata* sorcerer, Gerónima de Barahona, to wash herself, beat the water into a hot chocolate, and serve it to the man she desired to seduce. Similarly, Nicolasa de Torres, also a *mulata* servant, sought to attract her employer and was advised by an Indian woman, Petrona Mungía, to mix special ingredients into his chocolate drink. Such techniques were used by a Spanish woman named Doña Luisa de Gálvez in 1682 to end the abuse by her husband. The twenty-eight-year-old *mulata* slave of a nun, Rosa de Arrevillaga, served a priest (Padre Francisco de Castellanos) chocolate at confession during Easter in front of the other priests, as was customary. However, when she entered the confessional, he started to seduce her. She fended him off, and he accused her of "bewitching his chocolate with powders to gain his love."[6]

Inquisition records also disclose that chocolate drinking during church services had become customary in the New World. At least one priest protested that many of the *damas de sociedad* (elite women) disturbed the service as their entourage of slaves served steaming cups of chocolate. Furthermore, in approximately 1695, Pedro Rosuela, chaplain of the Santiago de Guatemala Cathedral, complained that the nuns drank chocolate in the pews, and he denounced them by name to the Inquisition. Ultimately, Santiago's city government enacted a prohibition against chocolate consumption in church.

The Jewish chocolate business, both trading and retail, also surfaced in the records of the Holy Office of the Inquisition. Many of those tried in the Mexican Inquisition for secretly practicing Judaism were cacao traders in the growing business with Caracas and Venezuela, importing and exporting cacao. That lucrative trade suffered due to the Inquisition trials. To supplement their earnings as seamstresses and embroiderers, Jewish women sold chocolate they had made.[7] When I asked scholar Stanley Hordes about these connections, he commented:

> I was not surprised to learn of the involvement of crypto-Jews in all stages of the importing and production of chocolate. Many of these folks pursued mercantile occupations of one sort or another.... Since chocolate was a much-sought-after commodity, it is not surprising that crypto-Jews, like other merchants, would have been heavily involved.[8]

Jews Make Their Cacao Fortune in New Spain

Indeed, from the Inquisition records we learn about several conversos on the chocolate trail in New Spain. In 1641 Manuel Álvarez de Arellano imported goods from Seville and distributed them throughout New Spain. That same year, he left for Spain with Mexican chocolate and other items, but he was arrested by Inquisition officials in 1642 and sent to Mexico for trial. Luis Núñez Pérez, a Portuguese converso and cacao retail merchant in New Spain, was arrested in June 1642, not long after he arrived. A vendor of cocoa beans, he was sentenced to reconciliation with the Catholic Church and life imprisonment at the age of thirty. Pedro de Campos became a successful cacao merchant in Campeche by the 1640s. In 1624 Francisco López de Fonseca, who spent his childhood in Portugal and Spain, sailed to Cartagena at the age of sixteen to help his uncle in his general store and then traveled to Venezuela, where he purchased a shipment of cacao and sailed for New Spain. Another Jewish cacao merchant, Duarte Castaño, operating out of Caracas, exchanged cacao for silver and products desired in Venezuela. During one expedition to Veracruz in 1645, he carried twenty-five *fanegas* (dry measure of about ½ bushels) of cacao belonging to Rabbi

Cacao in Central America

Mexican markets used cacao beans as coinage until Spanish currency became regularized. By the end of the sixteenth century, New Spain exported cacao to Spain, Mexican chocolate having become quite popular. Settlers in Guatemala shipped cacao for the American and European markets, with Oaxaca in southwestern Mexico serving as a transit point. Most of the Venezuelan cacao reached New Spain at Veracruz, in eastern Mexico, or Campeche, about 370 miles east of Veracruz, both along the Gulf of Mexico. From 1620 Venezuela exported large quantities of cacao to Mexico. Traders could double the value of cacao imported from Maracaibo and Caracas, reselling it in Mexico City. The success of the cacao trade invited controversies over taxing the lucrative commodity. King Philip IV sought to tax cacao to gain the income, while the viceroy in Mexico resisted, fearing that cacao taxes would generate an uprising from both local clergy and Indians, who were very fond of their chocolate. In the end, the local merchants succeeded in defeating a tax on cacao. Seeking to profit as well from cacao, Mexico City's Cabildo, the seat of colonial government, prohibited the import of Venezuelan and Ecuadoran cacao in 1624 and 1628. They prided themselves on their higher-quality Mexican cacao. The Cabildo further attacked a cacao monopoly in 1635, specifically targeting "a few rich *vecinos* [neighbors] of this city" for buying up all of the cacao at the ports and hoarding it to raise prices. In 1636 the Cabildo outlawed the mixing of cacao beans of varying quality because the practice confused purchasers.[a]

Benito Enríquez, eight *fanegas* sent by Pedro de Campos, as well as his own cargo of one hundred *fanegas*, all on consignment of converso Antonio Méndez Chillón. Francisco Franco de Moreira imported and distributed cacao from Venezuela. Manuel López Nuñez controlled the tax on cacao. Luis de Burgos, at age sixty-three or sixty-four, purchased a store that specialized in cacao, chocolate, and sugar. When he was arrested in 1645, his shop was sequestered by the Inquisition. They left its manager, Juan de Acosta, in charge. Even when Burgos was finally released, the Inquisition tribunal kept the store. The Burgos store inventory included cacao that had been sourced from Maracaibo, Venezuela; Guayaquil, Ecuador; and Soconusco, Mexico. Another crypto-Jew and chocolate retailer, Luis Núñez, acquired a chocolate store in 1642 and was shortly thereafter arrested. In the records of the auto-da-fé of March 30, 1648, we learn about a grower of cocoa beans in Zacatula, forty-year-old Melchor Rodríguez López, who had been born in Portugal and became a resident of Mexico.[9] Manuel Fernandez, whose father was accused of Judaizing by the Inquisition in Toledo in 1649, testified that a converso, Francisco Díaz,

> had a store of chocolate and luxuries on the plaza of Anton Martin.... Diaz brought him into a room behind the store, and being alone, offered him a *xic* (*jicara* [meaning "cup"]) of chocolate and then explained to him the rules of Moses.[10]

Antonio Méndez Chillón, one of the wealthiest Jews sought out by the Mexican Inquisition, carried on a very sophisticated cacao trade. He had come to Mexico from Angola in southern Africa in 1629 and settled in Veracruz, becoming a leading importer of Venezuelan cacao to New Spain. His crypto-Jewish agents and merchants in Gibraltar as well as Caracas and Maracaibo bartered for cacao and monitored the fluctuations in price, quality, and availability of the cacao beans.[11] Following his arrest, the Inquisition tried to confiscate a load of cacao from his manager, Orozco, but since it had not yet been transmitted into his ownership, the Veracruz *maestre* (master) would not turn it over to the tribunal, though the Inquisition kept trying until 1664.

When the Inquisition officials inventoried Méndez Chillón's home after his arrest, they found immense wealth, including 8,486 Mexican silver pesos, 349 gold Spanish doubloons, and trunks of silver, jewelry, tableware, gold, and pearls. Chillón had sought to protect his illegitimate children from the investigations against the Jews. He hid his seven-year-old daughter at the oldest convent in Mexico City, putting a house in Veracruz into her name to secure the payments to the convent. Perhaps because he had not been found to have networked with other crypto-Jews nor observed any Jewish rituals, his imprisonment was shorter than those of others. He was nevertheless deported to Cadiz, Spain, in 1647, and sadly, the Inquisition confiscated the monies he had set aside for his children.[12]

Jews Ritualize Chocolate

As I plunged further into these Inquisition reports about people such as Méndez Chillón, I saw that Jews not only took an active role in the cacao trade in the New World, but they also secreted it into their undercover Jewish ritual life. Mexican crypto-Jews used chocolate for welcoming the Sabbath because wine was scarce in New Spain. For Jews attempting to follow Jewish dietary laws, the pareve nature of the local chocolate drink prepared without milk lent itself to the separation of milk and meat; it could be enjoyed with a milk meal or a meat meal. Chocolate seeped into important Jewish customs and celebratory meals for holidays and life-cycle events. Beatriz Enríquez and her sister would not even drink their daily chocolate until they had prayed each morning. The same Beatriz recalled that following the private negotiations for an engagement, the entire family joined together for chocolate drinking.[13]

This chocolate use extended to sad times as well. Holding vigil for the dying Doña Blanca Méndez de Rivera, her daughters and granddaughters spent a day in reflection and prayer, fortified by a special meal of chocolate and pickled fish brought from Veracruz by the merchant Mathias Rodríguez de Olivera, as Margarita de Rivera recalled for the Inquisition (1644).[14] The proceedings of the trial of Gabriel de Granada (October 1642) report his testimony about the period of mourning for his father, Manuel de Granada:

> Gabriel sent to her the hard boiled eggs and chocolate which was eaten by the said widow and her children. During the six days preceding the said seventh, ... sent chocolate one day of the said six.[15]

At funerals, the Mexican Váez family (1630s) ate chocolate, raisins, almonds, salad, and homemade bread, but never any meat.[16]

Chocolate even accompanied meals associated with the beginning and end of the fast of Yom Kippur (Day of Atonement). This may have been the most frequently observed of the holy days, so much so that many secret Jews even risked writing down the exact date. The theme of atonement resonated for them, as they felt themselves constantly sinning through their public profession of Catholicism. On the other hand, Rosh Hashanah (the New Year) was rarely commemorated,[17] it being easier to hide a day of deprivation than Rosh Hashanah's celebratory meals and rituals. Gaspar Váez broke his 1640 Yom Kippur fast with chocolate, eggs, salad, pies, fish, and olives.[18] Isabel de Rivera testified on October 7, 1642, that a year before, on Yom Kippur, Doña Juana, who was married to the wealthy Simón Váez Sevilla, sent "thick chocolate and sweet things made in her house."[19] Around 1645 Gabriel de Granada and his family washed down their pre-fast meal with chocolate, having dined on fish, eggs, and vegetables. Others reported that they preceded the Day of Atonement with fruit and chocolate and that they broke the fast with chocolate and similar treats.[20] Beatriz Enríquez, at the age of twenty-two, testified that when her husband left for long business trips she took advantage of her sadness to hide her abstinence from chocolate and food on *día grande* (big day), or Yom Kippur:

> From the window she pretended to be crying over the absence of her husband and with this suffering she was able to hide from her *negras* (Negro servants) the fact that she ate nothing and did not drink chocolate that day.[21]

In order not to eat on fast days, Amaro Díaz Martaraña and his wife Margarita Moreira would stage a falling out with each other in the middle of the day. She testified under torture that when chocolate was brought to them, they would pretend to be offended and spill it on the servants. They reconciled in the evening.[22] Isabel Duarte told the Inquisition that she had tested Diego Díaz to see if he shared her religious secret of Jewish identity by offering him chocolate at different times, including on some fast days. When he refused, she asked him why. His reply, she told the Inquisition, was that "it was stupid to ask him why." To offer chocolate at times when it was proscribed and to receive a refusal in response was to communicate through a coded language.[23] Jews developed such subterfuges to avoid being outed for drinking chocolate on Catholic fast days or not drinking chocolate on Jewish fast days.

Crypto-Jews who marked minor fasts and penitential fasts established by the Jewish calendar may have been aware of the discussions in the Catholic Church as to whether the Lenten fast permits chocolate. These debates centered on whether to define chocolate as food or as drink. While drinking was permitted in Catholic fasting, it was not in Jewish fast observances. Jews generally sided with those of the Christian view that drinking chocolate broke the fast and maintained the Jewish view that it broke a Jewish fast.[24]

Such fasts were also framed with meals that included chocolate. Attempting a fast, fifteen-year-old Símón de León confessed to the Inquisition in Mexico in 1647 that he ran away from home because he had broken a fast that his father had ordered him to keep. When he could not bear the hunger any longer, he asked his sister Antonia for some chocolate.[25] One Juan de León and his Mexican converso friends preceded their fasts with chocolate and broke the fasts with chocolate, among other foods. They also followed local colonial Mexican custom and finished their meals with a cup of the festive drink, chocolate.[26] When, two weeks after Beatriz Enríquez married Tomás Núñez de Peralta in 1637, he left on a trading trip, she did an *ayuno* (fast) for him for the first time alone at the age of nineteen. She could not complete the fast fully, taking "a little bit of chocolate."[27]

Family members testified against each other using chocolate in their accusations. Fernando Rodríguez, a successful Jewish merchant who traded in cacao and slaves, owned a chocolate service of small silver spoons, silver saucers called *cestillos*, and deep clay cups known as *tecomates,* which he and his wife used for their daily chocolate drinking except on Jewish fast days. On such fast days, he dissembled to his servants that the price of cacao was too high and that he could not afford to drink it. As one of his adult sons testified to the Inquisitors, there were days when his parents skipped their daily chocolate: "I didn't see them eat all day nor drink chocolate as they always did on other days." Another son, Francisco López, testifying against his brother, mentioned that "a day before Holy Week," the brother had not had his chocolate "as was his custom" but went off and spent the day by himself in his father's warehouse on the beach, suggesting that he avoided the chocolate in order to observe some Jewish ritual, perhaps Passover's ritual of the fast of the firstborn son.[28]

Chocolate Nourishes Inquisition Jails

Even once Jews were arrested by the Inquisition, chocolate continued to be part of their experience during the capture and in jail. Muleteers hired to transport suspected crypto-Jews to trial drank chocolate and listed it as a reimbursable expense. Those who captured Rodrigo Serrano in Veracruz in September 1646 purchased chocolate in each place where they spent the night, planning ahead for the next morning's breakfast chocolate. The Holy Office mentions payment to Jesuits for "writing and occupying themselves with other internal business, ... they have been given some alms [for the purchase] of their chocolate."[29]

Chocolate lubricated jail life, according to Inquisition records, and was used commonly as a gift, bribe, barter, or jailhouse commodity. Jewish prisoners received chocolate, sometimes several times during each day, often delivered by servants or slaves. For some, this helped pass the time and broke up the boredom. Ana Suárez, who for a while shared a cell with her mother, Rafaela Enríquez, reported to the Inquisition that in the morning after their chocolate, Rafaela had carried on prohibited conversations with other prisoners. In other testimony, Simón Váez Sevilla repeatedly begged to see his son and his wife, Juana Enríquez, express-ing grave worry about her. When called again to appear before the inquisitors for his twelfth hearing in April 1644, he first requested some chocolate with sugar and only then asked to see his son and his wife. A slave, Francisco de la Cruz, fingered a prisoner to whom he had secretly delivered messages, identifying him as the occupant of the cell above the chocolate room. Beatriz Enríquez gave a Congolese slave, Sebastián Domingo, two pesos, explaining that he should buy her chocolate but intending to really pay him to help her deliver messages to her husband in jail. Yet another slave entered an Inquisition cell to find the prisoner perched on a bag of chocolate.

Chocolate Bribes

Chocolate smoothed life outside of the Inquisition jails as well. Diego Correa and his wife, Catalina de Rivera, who knew many of Mexico's crypto-Jews and could identify them, owned a small stall selling chocolate in the Cathedral Plaza. When the Inquisition arrested Blanca Méndez de Rivera and her daughters (May 17 and 19, 1642) to get their testimony, the Enríquez women called upon Correa, hoping to enlist his help in preventing his wife, her sisters, and their mother from selling them out. Correa testified that Juana Enríquez had given him a gift of six *libras* (pounds) of chocolate. Another woman, also worried about being reported to the Inquisition by Correa's wife, gave him "a little chocolate and a loaf of sugar."[30]

Chocolate continued to be important even after the Inquisition sentenced Judaizers to return to Spain to be dealt with by the Inquisition there. When Simón Váez Sevilla and his family emerged from penitential cells (1649), they were commanded by the Inquisition officials to leave Mexico City immediately. They departed for Seville with a cargo of chocolate, 5,000 pesos, jewelry, and silver.[31]

Mark and I found a plentiful trail of chocolate in Spain; it surprisingly led us to the complexities of Jews, religion, and chocolate in New Spain. Delving into the Inquisition records surfaced information about how chocolate both jeopardized the lives of Jews there and also enriched their businesses. It permeated their ritual observances and sustained them in jail. An authentic Spanish route of chocolate would explore the tensions between threat and nourishment for Jews represented by chocolate at this time. For Christians, chocolate pitted those who delighted in the treat against those who saw it as a source of pagan sorcery. This story of chocolate, Jews, and religion branched off into other destinations of the Sephardi migrations, including North America.

Chocolate Pudding

Based on the 1871 Esther Levy recipe from the first Jewish cookbook in America, this updated version transports our appetites to the American colonial period.[a] Warning: This is actually a cake.

Ingredients:

1 cup milk chocolate or dark chocolate, crumbled
5 large eggs, separated
1 cup sugar
1 cup graham cracker crumbs

Instructions:

Preheat the oven to 375°F. Lightly grease an 8-inch springform pan. Melt the chocolate in a large heatproof bowl set over a pan of simmering water; remove from the heat to cool. Beat together the egg yolks and sugar. In a separate bowl, beat the egg whites. Fold the egg yolks and sugar into the cooled chocolate. Fold in the graham cracker crumbs. Fold the egg whites into the chocolate mix. Pour the batter into the prepared pan. Bake for 30 minutes. Cool in the pan. To serve, cut into wedges.

Quantity: 6–8 servings

Chapter Three

Jews Dip into Chocolate in the American Colonial Period

Jewish shopkeepers specialized in cocoa and chocolate which they secured in large quantities from their co-religionists in Curaçao.... Chocolate in fact may have been a Sephardic Jewish specialty.[1]

THIS PASSING MENTION ABOUT THE SEPHARDI chocolate specialists in North America from the work of preeminent American Jewish historian Jacob Rader Marcus remained buried amid his many pages of writings. Perhaps chocolate was less popular. Or perhaps so much other fascinating material in Marcus's writings drew attention. In previous decades, historical themes of assimilation and anti-Semitism were certainly more compelling. Yet as Marcus noted, the Jewish chocolate trail winds deeply through the North American colonial period, and chocolate was in fact a Sephardi Jewish specialty. Here again the Sephardi trading network imported and shipped cocoa beans, as well as manufactured chocolate.

Hunting for Chocolate Up the Hudson

To trace the Sephardi diffusion of chocolate to colonial North America, Mark and I packed our barely awake Brooklyn-based adult kids into a rental car for what our daughter called a "family fun day" of chocolate research. It was a stormy New York June day, and our plan included an outing to the Gomez Mill House, the oldest extant Jewish homestead in North America that was built in 1714 as a trading post by the New York Jewish community's leading Sephardi family. In a perfect mix of history, chocolate, and family frolicking, we quibbled over the front seat, got lost, ate from each other's plates, and explored Gomez family chocolate roots in Newburgh, New York, about sixty miles north of New York City. The Gomez family members were among the several colonial and Revolutionary period North American Jews who engaged in the manufacture, retail, and consumption of cacao and chocolate, primarily in New York City and Newport, Rhode Island. Indeed, many of these pioneering Jewish chocolate endeavors preceded the beginning of the Baker's Chocolate Company, which has billed itself as "America's Oldest" and "evolved into the first branded 'Baker's Chocolate' product in 1780."[2] However, there were certainly many others making chocolate prior to Baker, including Sephardi cousins Gomez and Lopez.

The fort-like stone cabin in Newburgh, now listed on the National Register of Historic Places, was intended primarily for trading fur. This first Jewish settlement up the Hudson River—established by patriarch Luis (Lewis) Moses Gomez— was probably run by his sons Daniel and David Gomez. Born in Madrid, Luis and his mother escaped the Inquisition to France, possibly even Bayonne. According to Gomez family tradition, his father, Isaac Gomez, a Spanish nobleman and a favorite at court, was warned by the king that the Inquisition was about to arrest him and confiscate his estate. He quickly sent his wife and infant son, Moses, to France to secure their safety, along with "money, jewels and plate." It is said that the "Luis/Lewis" was added to Moses's name in gratitude to the French king for allowing him refuge in France. In 1706 Luis obtained a letter of denization (bestowing some privileges of a British subject) now displayed at the Mill House, which enabled him and his family to live in New York, where he purchased land and became a very successful merchant.[3] Luis bought the Hudson River plot at the intersection of several Indian trails leading to a holy site near a spring, which came to be known as Jews Creek. He built the house at least six miles from other habitations. The mill could have been used for grinding chocolate, but most likely the outpost's purpose was fur trading.

The Gomez Mill House in Newburgh, New York— the oldest Jewish house still in existence.

At least five members within two generations of the Gomez family enjoyed chocolate connections in New York City: Mordecai (1688–1750), his wife, Rebecca (1713–1801), his brother Daniel (1695–1780), Mordecai and Rebecca's son, Moses (1744–1826), and their nephew, Isaac (1768–1831).[4] In particular, Rebecca Gomez stands out not only for her retail advertising but also as the only known woman to manufacture chocolate in the colonies.

The Gomez family's chocolate business was built on a granular chocolate, which was plentiful and commonly imbibed as a beverage. There were no chocolate ice creams, chocolate candy bars, chocolate truffles, chocolate cakes, or chocolate chip cookies at this time. The proximity of the colonies to cacao bean sources in Central America kept prices reasonable while Britain levied high taxes on chocolate. Some countries, such as France, established monopolies on chocolate. By contrast, in the colonies there were fifty or more chocolate makers, with approximately twenty-four in Philadelphia by 1776. Surprisingly, America had more chocolate per capita than Europe did. Benjamin Franklin even sold chocolate in his Philadelphia print shop.[5]

Cacao beans first arrived in North America sometime in the seventeenth century. Colonial Williamsburg food specialist James Gay speculated that Jews may have brought chocolate to North America, arguing that conversos from New Spain, Brazil's Recife, or Amsterdam brought it.[6] Jews from these settings would have been exposed to chocolate, consumed chocolate, and traded chocolate. In Newport, Rhode Island, Aaron Lopez used chocolate at Passover and distributed it as *tzedakah* (charity) gifts. It was also thought that chocolate provided nutrition on a fast day during a cholera epidemic. Dr. Daniel L. M. Peixotto argued in August 1832 that Jews in New York should not observe the fast day of the ninth of

Jews Retailed Chocolate before Baker's

While the Baker's Chocolate Company counts its first recorded sale of Baker's-made chocolate in Boston on July 2, 1772,[a] there were many sales of chocolate by Jewish grocers and others prior to that, including by Nathaniel Abraham,[b] Hyman Levy,[c] Jonas Phillips,[d] as well as the following:

- [1752] Nathans and Hart included chocolate in the store price list for grocery items in their shop in Halifax, Nova Scotia.[e]
- [1760] Isaac Delyon, Savannah, Georgia, wrote to Barnard Gratz in Philadelphia requesting a number of items, including "25 lb chokolet."[f]
- [1761] Joseph Simon, Lancaster, Pennsylvania, ordered from Barnard Gratz "one barrel of good muscavado unrefined sugar, 24 lbs of chocolate, 25 lbs of good coffee."[g]

Av, Tishah B'Av, but rather "they should be permitted to take a light meal of coffee, tea, or cocoa with dry toast"[7] and thus build their immunity to the epidemic.

Jewish trading of chocolate began in New York. Since the first known business record of the Jew Isaac Marquez importing twenty-five pounds of chocolate in New York in 1701, Jewish merchants in this period profited from this chocolate culture.[8] Originally from Denmark, Marquez died in New York in 1706. New York customs records in the decade following 1701 list their cargoes as consisting mainly of "cocoa, rum, wine, fur, and fabrics." The customs records for cargoes in New York include cacao for the ten years after 1715.[9] Another Jew, Nathan Simson, engaged in significant trade of cacao, shipping more than thirty-three thousand pounds between 1710 and 1721. As early as 1728, the Jew Rodrigo Pacheco imported thirty thousand pounds of cacao through New York's port, the equivalent of approximately one-third of the total annual import through New York in the late 1760s in the period of what has been called the New York chocolate boom.[10]

These Jews imported cacao from distant as well as nearby ports. At times they ran into legal difficulties. Sometimes they did business with family. The cacao came primarily from Caracas, Venezuela, as well as Curaçao, Jamaica, and Haiti. It was also sourced from other colonies. Jewish merchant Rachel Luis imported cacao from Curaçao. Simson secured cacao that had been imported to South Carolina. In 1734 one of Rodrigo Pacheco's ships sailed from New York to Curaçao, where it loaded cacao that was exchanged for rice in Charleston, South Carolina. Then it continued on to Falmouth, England. He also traded to Jamaica, through New York, Lisbon, Genoa, and Barcelona. Between 1702 and 1704 the Jew Joseph Bueno, who was awarded his license to trade and traffic in New York in 1683, was buying large quantities of cacao in Newport, Rhode Island, dealing with

"24,000 wt (pounds) coko [cocoa]." Bueno shipped cacao to England from Newport on the sloop *Mary*. In at least one case, his captain attempted to circumvent the law. Claiming that his ship leaked, Bueno's captain unloaded in New York, storing the cacao in Bueno's warehouse rather than at the customs shed, purportedly awaiting an increase in the potential price of the cacao. Bueno was charged and fined. Another court case concerning cacao arose when Moses Levy sued Nathan Simson and Jacob Franks, executors of Samuel Levy's estate, claiming that Samuel Levy had sold him spoiled cacao with salt in it in 1722. In 1753 Daniel Gomez wrote from New York to Aaron Lopez in Newport inquiring about the price of cacao and at the same time notified Lopez of the death of his wife. Gomez's business with Lopez's father-in-law, Jacob R. Rivera, included chocolate.[11] Jews enjoyed a far-ranging, intercolonial, and intercontinental chocolate trade that was also familial.

What Did Alexander Hamilton Drink?

Our nation's founders—Washington, Jefferson, Adams, Hamilton, and others—fortified themselves for the battles of country building partly through their chocolate drinking.

Alexander Hamilton's rival, Thomas Jefferson, was quite a chocolate fan. Not only did he purchase chocolate in 1775, but Jefferson, seeking freshness, quality, and healthfulness in his chocolate, also hoped for greater cocoa imports. In 1785 he wrote to John Adams from Paris:

To increase its consumption would be to permit it to be brought to us immediately from the country of its growth. By getting it good in quality, and cheap in price, the superiority of the article both for health and nourishment will soon give it the same preference over tea & coffee in America which it has in Spain where they can get it by a single voiage [sic].[a]

He was so enamored of chocolate drinking that when he was president he commissioned a silver chocolate pot inspired by the design of Roman artifacts he had seen in France.[b]

John and Abigail Adams also loved the chocolate that they tasted in Spain. As Adams put it to his daughter, "I have never met with few Things more remarkable than the Chocolate which is the finest I ever saw."[c] His diary (for 1779 December 10 Fryday [sic]) records:

> *Breakfasted for the first time on Spanish Chocolate which fully answered the fame it had acquired in the World. Till that time I had no Idea that any thing that had the Appearance of Chocolate and bore that name could be so delicious and salubrious.*[d]

In 1779, in Spain, he observed, "Ladies drink chocolate in the Spanish fashion. Each lady took a cup of hot chocolate and drank it, and then cakes and bread and butter were served."[e]

In London six years later, Abigail Adams noted to their son, John Quincy Adams, that chocolate was served for breakfast.[f] The future president and first lady savored the European chocolate culture of their day.

President George Washington and his wife, Martha, were well acquainted with chocolate. He regularly purchased it, starting in 1757 when he ordered twenty pounds from Thomas Knox, a British merchant.[g] Over the years he bought quantities varying from one pound to the fifty pounds delivered three months before his death in 1799. Chocolate was part of each breakfast in their Mount Vernon home, with Martha dispensing the beverages of chocolate, coffee, and tea.[h] When Washington was elected to the House of Burgesses in 1774, the celebration featured chocolate.[i] That year the Washingtons ordered a silver chocolate pot from the London silversmith John Carter II as a wedding gift for Martha's son, John Parke Custis, and his bride, Eleanor Calvert.[j] In 1789, President Washington placed an order for Martha: "she will ... thank you to get 20 lb. of the shells of Cocoa nuts, if they can be had of the Chocolate makers."[k]

Martha's nephew by marriage, Burgess Ball, requested two or three bushels of chocolate shells for cocoa tea, mentioning how well it suits his wife Fanny's appetite. She "frequently drank Chocolate ... at Mount Vernon, as my Wife thinks it agreed with her better than any other Breakfast."[l]

Chocolate makers joined the five to six thousand craftsmen, masters, journeymen, and apprentices who marched in the Federal Procession of July 23, 1788, to celebrate the formation of the United States and the ratification of the Constitution. The chocolate makers carried a scroll decorated with two men drinking chocolate and a hand chocolate mill.[m]

With all of this chocolate consumption by his peers, it would be no surprise that Alexander Hamilton was likely enjoying it, too. Hamilton's chocolate doppelganger, physician Dr. Alexander Hamilton (1712–1756), imbibed breakfast chocolate. The Scottish-born Hamilton recorded his travels through Delaware, Pennsylvania, New York, New Jersey, Connecticut, Rhode Island, Massachusetts, and New Hampshire; his journal mentions drinking chocolate for breakfast at least six times over a couple of months. At one visit he gifted a pound of chocolate to his countrywoman, Mrs. Blackater.[n]

Certainly Alexander's circumstances would have made it politically correct to drink chocolate following the Boston Tea Party. While secretary of the Treasury, Hamilton raised tariffs on chocolate in 1792.[o] The local chocolate trade and drinking customs likely had permeated his work as a clerk at Kortright and Cruger import/export firm in St. Croix in the Caribbean. In those early years of our country, chocolate was foundational, and that was probably true for Alexander Hamilton as well.[p]

Colonial Chocolate Habits

This trade supported a daily chocolate habit throughout the colonies. Hot chocolate made from "cocoa nuts" or "chocolate nutts" (cacao beans) dressed up breakfast or supper, sometimes composing the full meal.[12] Coffeehouses and chocolate houses were as fashionable in the colonies as they were in England.[13] Ships' crews savored chocolate provisions on board, whether purchased by individual sailors, or the captain for his use, or provided for the crew. While the governments of England and Holland sentenced people to hang for stealing one pound of chocolate, it was so reasonably priced in North America that it was frequently dispensed to soldiers, prisoners, and poor people.[14] Chocolate drinking became even more popular in America around the time of the 1773 Boston Tea Party as an accessible and obvious alternative to politicized tea. James Green's advertisement reads, "Coffee and chocolate ... instead of tea, to which article we have bid farewell."[15] An English traveler reported in 1775, "Last Night [Twelfth Night] I went to the Ball.... A cold supper, Punch, Wines, Coffe [sic] and Chocolate but no Tea. This is a forbidden herb."[16] Philip Fithian, traveling in West Virginia as a Presbyterian circuit rider in December 1775, wrote, "Tea is out of the question; it is almost Treason against the country to mention it, much more drink it."[17] And, "Mr. Aaron Lopez, owner of the ship *Jacob*, Capt. Peters, has assured us in writing that said ship has not India TEA on board and that he thinks himself happy in giving such assurance."[18] In 1797, a group known as the Manufacturers of Chocolate appealed to the United States Fourth Congress complaining about the high duty laid on the import of cocoa. As a result, Congress repealed the additional two-cent duty on the cocoa.[19] This kept chocolate inexpensive and accessible to all as a common household item.

Our colonial chocoholics did not simply toss a packet of chemicals, sugar, and processed cocoa into boiling water. Painstaking preparation of this early American chocolate began with the import of the beans, which were then generally purchased at local dry goods stores.

James Gay explained the multistep, tedious process to me when I interviewed him in 2008. The tasks of tending and roasting the cocoa beans over a fire, shelling each one individually, grinding the chocolate nibs with sugar (sometimes along with cinnamon and/or other spices) while warming them over a chocolate stone with a roller, and then cooling the chocolate into hard tablets was often relegated to servants or slaves. It resulted in a drinking chocolate similar to that found elsewhere at that time and today in Mexico and Guatemala.[20] These solidified chocolate tablets, wrapped in used newspapers or in rags of questionable sources, were often stored randomly, likely absorbing the smells of sometimes fetid foodstuffs or rancid products.

Colonial Chocolate Recipes

Mars sought to reproduce the taste and look of colonial American chocolate in its *American Heritage Chocolate*, "Handmade chocolate inspired by an authentic colonial recipe."

To Make Chocolate: [1796]

Take six Pounds of cocoa-nuts, one of anise-seeds, four ounces of long pepper, one of cinnamon, a quarter of a pound of almonds, one ounce of pistachios, as much achiote as will make it the colour of brick, three grains of musk, and as much ambergris, six pounds of loaf-sugar, one ounce of nutmegs, dry and beat them, and searce [sift] them through a fine sieve; your almonds must be beat to a paste and mixed with the other ingredients; then dip your sugar in orange-flower or rose water, and put it in a skillet on a very gentle charcoal fire; then put in the spice and stew it well together, then the musk and ambergris, then put in the cocoa-nuts last of all, then achiote, wetting it with the water the sugar was dipt in; stew all these very well together over a hotter fire than before; then take it up and put it into boxes, or what form you like, and set it to dry in a warm place: the pistachios and almonds must be a little beat in a mortar, then ground on a stone.[a]

Larger fifty-pound chocolate quantities were generally sold in boxes.[21] Some households kept twenty-five to fifty pounds of chocolate on hand, which would have supplied a family of four with a customary daily hot chocolate for about a month. Before indulging, the hardened chocolate required further mixing with water and sugar using a special stirrer (*molinillo*, or mill) while heating in the chocolate pot, with its special opening in the top for the stirrer. The hot chocolate might have then been served in unique cups especially for drinking chocolate. Such specialized tools also were available at local dry goods shops. Colonial chocolate was very slow food.

These colonial chocolate experiences also leaked into religious life for better and worse. A vignette from this period relates that in 1690 Pilgrims traveled to Plymouth Rock via Amsterdam and stayed in a house near the city's biggest chocolate houses. The Pilgrims termed that chocolate "the Devil's food." Later, a chocolate cake became popular in Amsterdam that the local bakers named "Devil's Food." In this early American religious mind-set chocolate represented evil, perhaps because it indulged the senses and distracted from work and worship.[22] At least one New England moralistic ascetic charged "Serious Christians in the Professing Country to think of forgoing amongst other Things, Chocolate."[23]

Domestic colonial chocolate imbibing seeped happily into other ecclesiastical settings, perhaps influenced by the reports of British royal chocolate piety, as in this dispatch from London, 1761, about King George III:

An American colonial pantry boasts a chocolate pot.

> His majesty riseth at five o'clock every morning, lights
> his own candle ... dresseth himself, then calleth a servant
> to bring him bread, butter and chocolate. At six he goeth
> to chapel where he hath morning prayers in the most
> religious manner.[24]

Several ministers enjoyed their chocolate. Chocolate bolstered
the daily routine of Thomas Prince (1687–1758), reverend of
Boston's Old South Church and a historian of New England.
After his graduation from Harvard and his wedding, the
reverend's daily routine included rising at 5:00 a.m., reading
the Bible in his study, waking the rest of the family at 6:30
a.m., gathering all for family prayers, and enjoying "only the
Porringer [pewter dish] of chocolate for Breakfast."[25] Military
chaplains were rationed a certain amount of chocolate: "Chaplain of a brigade shall be entitled to draw only six galons of
Rum, either four pounds of Coffee or Chocolate ... monthly."[26]
The diary of Samuel Sewall—who studied for the ministry,
became a chief justice of Massachusetts, and was a judge at
the Salem witch trials—noted that his pastoral ministrations
bundled visits and sermons with gifts of chocolate.[27] Sewall
himself drank chocolate on occasion.[28] Chocolate was used in
houses of mourning as well. When Poulis Freer died in 1802,
his heirs served chocolate at the time of the funeral.[29] Another
minister complained that he could not maintain his standard of
living, including his customary chocolate drinking. His protest
to the *Boston Evening Post*, signed by "Your humble Servant,
T.W.," lamented:

> Upwards of 40 years ago I was ordained Pastor of a Church
> in ... and by the unanimous Vote of my People had settled
> on me ... with which I could buy ... Chocolate.... You will
> readily perceive by comparing these Accounts together
> that the same Articles one with another have risen more
> than seven and an half for one since my first Settlement
> with my People, whereas they could never yet be prevailed

on to raise my Salary more than three for one.... And I may
venture to say, this is the Truth of the Case with respect to
most of the Ministers throughout the Province.[30]

For these religious leaders financial challenges and shortages
were identified through the ability to buy daily chocolate
supplies.

Chocolate nourished these men of God and seemingly
enhanced their ministries. These chocolate customs were enabled
by the significant cacao trade and chocolate manufacturing of
people such as Aaron Lopez and the Gomez family members.

The Gomez Chocolate Dynasty

The Gomez family led the Sephardi and secular community
of New York. The state assembly met at Mordecai Gomez's
house.[31] Mordecai and Daniel served as Spanish interpreters
to the admiralty and supreme courts, Daniel serving for some
twenty years at this post.[32] The house of Luis Gomez was
taxed at nearly ten times the value of the Jews' rented house
of worship.[33] At New York's Congregation Shearith Israel,
the Gomez family enjoyed the most prestigious seats. Isaac
bequeathed silver ornaments for the Torah (scroll of the Five
Books of Moses) to his eldest son, Mordecai.[34] Moses Gomez
laid the first stone of the new synagogue, and Luis Moses
Gomez, along with his son Mordecai, signed the contract
with the mason. The affluent Gomez family's donation was
the highest from any single family.[35] Lewis Moses Gomez also
contributed the most generous gift from a Jewish community

Jews Traded Cacao from Philadelphia

[1801] Simon and Hyman Gratz worked as commission merchants,
as real estate brokers, and in the very successful shipping trade
out of Philadelphia. In their trade with Brazil they imported fifteen
thousand pounds of St. Domingo cacao.[a]

member to the Trinity Church steeple. Of the twenty-five Sephardi members of the leadership committee of Shearith Israel, twenty were part of the Gomez family.[36] Mordecai, Daniel, and David, along with father Luis Moses Gomez, appeared in the title for the Jewish cemetery in 1729. The northwest gallery of the synagogue's women's section, called the *banco*, was reserved for the Gomez family women, symbolizing their wealth and stature.[37]

Daniel Gomez engaged in a large and lucrative business in New York, trading with the West Indies, Madeira, Barbados, Curaçao, London, and Dublin, and sending 133 ships to Curaçao between 1739 and 1772. He corresponded and traded with Sephardi Jews in these locales.[38]

In addition to retailing chocolate,[39] Daniel Gomez imported more than 20,860 pounds of cacao to New York via Curaçao between 1728 and 1747.[40] In 1759 Gomez advertised boxes of drinking chocolate for sale at the corner of Bruling's Slip in New York City.[41]

When Mordecai Gomez died in 1750, he left several chocolate accoutrements in his estate inventory, including "16 chocolate cupps, whole and broken, 1 chocolate pott; 2 boxes Chocolate 50 lbs each and 6 Surnis (840 pounds) Coco [Surinam],"[42] suggesting his personal use in addition to his commerce.

For many years Moses Gomez earned his living as a chocolate maker. In 1788 he announced his hunt for his runaway "indented servant" who was "used to chocolate making."[43] Moses Gomez and company also advertised the private sale of "1 ton of Carracas cocoa."[44]

In 1815 Isaac Gomez's advertisement for smaller quantities of chocolate, "Isaac Gomez Jr. and Co 6 boxes chocolate," ran at least forty-three times.[45]

Rebecca Gomez sold chocolate, as did other women of the day. However, she was the only woman known to manufacture it. The youngest child of Abraham Haim Lucena, she married

Mordecai in New York on May 4, 1741.[46] Rebecca Gomez plied her wholesale and retail chocolate made at the "Chocolate Manufactory" through newspaper advertisements.[47] Rebecca used promotions such as these to further her endeavors:

[1779] Rebecca Gomez at the Chocolate Manufactory
Corner of Ann and Nassau-Street
HAS FOR SALE ...
Own manufactured Chocolate, warranted free from any
    sediments and pure.
Great allowance made to those who buy to sell again.[48]

[1780] Rebecca Gomez
Has for sale at the CHOCOLATE Manufactory
No. 14 upper end Nassau-Street between ...
SUPERFINE warranted CHOCOLATE, wholesale and
    retail ...[49]

[1781] Chocolate
Manufactured in the best manner, warranted fine and
    good, to be sold wholesale and retail,
by REBECCA GOMEZ at the Chocolate Manufactory,
    No. 57, Nassau Street between Commissary Butler's
    and the Brick Meeting ...[50]

[1781] CHOCOLATE
WARRANTED fine and good, wholesale and retail,
    at reasonable rates, by REBECCA GOMEZ, at the
    chocolate manufactory, No. 57, Nassau Street ...[51]

She reflected a mid-eighteenth-century interest in quality and increased focus on one product: "superfine, free from any sediments and pure."

Rebecca Gomez's business savvy led her to advertise about her unique chocolate, reflecting a growing sophistication about marketing. Using her family reputation and name to good effect, she not only ventured into business but also participated in a trend to specialization. Rebecca's manufacturing marked shifts in commerce toward industrialization in the decades of the 1770s and 1780s, perhaps using Mordecai's snuff mills and houses on Ann Street.[52] Overall, the Gomez family endeavors in chocolate trade, retail, and personal consumption exemplified the general popularity and availability of chocolate in the colonial period, as well as Sephardi interests in this market.

Aaron Lopez Sips, Sells, and Ships Chocolate

From his British wallpapered, wood-timbered office overlooking the wharf at Newport, Rhode Island, Aaron Lopez used labeled pigeonholes in the rafters to monitor his many vessels and related businesses, including that of chocolate.[53] There the multigenerational Gomez gusto for all areas of the chocolate business in New York mingled with that of their Newport cousin through their Sephardi roots, marriage vows, religious ties, and financial interests. Though Lopez's chocolate business differed from that of his New York coreligionists, he too was steeped in chocolate manufacturing, retail, and trade.

This prominent Sephardi Rhode Island trader of the eighteenth century was born in 1731 in Portugal. Known as Duarte in the Old Country, he and his family lived publicly as Christians and privately as Jews. Aaron abandoned Portugal to live a full Jewish life in America. He traveled to Curaçao to learn the sperma (whale sperm) process and introduced it to America for the purpose of candle making, arriving in Newport, where his older half-brother, Moses, was already living and setting up shop in 1750. Another Newport merchant, Jacob Rodriguez Rivera, became Aaron's father-in-law in 1763. Although he was refused citizenship in Rhode Island, Aaron became the first Jew to be naturalized in Massachusetts. Until 1765 Lopez's trade was mostly coastal, between Boston, New York, Philadelphia, and Charleston. He expanded across the Atlantic, importing from Bristol, England, to satisfy the American desire for British products while avoiding London prices. By 1767 Lopez had sent at least nine vessels to the West

Indies, shipping livestock, poultry, pickled oysters, candles, naval stores, bricks, lumber, and even silverware; return cargoes brought cocoa, molasses, rum, coffee, and sugar. In 1768 he ran thirty-seven coastal voyages.[54] Lopez's success boomed so that by the time of the American Revolution, he had financial interests in nearly thirty of the one hundred sailing vessels associated with Newport and the transatlantic trade. By the middle of the 1770s, Lopez was the highest taxpayer in Newport and the richest man there.[55] His trading ventures and volume put him on par with the Browns of Providence, benefactors of Brown University.[56]

Even with all of the demands of his business, Lopez maintained his Sabbath observance. He "rigidly observed ... Saturday as holy time," closing from Friday afternoon to Monday morning. Over a three-year period none of his ships left port on a Saturday. He customarily ended his letters, "Sabbath is coming on fast."[57] When he died prematurely in a freak drowning accident, Reverend Ezra Stiles, the president of Yale University, wrote about him:

> In honor and aptitude of commerce there was never a trader in America to equal him. In business he dealt with the highest degree of seriousness and clear-sightedness, showing always an affability in manner, a calm urbanity, an agreeable and sincere courtesy of manners. Without a single enemy, no one is known who was more universally loved.[58]

Lopez's expansive business interests included the cacao bean trade and chocolate manufacturing. As historian Jacob Rader Marcus put it:

> Aaron Lopez ... saw food-processing as ancillary to his involvement in the coastal and West Indian traffic.... The chocolate he secured through outwork was destined for local and North American consumption.[59]

Captains and agents represented Lopez in these endeavors, selling chocolate on his behalf, paying off accounts in cocoa beans, and buying chocolate from others. Lopez also often sold chocolate at his dry goods shop on Thames Street in Newport. His Jewish and non-Jewish customers bought chocolate there every few months, purchasing periodically in small quantities of about one or two pounds and paying about two pounds sterling.[60] Lopez was also buying larger quantities of chocolate, perhaps for his personal use. After the American Revolution, Samuel Wallis of Boston received from Mr. Ezekiel for the account of Mr. Aaron Lopez "five boxes of Chocolate weighing 110 pounds, 110 pounds, 110 pounds, 102 pounds, and 108 pounds totaling 540 pounds ... forty pounds of Chocolate over to fill the Boxes."[61]

There were some Jewish connections to chocolate for Lopez as well. In Newport the reasonably priced chocolate made its

Jewish Estate Inventories: Personal Chocolate Usage

[1708] Jacob Bueno, New York: One hundred bags of cocoa as well as chocolate grinding stones.

[1709] Isaac Pinheiro, New York: Thirty pounds of chocolate, a copper chocolate pot, and ten chocolate cups.

[1725] Abraham de Lucena, New York: One copper chocolate pot.

[1750] Moses Louzada, New York: Four "baggs cocoa."

[1750] Mordecai Gomez, New York: One chocolate pot, sixteen chocolate cups, two boxes of chocolate of fifty pounds each, and six "srunes [British measure of approximately 140 pounds] coco."

[1782] Aaron Lopez, Newport: Fifty pounds of chocolate, eight brown china chocolate bowls, eleven turtle-shell chocolate bowls, and four and a half dozen chocolate and cake pans.

[1813] Michael Gratz, Philadelphia: Plate chocolate pot.[a]

way into *tzedakah* gifts, which Lopez distributed on behalf of the Jewish community. In March 1765 he organized "*sedakah* [charity] ... delivered [to] Mrs. Lazarus towards her support 14 pounds of rice, a pound of tea and 2 pounds of chocolate."[62]

Again in 1770 the Aaron Lopez account against the synagogue's treasury itemizes "Sedakah Sunries for Judah Abrahams, 28 pounds of bread, an iron pot, a pound of tea, and two pounds of chocolate."[63]

Also, Lopez may have been the first to connect chocolate with Passover. In April 1772, Lopez paid Joseph Pinto for "6 lb Chocolate for Pesah."[64] Maybe he dunked his matzah in it!

The American Revolution caused Lopez significant business losses. In 1779 he described the wartime hardships of the inhabitants of Leicester, Massachusetts, and Newport to a Captain Anthony, noting that they lacked basic food but at least had chocolate:

> The Jews in particular were suffering due to a scarcity of kosher food. They had not tasted any meat, but once in two months. Fish was not to be had, and they were forced to subsist on chocolate and coffee.[65]

Newport and Providence Compete Over Chocolate

Lopez competed in the chocolate manufacturing business with Obadiah Brown of nearby Providence, Rhode Island. Figuring that he could make some extra money by grinding chocolate for his grocery customers, Brown built a water mill in Providence to increase his production and quality, as well as to lower costs. It may have been the first of its kind in Rhode Island or even in America. Brown's mill preceded Dr. Baker's 1764 water mill on the Neponset River by twelve years. When Brown announced this "chocklit" processing to his customers in 1752, he noted his competition in Newport:

> I have been at considerable charge to git a chocklit mill
> going by water which have now completed. I am advised
> ... that you have occasion for a considerable quantity of
> chocklat in your way. I shall be glad to supply you with
> all you have occasion for at ye cheapest rate you can have
> it at New Port or any whair else.[66]

Lopez also had difficulty keeping up with the chocolate makers
of Boston. He was warned in 1780 by Joseph and William
Rotch, his contacts in Boston and Nantucket, that his chocolate
was inferior: "Massachusetts folks not buying Rhode Island
Chocolate as Boston's is better and cheaper."[67] This may have
been because Lopez's chocolate, never branded as uniquely
his, had been hand ground for him by slaves and others in
Newport, resulting in a less finely processed chocolate than that
of machine milled. While the Gomezes and others advertised,
neither Lopez nor Brown offered their chocolate in newspapers.
Nor did they seem concerned with quality or with branding.

Jews and "Negroes" Grind Chocolate

In Newport, several people ground chocolate for Lopez, some of
them Jews and others, per the original documents, "Negroes."
Lopez paid local Jews such as Joseph Pinto and James Lucena
to grind his chocolate by hand. Lopez also hired "Negro
chocolate grinders" Prince Updike, Cornelius Casey, and
Abraham Casey,[68] paying them four to five shillings per pound
of ground chocolate.[69] These "Negroes" were probably freed
slaves or possibly were working to purchase their freedom, as
was customary in Newport.[70]

Rhode Island merchants controlled a significant portion of
the slave trade, though a very small segment of Lopez's trade
was in slaves.[71] Lopez's chocolate grinder, Prince Updike,
derived his name from the family for whom he worked, the
Updikes of Wickford (also known as North Kingstown),
Rhode Island. In 1744 the Updike family may have owned
eleven slaves; one of them, Prince, died in January 1781 and

"Negroes" working for Aaron Lopez probably ground chocolate in this manner.

Jewish Chocolate Grinders Working for Aaron Lopez

[December 1770–August 1771] Joseph Pinto paid off his debts for clothes and food by grinding chocolate.

[1770] Pinto's Negro Cezsar ground in twenty-five, fifty, and one hundred pound amounts.[a]

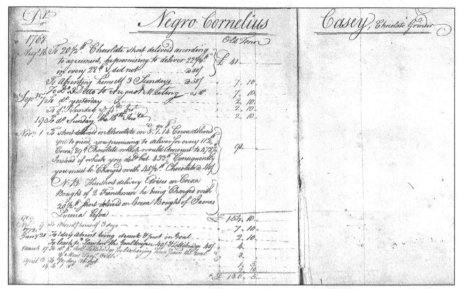

"Negroes" specialized in grinding chocolate for Aaron Lopez and others in colonial Newport, Rhode Island.

was buried in the God's Little Acre section of the Common Burial Ground of Newport.[72]

Chocolate grinders Abraham and Cornelius Casey took the Casey name from a family located in South Kingstown. The Casey chocolate makers were occasionally reprimanded by Lopez for inferior work. Lopez withheld payment to Abraham or Abram for one batch of chocolate in 1768 "as it was only melted over." In 1768 "chocolate grinder" Cornelius Casey was fined by Lopez because he short delivered a couple of times, he absented himself on occasion, and he was one day "being drunk and put in gaol [jail]."[73]

The easy access to slaves and cheap labor in the port of Newport meant that the use of hand grinding prevailed there, while in other communities, such as New York and Providence, alternate milling technologies took over. Newport's few mills served primarily for grinding corn. Had Lopez been using more advanced equipment, he would have probably generated larger quantities and higher quality. Increased opportunities for mechanized manufacture of chocolate in this period paralleled the industrialization that occurred after the American Revolution and accompanied the focus on quality of the product. Nonetheless, chocolate grinding, retailing, and shipping made up a part of his business and apparently his own daily pleasure.

Jacob Rader Marcus was quite correct in calling chocolate a "Sephardic Jewish specialty." Jews of North America's colonial period joined Sephardi Jews in other locales along the route of chocolate's dispersion. These eighteenth-century North American Jewish entrepreneurs dipped deeply into the chocolate concerns of their day. They benefited from cacao, enjoying the personal consumption of the beverage and economic profit from it as a commodity. Long before the Baker's Chocolate Company, these merchants and others, including religious leaders, made and relished their chocolate. Overall, these Jews reflected the commercial interests and technological advances in chocolate of the day, contributing to the pioneering cacao and chocolate enterprises of the colonial period in North America.

Peanut Butter Gelt Cookies

This easy recipe incorporates and maintains the shape of the gelt on top of the cookie. Not only is the cookie delicious with the chocolate, it also highlights the gelt.

Ingredients:

1 cup peanut butter (crunchy or smooth; do not use old-fashioned or freshly ground)
1 cup sugar
1 large egg
Approximately 35 chocolate Chanukah gelt (preferably organic, fair trade)

Instructions:

Preheat the oven to 350°F. Lightly grease two baking sheets. Beat the peanut butter, sugar, and egg together. Shape the dough in rounds with flat tops the size of the gelt. Bake for about 12 minutes. Remove the cookies from the oven, cool slightly on the pan, then gently press one piece of gelt into the center of each cookie. Cool the cookies on the baking sheets for 10 minutes before transferring to a wire rack to cool completely.

Quantity: About 35 cookies

Chapter Four

Chanukah and Christmas Chocolate Melt into Gelt

HAVING FOUND INTERSECTIONS OF THE TRAIL OF chocolate, Jews, and religion in France, Spain, Mexico, Newport, and New York, we hoped to revel in more of it in the chocolate haven of Belgium. We would have been satisfied just to eat chocolate and visit Belgian chocolate museums, yet we suspected that with all of the chocolate there had to be something Jewish and/or religious. We just had no idea what that might be.

To find one of the four chocolate museums in Belgium, Mark and I drove from Brussels about fifty miles southeast to Liege, Belgium, in early December. As we descended the hilly road into the downtown square, we stopped at a red light, where several young adults wearing plasticky white jackets covered with handwriting in many colors of marking pen approached the car window, jiggling cups at us. They said a few words in Flemish, shrugged, and walked away. We did not understand a word, but we were in Europe so we were, perhaps mistakenly, not frightened. As we wandered in town later that night, we were approached repeatedly by similar groups, again wearing the white jackets, again shaking the cups. This time we heard coins clinking in the cups. Perplexed by what was happening, we inquired at the tourist office the next day. The clerk

Chocolate molds of St. Nicholas for the celebration of the festival of St. Nicholas.

patiently explained that we had arrived during the feast day of St. Nicholas, December 6, when college students customarily roam the streets begging for gifts to buy beer to observe the holiday.

Throughout Belgium we had noticed, in both the best and the junkiest of chocolate stores, chocolate molded in the shape of the tall, lanky St. Nicholas in his Episcopal robes. That made sense. We knew that St. Nicholas provided the prototype for Santa Claus. To find either one in chocolate did not surprise us. After all, we had seen, and probably eaten, our share of chocolate Santas over the years. Something else clicked for me. I began to wonder about these coins and how they might relate to Chanukah coins, since Chanukah and Christmas usually coincide in December. And, most importantly, what about the gold-covered chocolate for Chanukah, also known as gelt, the Yiddish word for money?

Chanukah's Money

As I dug further into the literature about Chanukah's connection to coins, I found many associations. Chanukah recalls the victory of the ancient Maccabees over the Syrian Hellenists and renewed access by the Jews to their ancient Temple in Jerusalem (165 BCE) after its desecration. The gelt of Chanukah recalls the booty, including coins, that the Maccabean victors distributed to the Jewish widows, soldiers, and orphans, possibly at the first celebration of the rededication of the Jerusalem Temple.[1]

In ancient Israel, striking, minting, and distributing coins expressed Chanukah's message of freedom. The Maccabee's descendants, known as the Hasmoneans and who ruled Judea, started to strike coins. As the book of 1 Maccabees records,

Syria's King Antiochus VII said to Simon Maccabee, "I turn over to you the right to make your own stamp for coinage for your country" (15:6).

Unfortunately, few Jewish coins were produced between the time the Romans destroyed the Second Jerusalem Temple in 70 CE and the establishment of the modern State of Israel in 1948. Since 1958, Israel has minted commemorative Chanukah medals, reforging this connection of coinage, freedom, and the holiday, most appropriately because Chanukah celebrates political independence and religious freedom.

Money and Chanukah go way back in other ways as well, including the very observance of the holiday. As early as the sixth century, the legal text known as the Talmud taught that the poor must celebrate Chanukah even if they had to wander door to door to beg for the money to pay for the lighting materials, which in those days were probably oil, clay lamps, and wicks. Later, in Sephardi and Oriental (following the customs of Jews from North Africa and the Middle East) Jewish communities, people walked through their neighborhoods burning special grasses to ward off the evil eye in exchange for gifts or money at the Chanukah season. Yemenite Jewish children were given coins to purchase sugar and red food dye to make a special Chanukah wine.[2]

With time, additional customs evolved related to giving coins at Chanukah. The Hebrew word *Chanukah*, which refers to the rededication of the Jerusalem Temple after the Syrian Hellenists

Ancient Israelite Coins

One of the early Israelite coins, produced during the rule of Antigonus Matityahu (40–37 BCE), the last in this line of Hasmonean kings, portrays a seven-branched menorah (candelabrum) on one side and the shewbread (offering) on the other, each symbol a reminder of the centrality of the ancient Jerusalem Temple to the Jewish people and the victory of the Maccabees over the Hellenists.

had desecrated it, came to be associated with the Hebrew word for education, *chinukh*. The gelt or money for Chanukah supported Jewish learning. In the days of the Chasidic leader, the Ba'al Shem Tov (1698–1760), rabbis often traveled to distant villages to give instruction to impoverished and illiterate Jews, generally refusing payment. However, at Chanukah time, the instructors accepted coins and food as tokens of gratitude. Chanukah gelt signified appreciative, though modest, compensation for dedication to Jewish education.[3]

In addition, coins came to be an expected part of the Chanukah festivities in the home. One such custom involved giving gelt on each night of Chanukah, except for Friday evening, the Sabbath, when the use of money is prohibited. The normative legal code, the sixteenth-century *Shulchan Aruch*, stipulated that the light shed by the Chanukah candles may not be used for benefit, not even for counting money. It therefore became customary to play games, some of them using money, while the candles burned (*Shulchan Aruch, Orach Chayim*, chapter 46; *Chanukah* 671:5, 673:1). In dreidel, the popular children's game of Chanukah using a spinning top, the winner is also sometimes paid in coins.

In recent years, some Chasidic rebbes have given gelt to their followers, a much-cherished Chanukah gift for the recipient. Gifts are counted into the income of the 10 percent that is given away as the tithe. Many older people today remember

Gelt and Gold

Gelt and gold are also connected linguistically. With the development of the Yiddish language, the Judeo-German dialect of the eleventh century, we first find the word *gelt*, meaning "money." This word is related to the Dutch and German *geld*, which also means "gold." The first recorded appearance of the word *gelt* may have been in 1529, gelt coming to be identified with Chanukah money.

receiving no gifts at all at Chanukah, only a few coins of gelt, suggesting that gift giving has only recently become customary.

Money Grows on Cacao Trees

With so many ties between coins and Chanukah, it would not be surprising to find chocolate in the mix. After all, there was an early and fundamental joining of money and chocolate. Cocoa beans served as currency for the pre-Columbian peoples. Columbus and his crew soon learned that those mysterious-looking "almonds" they first saw in the bottom of a canoe were used by the indigenous people of the Americas as coinage. For example, in 1513, Hernando de Oviedo y Valdez paid one hundred cocoa beans to purchase a slave. So valued were cocoa beans that counterfeiters were known to fill empty shells with clay or earth.[4] In the New World, cacao was gelt and it grew on trees.

Why Chocolate Coins?

Opinions differ, however, as to how chocolate came to be associated with coins for Chanukah. According to Tina Wasserman, food writer for *Reform Judaism* magazine, eighteenth- and nineteenth-century Jews became prominent in European chocolate making and started the Chanukah chocolate coin custom. Jenna Joselit, in her book *The Wonders of America*, notes that with the increased purchasing capacity in the American Jewish community in the 1920s, Loft began producing Chanukah chocolate. Gelt may have roots in a Polish custom that informed Israel's Elite's production of chocolate coins.[5]

Certainly, gold foil chocolate coins unfailingly appear every December in many commercial and residential Chanukah displays. My mother used to put bags of chocolate Chanukah gelt into large plastic dreidels. Some people scatter gold Chanukah gelt on the holiday table. While President George W. Bush's White House chief of staff, Joshua Bolten shared chocolate gelt at senior staff meetings in December. An online search yields comparisons of quality and costs of chocolate Chanukah gelt. A rap song lauds Chanukah gelt.[6]

Finding Good Gelt

Author and chocolate maven Francine Segan brags that her children refused to eat "traditional" chocolate Chanukah gelt. They begged her to recycle it or to leave it on the table for glittery decoration. As Segan explains:

> Good chocolate needs to contain 100% cocoa product, without cheap substitutes or additives, along with quality sugar and flavorings. Just as we want to be feeding our children real food, we should be giving them real chocolate.[a]

The flavor of gelt further improves when hazardous child labor and slavery are not ingredients (see chapter 11). Unfortunately, there are very few chocolate coin purveyors that adhere to fair trading commitments even while children perform dangerous work in the cocoa growing of West Africa. Selecting fair trade chocolate gelt or a chocolate produced with comparable commitments complements Chanukah's messages about freedom from oppression.

The phrase "freedom and justice," a perfect message for Chanukah, encircles the cocoa tree embossed on the fair trade, organic-certified, foil-wrapped chocolate coins produced by Divine Chocolate. As Ilana Schatz teaches at the Fair Trade Judaica website, "The gelt we eat on Chanukah is a reminder of the freedom our people won many years ago."[b] A collaboration among the Jewish organizations Fair Trade Judaica, T'ruah, and the Divine company furthers this effort with Guilt-Free Gelt.[c]

St. Nick's Coins Save Family

I realized that this St. Nicholas miracle tradition we happened upon in chocolate-suffused Belgium may explain Chanukah gelt. As we continued to savor Belgium, we learned that St. Nicholas, the patron saint of sweets, journeys from distant Spain to reward children with gold-covered chocolate coins! The feast day associated with St. Nicholas has been relished in Europe since the thirteenth century. One of the several St. Nicholas *Golden Legend* miracle stories, written in 1275 by Jacobus de Voragine, archbishop of Genoa, records that Nicholas tossed bags of gold coins to an impoverished father in order to provide his daughters with dowries, thus saving them from lives of prostitution.

Chocolate coins of St. Nicholas for the holiday of St. Nicholas.

Rituals related to the celebration of the feast day of St. Nicholas in Belgium, the Netherlands, Germany, and the United States use gold-covered chocolate, *geld*. Youngsters collect chocolate coins from their shoes on the morning of December 6, following the previous night's visit by St. Nicholas, or as the Dutch call him, Sinterklaas.[7]

While Chanukah chocolate initially seemed pretty remote from Liege that night in December, St. Nick's *geld* surprisingly and sweetly flowed right into Chanukah's gelt. Gold-covered chocolate coins for the Christmas season commemorating the miracles of St. Nicholas may very well be the basis for the gold-covered chocolate gelt celebrating the amazing events of Chanukah, or possibly the other way around. These Christian and Jewish golden coin stories, each originating from the Mediterranean area, each of them centuries old, each with inspiring accounts of courage and liberation, also indulge and nurture a love of chocolate. Jewish and Christian customs melt together on this fork of the chocolate trail.

Cognac Truffles

Refugee Lisa Hoffman, whose story is featured in this chapter, fled Germany in 1939 with this recipe. Her chocoholic assessment of it: "These truffles make a wonderful present and are the ultimate in chocolate richness. When making them, always use the finest ingredients."[1]

Ingredients:

2 ounces unsalted butter
3 tablespoons superfine sugar
1 pound bittersweet or dark chocolate, broken into pieces
½ cup heavy cream (fresh, not ultra-pasteurized)
½ cup quality Cognac (or rum or a liqueur)
Cocoa, finely chopped nuts, or powdered sugar, for rolling

Instructions:

Line a baking sheet with waxed paper. In a large heatproof bowl set over a pan of simmering water, heat the butter and sugar until melted and dissolved. Add the chocolate and stir continuously with a wire whisk until it starts to melt. Add the cream and continue to stir with a whisk until the chocolate is completely melted. Add the Cognac. Stir until thoroughly integrated.

Cool in the refrigerator overnight, or set a bowl over an ice bath and continue whisking until cool (this technique creates a lighter truffle and allows you to complete them sooner). Use two teaspoons to form chocolate balls, and roll in cocoa, finely chopped nuts, or powdered sugar. Place the chocolate balls on the prepared baking sheet. Store in a cool place in a covered container.

Quantity: About 30–35 truffles

Chapter Five

Chocolate Revives Refugees, Survivors, and Immigrants

AS I DELVED FURTHER INTO THEMES OF JEWS AND chocolate, I began to hear various stories about the potency of twentieth-century wartime chocolate for refugees, survivors, and immigrants. These accounts spanned from deprivation to comfort, from degradation to rescue, from despicable to artful, from Europe to America. For some, chocolate soothed and fortified refugee and immigrant passages and evoked sweet opportunities, loving reunions, renewal, and hope. For others, chocolate-making skills meant survival. Chocolate companies launched some chocolate makers into leadership of their wartime Jewish communities and beyond.

Immigrants Pave America's Streets with Sweets

Jewish immigrants have a long history of succeeding in the chocolate and candy business in the United States, dating back to the late 1800s. Immigrant Louis Auster developed the chocolate egg cream in his candy store in New York's Lower East Side in 1890. He made the drink using his secret recipe, including a chocolate sauce that he developed, and sold it for three cents a glass, averaging three thousand sales on a summer day. Ultimately he opened four additional locations, until his business closed down in the 1960s. In 1895 Herman and Ida Fox, also New Yorkers, developed Fox's U-bet Chocolate Syrup in Brooklyn, offering a kosher-for-Passover version as well. The Fox family–owned company is still located in Brooklyn.[2]

In New York City in 1896, Leo Hirshfield started a small candy shop, having learned the confectionary business in Austria from his family. His special taffy-esque formula of Chocolate Tootsie Rolls—named for his daughter—avoided the cost of actual chocolate by using cocoa powder instead. This, plus the individual wrappers separating the candies, made them easily portable even in the summer.[3]

David Goldenberg immigrated to Philadelphia from Romania in 1880 at the age of eighteen, the youngest of seven children. He changed his name on the boat, having heard that it would be preferable to be a Goldenberg than a Seltzer. He developed a chocolate ration bar for the army using molasses and peanuts as a substitute for more expensive almonds. This candy bar came to be known as Peanut Chews. His children, Sylvia and Harry, introduced the individually wrapped Peanut Chews for retail sale in 1921, and the brand was sold to Just Born in 2003, yet another immigrant candy story.[4] They produce the popular Peeps for Easter.

When he was twelve years old, Edmond Opler Sr. went to work in the Runkel Brothers Chocolate Company to help support his seven siblings after the death of his father just a year before. He worked his way up to salesman. After World War I, he and his brother Arnold moved to Chicago and opened a bulk cocoa packing company that ultimately became World's Finest Chocolate, Inc.[5]

A number of sweets makers and appetizing stores were located on Franklin Avenue in Brooklyn, including JoMart Chocolates, which was founded on April 15, 1946, by Martin Rogak with his cousin Joe. Their grandfather had made candy in Brownsville, Brooklyn, in the 1920s. Martin explained that he started the company after World War II seeking a business that would focus on life after so much sadness and suffering. Martin's son, wife, and family still run the company.[6]

Koppers Chocolate, now in its third generation of family ownership, was founded in 1937 in New York City by Fred Stern and claims to be the "first U.S. chocolate officially certified Kosher."[7] Morris Cohen opened Economy Candy in New York that same year. One of many typical candy stores of the time, it survives today on the Lower East Side. Carl Mondel arrived in Ohio from Hungary in 1923. He said, "When I first started out, all I knew about candy was how to eat it. I've always loved candy and I always wished to have a candy shop."[8] As his experiments with chocolate improved, he sold to his friends and relatives. In December 1943, he opened his store, Mondel Chocolates, in New York at Broadway and 114th Street, where his specialties were, and still are, handmade.

Refugees Make It by Baking It

Candy making wasn't the only sugary opportunity awaiting immigrants to the United States. In two American cities, refugees from Europe's war were hired in bakeries specially created to give them jobs. The Window Shop Bakery on Brattle Street in Cambridge, Massachusetts, was started by Bostonians to help German refugees during World War II. The Bake Shop in Cincinnati was started by the Jewish community specifically to assist refugees.[9] Holocaust refugee Ernest Weil opened his own bakery, San Francisco's beloved Fantasia, in 1948.

Weil, born in 1924, learned to bake and work chocolate from his mother in Landau, Germany. The proudest aspect of his Bar Mitzvah, he recollected, had nothing to do with the Hebrew, the Torah portion, or his speech. It was instead that he baked all of the pastries himself. When he was only fifteen, he escaped Germany and ended up in a French orphanage. There he won a scholarship to study at Le Cordon Bleu Culinary Arts Institute in Paris. Finally in the United States at the age of sixteen, he worked in a New York bakery. He hoped to have his mother's affidavit papers signed by a senator in Washington, to allow her to enter the United States, but the owner of the bakery would not allow him the day off. Only when the rest of the crew threatened to walk off the job on Ernest's behalf did the boss permit him to go. When Ernest's mother finally arrived in America, the two joined his older brothers in California. There, through one brother who knew someone who knew someone, Ernest landed a job at the elegant Blum's restaurant and café, which was decorated completely in pink. After his release from the U.S. Army, Weil launched his Fantasia bakery using many family recipes, including those of his mother and mother-in-law. When his longtime sweetheart and later wife, Margo, was confirmed, he made her a box of marzipan-filled chocolate called Mozartkugeln. Fantasia made those, as well as Sacher torte and chocolate truffle roulade, among many other international treats. While Fantasia did not have a formal plan to hire refugees, they did engage several. Their first pastry chef was born in Germany and studied in Switzerland. They also employed an elderly German-Jewish man from Shanghai who had difficulty finding a job and who had been a manager in a department store in Shanghai.[10]

World War II and Chocolate's Dark Side

While sweets and chocolate shops were opening and, in some cases, thriving in the United States, wartime Europe cast some darkness over chocolate. European Jewish businesses, including a number of Jewish chocolate enterprises, were forced to shut down during the Nazi period of World War II. Nestlé's chocolate subsidiary, Maggi, employed thousands of war prisoners and Jewish slave laborers in its factory in Germany near the Swiss border. As recently as 1997, it refused to open its Nazi-era records.[11] Nazis used chocolate bars to lure Jews onto cattle car trains to concentration camps.[12] German saboteurs designed a chocolate-covered, sleek, steel bomb intended to explode seven seconds after breaking off a piece.[13] Other Nazi schemes sought to poison Allied officers through chocolate.[14]

THE BOMB IS MADE OF STEEL WITH A THIN COVERING OF REAL CHOCOLATE. WHEN THE PIECE OF CHOCOLATE AT THE END IS BROK' OFF THE CANVAS SHOWN IS PULLED, AND AFTER A DELAY OF SEVEN SECONDS THE BOMB EXPLODES.

CANVAS

STEEL ENDS

Booby trap chocolate bar developed by the Nazis during World War II.

Israeli author Haim Gouri's fictionalized chocolate's bitter layer in *The Chocolate Deal*, a depiction of the ruin, revenge, and recovery of post–World War II Europe. The main character, Rudi, a Holocaust survivor, paid his prostitute with chocolate. Rudi hatched a scheme premised on the abundance of surplus military chocolate, conspiring to spread rumors that the chocolate contained tranquilizing ingredients that were intended to pacify military men. Prices would drop, the false reports about the tranquilizer would be denied and corrected, and a fortune would be gained from the increased value. Rudi predicted, "You take what's yours and go far away."[15]

World War II Spurs Chocolate Innovation

While its dark side is very dark indeed, chocolate also played a positive role in World War II, sparking innovation, heroism, and the development of survival skills for citizens, the military, and business. Chocolate companies accommodated to

Camille Bloch developed these bars using hazelnuts to save the cost of chocolate during World War II.

restricted food supplies and the severe rationing of the period by modifying their products. For example, to make up for the shortage of cocoa in Italy in the 1940s, Pietro Ferrero developed Nutella spread, using the abundant local Piedmont hazelnuts. Similarly, the Swiss company Camille Bloch created its popular Ragusa line, replacing unattainable chocolate with hazelnuts. Cadbury Dairy Milk, which depended heavily on fresh milk, could not be produced during the war, so the company substituted powdered milk in what came to be called Ration Chocolate. Home recipes were modified to accommodate chocolate shortages, as in the Wacky Cake recipe in this book.[16] To satisfy government orders for chocolate in wartime, companies helped each other. For instance, Nestlé would produce a bar for Cadbury, or Cadbury would make a Nestlé product.[17]

While many chocolate companies and civilians were chocolate deprived during World War II, the U. S. military put chocolate to good use in rations. Hershey developed its Ration D Bar to very clear specifications at the government's request. These bars needed to be nutritious, portable, and temperature resistant, yet not so appealing that soldiers would devour them as snacks.[18] The final ingredients included chocolate mass, sugar, skim milk powder, cocoa butter, oat flour, and vanillin. Sugar was decreased and chocolate mass increased to give the bar a less pleasing taste than normal chocolate bars. The formula created a heavy paste that had to be pressed rather than poured into molds. A four-ounce bar contained six hundred calories. The original formula and shape of the ration bar were altered slightly when thiamine hydrochloride was added as a source of vitamin B^1 to prevent beriberi, a disease likely to be encountered in the tropics.

While the calories and nutrition from chocolate helped sustain members of the military, the skills of chocolate making and homemaking assisted Jewish civilians under the deprivation of Nazi rule. In the late 1930s in Frankfurt, Germany, at the age of fifteen, Lisa Hoffman and two other classmates were told they could not return to school because they were Jews. Lisa had already been forced to greet the teacher with the Nazi salute and had been required to sing Nazi songs, which spoke of murdering Jews. When the Nazis closed her father's department store, her mother, Elsa, took boarders into their large apartment. Hoping to send Lisa to England as a domestic, Elsa trained Lisa along with other young Jewish women, some of whom were her lodgers, in homemaking skills. Unemployed Jews who had worked as waiters, cooks, and bakers also gave lessons.

The person who was to serve as chocolate instructor was arrested by the Nazis just days before he was scheduled to teach his specialty. Since Lisa had only weeks before begun an apprenticeship with a famous chocolate maker, she coached the group instead, staying one week ahead of the group's lessons. Lisa, a self-diagnosed chocoholic, taught them about chocolate fillings and how to use special dipping forks to form perfectly shaped and delicious truffles, including the truffle recipe included in this chapter.

Finally with a visa in hand, she departed Germany for England on August 18, 1939. Only two weeks later, war was declared between Germany and England. Looking back on that time when she was without family and classified as a foreign alien, she wrote:

> I carried inside of me all of the lessons my mother had worked so hard to get for me. I could make chocolate, cook for large families and carry soup without spilling.

But more importantly what she'd given me was a belief in myself. It's stood me well through the years, this gift from my mother Elsa Hoffman.[19]

Chocolate Smuggles Jewelry

Jill Soloway's television show *Transparent* aired a scene in its second season in which a Berlin family member melted chocolate over jewelry to smuggle it out of Germany in the 1930s. Soloway based that segment on the true story shared with her cast by the actor Henry Winkler. His father had hidden their family's gems in warmed chocolate. When the Nazis searched for valuables, he denied having any, all the while clutching the candy box under his arm.[a] That recalls the escape story of my father and grandparents from Danzig.

In the summer of 1937, my great-uncle George and his wife, Margaret, together with my grandmother, Toni Prinz, and my father, Ray, boarded a ship for Copenhagen. My great-aunt Selma and her husband, Mor, escorted them to the ship to wave goodbye and at the very last minute gifted them with a box of local MIX Konfect chocolates.

George and Margaret happily accepted the box with its concealed $10,000 worth of gold coins. My father, just twelve at the time, had gold pieces amounting to $3,000 sewn into his suitcase and coat hem. The *mishpucha* (family), ostensibly on vacation, traveled overnight to Copenhagen, where they visited Tivoli Gardens, and after a couple of days returned to Danzig. While in Copenhagen, Toni and Ray wired their money to Union Bank in Los Angeles, California, where other family members had already settled. George and Margaret similarly wired funds. By the time of the excursion to Copenhagen, my relatives were applying for affidavits to the United States and ordering clothes for their desired departure.

In September of 1938, members of the Nazi Party hunted for my grandfather, Sigfried, at their Pfefferstadt 52 flat. Omi Toni, as I came to know her, sent their maid to wait for Sigfried at the building's entrance to tell him to meet her immediately at the train station. Toni explained to the Black Shirts that she knew where to find him and that she would bring him back. Fortunately she had stowed their passports in her purse, which she grabbed before hurrying to the station in her bedroom slippers. The two of them boarded a train to Orlovo, a nearby seaside resort, where they rented a room. The landlady there was suspicious, curious that they had arrived after the summer season.

My grandparents then called Jewish neighbors in Danzig to contact their sons, Arno (my uncle) and Ray, to urge them to join them. The boys quickly packed a few things from the apartment and ran to catch a train. A few days later, they returned to the apartment to retrieve more. They managed to take the Shabbes candlesticks but had to leave behind a brass menorah, which Ray says he has never forgotten. On yet another trip to the apartment, they found that Nazi Party members had vandalized everything.

Meanwhile the family's haberdashery store and its inventory had been impounded. To try to secure some income, the family snuck into the store in the middle of the night and bundled as much as possible. A former employee named Roeschel, a Catholic, helped carry it off to his apartment. He later mailed the stock to family members, the Holsteins, in nearby Soblevo. Proceeds from that dangerous escapade supported my family from September 1938 until January 1939.

Luckily, fifteen-year-old Arno had received his visa on the Danzig quota, which came up in 1938 before the rest of the family received theirs. He redeemed store IOUs at discount so that he could clothe himself for the trip. He traveled through the "corridor" in a "sealed" Polish train (neither German nor Polish police could search it) to the port of Gdynia, where he boarded the MS *Batory*, Poland's only luxury steamship.

Because the Danzig consulate had sent my father's and grandparents' papers ahead to the Warsaw consulate, they finally were able to leave Danzig on the Polish quota. In January 1939 the three of them took a sled through Danzig to the train station in Gdynia in order to board a ship to America.

What started in Danzig with a small box of chocolate produced by MIX Konfect helped support my family's four-generation love of See's marzipan candies in Los Angeles—and the sweet freedoms of America.[b]

An Even Sweeter Freedom

Chocolate's role in the war extended to the liberation of the concentration camps, serving as a symbol of the caring world beyond the walls of the camps. Chocolate forged friendships as well.

Soldier Harry J. Herder Jr. connected with a very young survivor through chocolate at the liberation of Buchenwald concentration camp. Herder pulled a chocolate bar out of his pocket. The boy had no recognition of what it was. While the

Childhood Chocolate Losses

Albert Einstein and his sister, Maja, were given chocolate cups as children by their parents in Munich. Each cup, fabricated by Staatliche Porzellan-Manufaktur Nymphenburg, bears an image of each child. When Einstein immigrated to the United States, he brought the cups with him. He was able to keep his chocolate memento in his home in Princeton, New Jersey.[a]

Albert Einstein's childhood chocolate cup accompanied him to Princeton. Courtesy of the Leo Baeck Institute

Writer and film director Leon Prochnik unfortunately lost his childhood chocolate when he was six years old in 1939. The Nazis expropriated his family's franchise of the Swiss Suchard chocolate factory located in Kraków, Poland, while they were on vacation. It took fourteen months for the family to flee to Chelm, to Lithuania, to Siberia, to Japan, to Vancouver, to Toronto, and ultimately to New York City. Dreams of his family's chocolate tub appeared to him throughout the escape. Recollections of how he used to dunk his arm into the vat of melted chocolate to lick it off helped him fall asleep at night. In New York City, the family was able to open the Marlon Chocolate factory on Fifty-Fourth Street.

Around the time of his eightieth birthday, Prochnik started sharing his Holocaust story publicly. Following his talks at the Museum of Tolerance in Los Angeles and in local Los Angeles schools, children child practiced the pronunciation "candy" and "chocolate," Herder removed the chocolate wrapper. As he watched the youngster's puzzlement, Herder realized that he had probably never tasted chocolate! Herder showed him how to break off a piece, put it in his mouth, and chew it. He slowly ate the entire bar "with wonderment" in his eyes. They drank hot cocoa from Herder's K rations. At the end of his tour, Herder emptied his pockets of all of his candy bars for his new friend.[20]

draw pictures of his story, many of them featuring the chocolate tub. He hopes to develop their stories into a Holocaust education project.[b] The chocolate factory was one of many things Leon lost in the Holocaust. Sharing that part of his story helps his young audiences understand more about the Holocaust and the many deprivations Jews experienced at that time.

Francine Christophe, also a child during the Holocaust, surrendered her chocolate as well. At the age of eight, she was interred at the Bergen-Belsen concentration camp with her mother, who had smuggled a couple of pieces of chocolate into the camp. She explained to Christophe, "We'll keep these for a day when I see you've collapsed completely and really need help."

Because Christophe's mother was the barracks' chief, she accompanied a very weakened woman, Hélène, to the camp hospital when she went into labor. Christophe recounts that her mother said to her, "Remember that piece of chocolate I was saving for you?"

"Yes, Mama," Christophe replied.

Her mother asked, "How do you feel?"

"Fine, Mama," Christophe replied, "I'll be fine."

So Christophe and her mother gave the chocolate to Hélène, who gave birth to a daughter. According to Christophe, the baby did not make any sounds until the liberation six months later. Years after, Christophe told her story at a conference about the necessity of psychiatric support for camp survivors. Another presenter followed her to the podium to give her talk, reached into her pocket, pulled out a piece of chocolate for Christophe, and said, "I am that baby."[c]

Mike Jacobs tasted his first Hershey bar at the liberation of Mauthausen. Born in Konin, Poland, and named Mendel Jakubowicz, he was nineteen and a half years old and weighed seventy pounds in 1945. Having been sent to Mauthausen when Auschwitz was evacuated, he saw tanks approaching the camp and wondered why the Germans had switched the customary swastika to a star. Hours later, more star-studded tanks arrived, and a soldier tossed him a little package. "I grabbed it and run [sic] into the barracks and say, 'Hey, guys, look—I got a bar of chocolate. And can you imagine! The name of the chocolate is Hershel!' [Hershel is a common Yiddish name.] I didn't read the wrapper properly, so the first American food I eat is a Hershel bar."[21]

Chocolate Pilot Wiggles His Wings

Children in the ruins of postwar West Berlin were deprived of chocolate and candy. The Berlin Airlift sent in 1,535 tons of food, only enough necessary to maintain the city at minimal nutrition during the Soviet Union's blockade.[22] In 1948, after his first airlift flight into Berlin through Templehof airfield, U.S. Air Force pilot Gail S. Halvorsen, a Mormon, glimpsed a group of children gathered at the fence watching the flights of the airlift. He was impressed that they did not beg. Unsure how to distribute the two sticks of gum he had, he divided it for the four children who had translated for him and then decided to share the wrapper with the others, as he had nothing else to give them. They happily pocketed the scraps. On the spot he promised them that he would drop goodies for them the next time he flew into the field. As they questioned how they would know which plane was his, he promised to wiggle the wings of the plane, thus becoming known as Uncle Wiggly Wings, the Chocolate Uncle, or the Chocolate Pilot. He quickly enlisted his teammates to donate their rations of chocolate and gum as well as their handkerchiefs to serve as mini-parachutes to ferry the chocolate to the waiting hands on the ground.

Many successful drops followed in what came to be known as Operation Little Vittles, and the children began to write heartwarming and funny letters to Uncle Wiggly Wings.

One youngster, Peter Zimmerman, hoped that the pilot would aim the chocolate right into his backyard. He wrote, "Fly along the big canal ... at the second bridge turn right. I live in the bombed out house on the corner. I'll be in the backyard every day at 2:00 PM. Drop it there." When his packages did not arrive, he wrote back, "You are a pilot? I gave you a map. How did you guys win the war anyway?"[23]

The Chocolate Pilot received a letter from Elly Muss on October 15, 1948: "For days and days, four small brothers without a father have run to the airport in vain to get their hardworking mother a piece of chocolate. Is there another way to fulfill this request for five hungry souls?" And it was fulfilled when Halvorsen sent them a package of treats by mail.

Another child marveled:

> Suddenly out of the mist came a parachute with a fresh Hershey chocolate bar from America. It took me about a week to eat that candy bar. I hid it day and night. The chocolate was wonderful, but it wasn't the chocolate that was important. What it meant was that someone in America cared.... It represented hope.[24]

Based on her Berlin Airlift experiences, Mercedes Simon became the focus of a recent children's book about this chocolate operation. Mercedes was only seven and could not go to the airfield unless accompanied by her mother. When she finally did get there, a bigger boy grabbed the closest chocolate bar before she could. Instead of trying again at the airfield, with her mother's help she too wrote a letter to the Chocolate Pilot. In return, Halvorsen mailed her a package of candy and chocolate with a personalized note signed, *Dein Shokoladenonkel*, "Your Chocolate Uncle." Years later, Halvorsen and Mercedes met at her home, where she still kept the handwritten letter, which she had savored over the years as much as—or possibly more than—the chocolate.

When Halvorsen was sent to New York in 1948 on a tour that celebrated "Operation Little Vittles," which was headquartered at Westover Air Force Base in Chicopee, Massachusetts, he met with "John Swersey, a Jew," of the National Confectioners Association, which had sent thirty-five hundred pounds of chocolate and gum for the operation. These chocolate missions alleviated the bitterness of these war-torn children's lives.[25]

Chocolate Fuels the Fight after the War

While chocolate sweetened the lives of children affected during the war, it played a vital role in healing for Jews long after the war was over. The Swiss chocolate company Camille Bloch is soaked in the Swiss Jewish and Holocaust story, and today it is also one of the very few third-generation Jewish-owned chocolate companies. As explained to us in an interview with company CEO Daniel Bloch, the company's founder, Camille, Daniel's grandfather, was initiated into the chocolate business at a very young age. As a teen, he apprenticed at Tobler, another famous Swiss chocolate maker and creator of the patented Toblerone bar. He eventually went into sales for the company. At the same time, he began experimenting with his own private-label chocolates at home in Bern, Switzerland. When Lindt was bought by Sprüngli, Camille purchased their chocolate-making equipment. In 1929 he started his business, principally serving the Bern area, and business went well.

Needing more space, Camille moved the factory from Bern about twenty-six miles northwest to the farmlands of Courtelary, taking over a former paper factory in a depressed area of significant unemployment in 1935. During World War II, Camille's son Rolf was expelled from the Scouts, and his friends stopped speaking with him because he was Jewish. However, the factory continued to function, and Rolf focused all of his energies there, rising to become a leader of both the business and the Jewish community.

Rolf later became president of the Swiss Federation of Jewish Communities, an eighteen-thousand-member Jewish organization, from 1992 to 2000.[26] During his tenure, information leaked out about Swiss deceit and theft during World War II. While Switzerland had claimed neutrality, it actually profited in several ways from collaboration with the Nazis during the war through sales of Swiss products to Nazi Germany, purchase of Nazi gold, stockpiling of art stolen from Jews, investments of approximately $3 billion in Nazi Germany, and secret Nazi holdings in Swiss banks. Worse, Switzerland closed borders to thousands of Jews seeking refuge beginning in August 1942. After the war, accusations surfaced of Swiss profiteers who committed fraud through the disappearance of accounts belonging to families of Holocaust victims and the refusal to pay insurance policies to beneficiaries of deceased Jews. Counterclaims from some Swiss bankers that the Jewish community was blackmailing and seeking ransom money from them generated a backlash of anti-Semitism, including hate mail, graffiti attacks, and verbal harassment.[27] Subsequent investigations of the dormant Swiss accounts in the names of Holocaust victims raised doubts about the integrity of Swiss banks, insurance companies, and government policies as they repeatedly claimed no responsibility.

When Rolf Bloch noticed a change in the mood of Switzerland on these issues with the collapse of communism and the publication of a new study of Swiss attitudes toward Jews during the war, he encouraged Edgar Bronfman Sr., then president of the World Jewish Congress, to fly to Switzerland in 1995 to pressure the Swiss government to investigate. Kaspar Villiger, then Swiss president, called upon the country to apologize to its Jewish victims, pleading, "We can only bow our heads in silence before those whom we led into suffering and captivity, even death."[28]

Jewish leaders prior to Rolf Bloch had been reluctant to push and had made no progress. Rolf Bloch's very Swiss manner—reserved, very formal, always in suit and tie, nicknamed the "Ball" by his staff because of his build—was able to move things forward.[29]

> He is the perfect incarnation of a Swiss Jew, committed to Judaism in private and blending in publicly. When the Holocaust assets debate broke out, Swiss Jews could not maintain this peaceful dual identity. The fact that they were Jewish had become a public matter. Many felt anti-Semitism for the first time or felt uneasy in the boards, country clubs, and other societies they were part of. Bloch managed to walk on that tightrope quite brilliantly. He looked and sounded Swiss and did Swiss "things" (chocolate, which was better than banking in those days). He was Jewish, but not a "visible" Jew.[30]

"Justice for the victims and fairness for Switzerland," a phrase Rolf Bloch coined before a hearing of the United States Congress Banking Committee in December 1996, captured this simultaneous resolution and discretion.[31] Later Bloch chaired the Special Fund for Holocaust Victims established by the Swiss government and funded by Swiss companies. Bloch's leadership furthered post-Holocaust healing.

Barton's Founder Flees Vienna

While Camille Bloch was upholding Jewish ideals and seeking justice for Jews in Europe, Barton's Bonbonniere was doing similar work in the United States by creating refuge for those seeking to flee the ravages of the war. Stephen Klein fled Vienna the day after the 1938 Nazi march into Austria known as the Anschluss. His soon to be vastly successful American company, Barton's Bonbonniere, in turn assisted other World War II refugees seeking to immigrate to America.

In Vienna, Klein had owned one of the city's largest commercial suppliers of chocolate. A Nazi competitor marched into Klein's offices and seized ownership of Klein's company the day after the Anschluss. To escape likely arrest, Klein hurriedly left his two children and pregnant wife behind, spending five months in Belgium before arriving in the United States. A few months later he brought the family to New York via Belgium, subsequently to be joined by his five brothers and two sisters. From the small New York apartment that he shared with about ten family members, he prepared chocolates, which relatives then sold from pushcarts, catering to the varied tastes of the ethnic neighborhoods. Commenting on his product, Klein claimed that he knew which chocolates to blend and how to control taste. As he put it, "All the pieces should look good—no *chazerei* [junk]...."[32] Barton's sought to produce excellent bonbons, using the best Swiss and Belgian chocolate. The Viennese style in the product as well as in the décor mixed with the Orthodox values Klein held dear.

As his enterprise grew, so did his aid to numerous Jewish immigrants, refugees, and Holocaust survivors. For instance, Klein supported Jack Gold and Henry Kaye, Polish survivors, in opening their own shop to make boxes for chocolate on West 18th Street in Manhattan. Gold and Kaye started working in chocolate on their own in 1949 at Madelaine Chocolate Novelties. Madelaine is still family run and thriving thanks to the boost they received from Barton's. The Gold and Kaye families, also adherents of Orthodox Judaism, affiliated with local synagogues, making seasonal mold confections with the Orthodox Union, or OU dairy *hechsher* (certification of kashrut, Jewish dietary requirements).

Never forgetting his European community of origin, despite his success in America, Klein helped to further the work of the American Orthodox relief agency Vaad Hatzala, a body originally established to rescue rabbis and yeshivah students and eventually expanded to assist all Jews during World War II.

Initially the Vaad sent packages of religious articles, food, cloth-ing, household goods, and Barton's chocolate via a loophole through Tangier to Nazi-occupied countries. After the war this Jewish charity continued its support of the religious rehabilita-tion of Jewry through educational and religious endeavors.[33] Klein also volunteered for a six-month stint in 1946 in Europe with the United Nations Rescue and Relief Agency (UNRRA). Klein's Barton's headquarters housed an office of immigration for assisting with the technical details of bringing over displaced Jews. His company hired many of those approximately fifteen hundred individuals he had assisted. While the payroll included Orthodox Jews, it was a very pluralistic, multi-ethnic work line. No strikes disrupted the flow of chocolate, and there were no complaints about closing on Saturdays. Perhaps this was

Chocolate Recovery

Estee Farber, Madelaine Chocolate Company's marketing direc-tor, reflecting on the destruction of their factory equipment during Superstorm Sandy, said, "There's a resiliency to our family from its Holocaust background."[a]

During the Holocaust, the Nazis imprisoned Estee's grandmother, Helen, in a labor camp in Poland, her great-aunt, Esther, in a labor camp in Czechoslovakia, her grandfather in Buchenwald, and mur-dered a great-uncle in Auschwitz. Family tales of narrow escapes and luck were always at the forefront of the Farbers' minds, not in a sad way but in an uplifting way. Estee's grandmother often told sto-ries about maintaining humanity, even in the concentration camp.

After the war, Esther married Jack Gold, and Helen married Henry Kaye. Gold and Kaye had been sponsored to come to the United States by Stephen Klein, who employed them at his company, Bar-ton's Bonbonniere. Klein further assisted as Gold and Kaye opened a chocolate packaging plant on West Eighteenth Street in Manhattan.

In 1949 the Golds and Kayes developed a line of European-style foil-wrapped chocolate novelties for holidays and special because employees were allowed to eat as much chocolate as they wanted.

Klein's commitment to Orthodox Judaism began very early in life and was apparent at every turn thereafter. In 1923 his father, Reb Simcha Klein, had taken Stephen to meet the illustrious rabbi and ethicist known as the Chofetz Chaim. The esteemed rabbi pronounced this blessing on Stephen: "May you be successful and in all of your endeavors, sanctify the Name of *Hashem* [God]." Klein seemed to embody these words in his workplace, in fulfillment of the Jewish law to rescue the captive and also in his inclusion of Jewishness in the workplace. As he once explained, "I am a devoted and conscientious member of the Orthodox Jewish community."[34] At least six hundred

occasions, calling it Madelaine after a popular British actress of the time. Ironically, this religiously observant family's first products were kosher-certified chocolate Easter eggs. Just as Barton's created a refuge for many World War II immigrants, today Madelaine hires newcomers to America.

Estee ponders her family's journey through trauma and most recently through Superstorm Sandy, which destroyed most of the factory's equipment in Rockaway Beach, Queens.

If our grandparents' generation could get through the Holocaust, we could get through the storm in 2012. It represents more than a business. It represents a family coming with nothing, after having lost so much, and building so much to provide for so many, creating a better life for them and for so many people.[b]

For the Rockaway Beach–headquartered Madelaine Chocolate Company, gratitude for recovery is embedded in each piece of chocolate flowing off the conveyor belt.[c]

organizations, several of them Orthodox, benefited from Klein's generosity, including Young Israel and Yeshiva University.

While he had a broad customer base, Klein saw the Orthodox population as a niche market and proudly declared, "The competitors are just sitting around kicking themselves

What Makes Chocolate Kosher for Passover?

Several factors contribute to the complexities of kosher-for-Passover chocolate. Certifications in America generally promote the Ashkenazi prohibition against eating legumes (*kitniyot*) or leavened breads during the festival. This precludes the use of soybean lecithin as an emulsifier, which is often added to smooth the chocolate texture. In some situations, this restriction about *kitniyot* divides Ashkenazim and Sephardim whose Passover diets diverge. Sephardi custom permits *kitniyot* and would not prohibit the soy lecithin in chocolate. In Israel, a culture war sometimes erupts at Passover between Sephardim and Ashkenazim, each group adhering to a separate Passover certification system. On occasion Ashkenazim have been prohibited from visiting Sephardi homes during the holiday lest they eat *kitniyot*.[a]

Because of *kitniyot* restrictions applying to beans, some have thought that chocolate from cocoa beans could not be eaten during Passover at all. Actually cocoa beans are seeds and permissible. Barton's Chocolate issued educational materials, including a haggadah for Passover. This subtly conveys messages about the permissibility of chocolate at Passover and also advertises their kosher-for-Passover chocolate products. In the Barton's Haggadah issued in 1944, the Orthodox company founder and president Stephen Klein explained, "This haggadah is part of Barton's program of presenting useful and informative literature for each Jewish holiday placed in every box of Barton's confections."[b] Barton's produced many fondly remembered treats for the holiday.

Passover's chocolate layers new causes onto the festival's age-old themes of freedom, peoplehood, and monotheism. Until Passover of 2013 it was not possible to find a fair trade kosher-for-Passover chocolate, which meant that chocolate consumed during for having overlooked it." In order to cater to this traditionally observant clientele, he had to follow particular business practices that cohered with Jewish law. For example, he had the chutzpah (courage) to close his offices and all stores on Shabbat and Jewish holidays. This meant that in the fall Jewish

Passover likely included beans sourced from farms in West Africa, where over two million children work in hazardous conditions. Thousands of them are enslaved.[c] Due to the efforts of Ilana Schatz, Fair Trade Judaica's founding director, and the decision of Rabbi Aaron Alexander of Adas Israel Congregation, one fair trade chocolate brand was also deemed kosher for Passover. That chocolate company has since switched from formal fair trade certification to using chocolate from fair trade certified co-ops (see chapter 11). Schatz explains her passion for fair trade Passover chocolate this way:

In 2010 ... I was stunned to learn that this most delicious and heavenly food was being produced by slave labor! Two things were immediately obvious: the connection to a contemporary Pesach story and the fact that there was no chocolate we could eat on Passover that wasn't probably tainted by child labor.[d]

To further awareness of slavery in our chocolate, Schatz also developed a "Virtual Fair Trade Chocolate at Seder" campaign. This decorates the Seder plate with cocoa beans or photos of cocoa beans, cocoa pods, and/or cocoa trees.[e]

The text accompanying the chocolate ritual foods in "A Haggadah for a Socially Responsible Chocolate Seder" (free download) unwraps themes of ethical kashrut, worker equity, and food justice. It elevates Passover's underlying messages of freedom, dignity, and fairness through chocolate.[f] The text recognizes those who labor, often in great poverty, to grow and harvest cacao, including children and adolescents working in bondage on the cocoa farms of the Ivory Coast and Ghana.

This year: chocolate. Next year: more chocolate.[g]

holiday cycle, the operation might have been shut down for ten working days. With time Barton's even publicized Shabbat and holiday closings in newspaper advertisements. Some think that doing so strengthened the Jewish identity of others to prioritize Shabbat observance over the workplace. A Brooklyn Catholic priest was reportedly so taken with this piety that he urged his flock to be as observant of Sunday's Sabbath as Barton's was of Shabbat. Still, calculations of the financial benefit or loss due to Bartons' Orthodox practices were never made and perhaps could not really be calculated.

Klein used his business to further educate Jews in their faith, albeit in a very sweet way. Barton's produced Jewish-themed chocolate, including Hebrew letter *aleph-bet* shapes. Other special Jewish products included chocolate matzah; matzah balls, which were chocolate covered coconut or marzipan; chocolate-covered hamantaschen; and chocolate-shaped latkes, which were chocolate disks with candy fillings. My audiences fondly recall the Passover Chocolate Pops and the Almond Kisses. Advertising emphasized education, with materials such as games and stories about the various Jewish holidays included in the boxes. Approximately one million of these informational resources a year were published, half of them for the boxes of candy. Jewish subject matter often filled the full-page ads in major newspapers.[35]

The commitment to Orthodoxy also meant a dedication to kashrut. Bartons' supervisor for implementing kosher requirements was Rabbi Nachum Kornmehl, the brother-in-law of Stephen Klein. Rabbi Kornmehl traveled once a year from Albany to check ingredients, to review suppliers, and to oversee the two-week closing for thorough cleaning prior to Passover. Until a vegetable gelatin could be developed for use in marshmallows and Klein had approval from his rabbi, Barton's did not use marshmallow. Even the seasonal Santa Clauses and Easter eggs were kosher.[36] In fact, while business increased at Passover, Christmas sales exceeded all. Though it is difficult to know exactly how much of the Bartons' client base was actually Jewish, estimates suggest that more than fifty percent of sales were to non-Jews.[37]

Barton's played a significant role in the kosher food industry. Not only did it initiate kosher-for-Passover lines and mass-marketed kosher chocolates, cakes, and ice cream, Barton's also actively engaged in discussions about OU (Orthodox Union) kosher certification, initially rejecting it as arbitrary and overly demanding. When the competing chocolate company, Barricini, attempted to acquire a *hechsher* from the Orthodox Union, Barton's tried to stop it. Barton's resorted to advertisements, claiming, "If it isn't a box of Barton's, is it right for a Jewish home?" In the end the OU certified Jewish-owned Barricini, even though its franchises were open on Shabbat, which was generally not permissible. Originally located at West 158th Street, it was meticulously clean. Founded in 1931, Barricini's had 250 outlets at one point. The OU had determined that ownership was really held by a corporation. Ultimately, Barton's also used the OU certification.[38]

The family sold this immigrant start-up company in 1978, and since then Barton's has been owned by three companies. This proudly Jewish company contributed to the growth of the kosher food industry and aided many refugees.

Mark and I kept this chocolate survivor in mind as we passed a shabby Barton's storefront sign in our neighborhood on Second Avenue between Sixty-Third and Sixty-Fourth Streets. One wintry day we noticed the demolition of what we thought might have been one of the last, if not the last, extant Barton's sign. As the sign was hauled away to the junk heap, it felt as though an era of refugee and immigrant chocolate that had aided so many people battling loneliness, dislocation, and trauma had ended. However, remembrances of the liberating essences of World War II–era chocolate endure.

Israeli Chocolate Spread

Chocolate spread permeates Israeli meals and experiences as it is eaten for breakfast, served on bread at teatime, toted in a lunch bag, and packed in army supply kits. The original version from the *Tzena*, the period of food scarcity in Israel between 1949 and 1959, would have used margarine.

Ingredients:

1 cup unsalted butter
1 cup sugar
3 large eggs*
1 teaspoon vanilla extract
5–6 heaping tablespoons unsweetened cocoa powder

Instructions:

Cut the butter into small pieces and put in a blender. Add the sugar, eggs, and vanilla, and blend well. Add the cocoa powder and blend well again. Put in a container and refrigerate. Serve on bread or toast, with fruit, or in a sandwich.

Quantity: About 1½ cups

* Caution: It may be best to use pasteurized eggs.

Chapter Six

Israelis

Meshuga for Chocolate

THE RAIN FLOODING THE STEEP STREETS OF NAZARETH could not deter us from reaching the pinnacle of Elite's factory to continue the chocolate *shvil* (trail) in Israel. We walked into a fantasy come true, an office bedecked with volumes of Talmud and piled high with boxes of chocolate. Haphazardly teetering Elite bittersweet bars, packets of popular Israeli candies Pesek Zman and Mekupelet, jars of chocolate chips, an alcohol-preserved cocoa bean—just the right assemblage for Haim Palgui, whose business card reads, "Chocolate Chief." I jealously noted the title before catching the next line, "Technologist." So it was that we met the affable Palgui, the Elite Chocolate Factory's secular-minded, mezuzah-kissing, Talmud-studying, shul-going chocolate expert, only one of our several fun chocolate visits, west, east, north, south (Genesis 28:14). Chocolate establishments dot Israel's countryside as abundantly as *sabra* (cactus) plants. Tourists soon discover the impossibility of seeing all the sites, and the same applies to chocolate shops. However, layering fun chocolate experiences onto the serious menu of holy sites makes for a tasty mix.

Make It Milk Chocolate

As Janna Gur, chief editor of Israel's *Al Hashulchan* [On the Table]—*The Israeli Gastronomic Monthly*, explained to me in a phone conversation, Israelis love chocolate, with a distinct preference for milk chocolate.

Most Israeli chocolate experts were trained in Belgium. At one time Elite licensed with Swiss companies Maestrani and Camille Bloch, which may explain that Israeli proclivity. Only one small Israeli chocolate company, Holy Cacao, currently roasts beans for their various bars. Gur also told me that for Israelis, local chocolate rates over imported chocolate, and chocolate remains the most popular restaurant dessert offering. Between 2003 and 2008, as the Israeli economy improved, chocolate eating in Israel increased 100 percent. Climate differences may explain why Israeli consumption (about seven pounds per person per year) remains significantly less than that of the Swiss (about twenty pounds per person per year). The desert temperatures in Israel's summer make transporting chocolate difficult and may make it less appetizing, while Switzerland's more moderate climate would keep chocolate appealing all year long. Nevertheless, chocolate is a hot commodity in Israel, as may be seen from the theft of one hundred tons of chocolate from a factory in Haifa in 2008.[1]

Israel is a child-centered culture, so it is not surprising that the marketing of chocolate in Israel focuses on children. This is certainly evident in the playful kiddie menu at branches of Max Brenner and the children's chocolate workshops at establishments such as Ornat, Galita, and De Karina. Strauss-Elite launched a milk chocolate confection named Etzbaot (fingers) aimed at children to compete with the Italian company Ferrero's Kinder (German for "children") line of chocolate. To entice Israeli children, Elite added popping candy, cookies, and Israeli-style "M&M's" (called *adashim*, or lentils).

As Israelis know full well, regarding taste and smell there is no arguing. In my experience, Israeli hot chocolate tends to be tepid, both in temperature and in flavor. Unusual local chocolate treats in Israel include honey and chocolate liquor (De Karina) and honey mixed with chocolate nibs (Roy), wonderful add-ons that could sweeten the first year of any newlyweds' marriage, following the custom of honey dripped onto the Shabbat challah bread.

Spread It, Bake It, Drink It

Israelis also adore chocolate-flavored spread. Around the time that Nutella unveiled its first modest version in 1946, Israelis developed a local formula minus the hazelnuts.[2] Palgui at Elite explained its popularity to us: "It spreads easily on bread, it does not spoil, it is cheap and sweet." In the austerity period of the 1950s called the *Tzena,* his mother, *z"l* (of blessed memory), whipped up the spread using margarine, powdered sugar, and cocoa powder. One former Israeli army reservist recalled that chocolate spread was often served at meals in the army, its pareve nature making it an easy addition that caused no conflict with Jewish dietary laws. Also, night patrols fortified themselves with sweet tea, bread, and chocolate spread, both going out and returning, as my kibbutznik brother-in-law Jay recalls. In a sweet irony, our local Upper East Side, Egyptian-owned bodega used to sell the Hashachar brand of Israeli chocolate spread. Why? Isaac El Neggar said, "Just to have. Some people crave it because it relates to their childhood." He prefers the taste of Nutella.

Birthday parties in Israel often feature the evocative cocoa-based cake nicknamed *ugah kushit* (black cake). This un-PC name actually comes from the word *kushi,* referring to a black person, based on the biblical text mentioning Moses's wife's land of origin in the Kingdom of Cush in Africa, "And Miriam and Aaron spoke against Moses because of the Cushite woman whom he had married; for he had married a Cushite woman" (Numbers 12:1). Some call it *ugat yomledet,* "birthday cake." In 2017 a large industrial Israeli bakery stopped calling their chocolate cake by this name in response to customer complaints on social media. Israeli-born Yigal Ben Aderet remembers his Turkish-born mother baking this "big deal," spongy, moist, chocolaty cake, sometimes frosted, sometimes with whipped cream, and not just for birthdays. This "incredible" treat was eaten with milk and/or dunked in milk. Yigal Rechtman recalls that the class mothers responsible for special occasions who were expert bakers on his kibbutz occasionally made the very dark, unfrosted, somewhat coarse, round cake with a hole in the middle. Cheesecakes and white cakes were common enough, but this *ugah* was unusual, likely requiring a trip to Jerusalem to acquire the right ingredients. The last time he tasted it may have been when he became Bar Mitzvah in 1979. Winners of the Purim lottery might have won such a cake, as he recalls.

Black cake is not the only chocolate infused form of celebration. Another kibbutznik, now living in Cincinnati, suspects that her family birthday custom of creating a themed chocolate table for the early morning of the special day started at her kibbutz. For her daughter, it might be a seashore with chocolate seashells; for her husband's birthday, truffles with some erotic innuendos.

Surprisingly, we frequently saw private-label chocolate liqueurs in Israeli chocolate shops, especially given the stereotypes about Jews not drinking alcohol. While we enjoyed such liqueur in Italy and Belgium, it is not easily found in other countries; even in New York City our search yielded only a mediocre American brand. This Israeli affection for chocolate liqueur may have been inspired by Sabra, which was developed by Edgar Bronfman Sr. in 1963. Intended to be a unique Israeli product, the Sabra bottle resembled an ancient Phoenician flask. When the original *sabra*-flavored recipe failed, chocolate combined with orange replaced it. For many years Sabra was readily available at duty-free shops and other stores. However, ask Israelis today about Sabra and many of them have no clue. While Sabra's popularity has waned, something in the Israeli psyche still demands chocolate liqueurs.

Chocolate Levels the Army

One fondly remembered line of chocolate made by Elite, Hayal-Hayelet, a fifty-gram milk chocolate bar, was sold to

A Jerusalem chocolate shop shelf swells with chocolate liqueurs.

Israeli soldiers at subsidized prices at canteens. Since the great majority of the Israeli population served in the military, they would have experienced Elite this way, if not earlier in their lives. Chocolate eating in the Israeli army provided immigrants from Morocco, Yemen, and Ethiopia another means of engaging Israeli society. The antiwar song "Chocolate Soldier" (*Chayal Shel Shokolad*) sung by the High Windows, an Israeli group of the late 1960s, was rejected for radio play then but may be heard today. It speaks to the challenges of fighting and turning into a chocolate soldier, one who may melt in the heat of danger, dying in the battle due to cowardice.[3]

Exploring Elite Firsthand

While Elite attempted to capitalize on the culture of the military, its Para brand captivated the general Israeli population. Israel's boutique chocolate purveyors of today compete with this long familiar taste.[4] Elite's pioneering Para (cow) brand, originally known as Shamnonit (fat), is wrapped in distinctive red paper imprinted with a cow. Israelis fondly identify it as Para or Para Adumah (red cow), or Shokolada Para (chocolate cow). To find out more about Elite and its Para, I tracked down a phone number for the Strauss Group (which bought Elite in 1996), expecting an ordeal to connect with the right person in the chocolate department and hoping to confirm an appointment during my limited time in the country. The receptionist responded with typically hospitable Israeli informality and immediately offered to gift me a book from her home about the history of Elite. The next morning Mark and I drove to the company headquarters in Petach Tikvah to find Tzila Gilbert at her desk with the large commemorative picture book about the sixtieth anniversary of Elite tucked carefully into a white envelope. Not only that, Gilbert then encouraged us to enjoy a drink at the Elite café at the other end of the hall. As I downed my hot chocolate with Mekupelet (bars of thinly folded milk chocolate produced in Israel since 1935, originally by Elite, similar to the Flake Bar of Cadbury, developed in 1920), Gilbert contacted the director of the Chocolate Division. Within just moments we were chatting with a very pregnant Hila Elad, director of the Chocolate Division of the Strauss Group, and her assistant, Lior Offer. They, in turn, referred us to Haim Palgui in Nazareth. We managed to squeeze a meeting in between his international travel and our remaining days in Israel.

As we sat in his office perched over the chocolate plant, Palgui explained, "The Israeli customer likes more [sic] the Elite product. They are used to it and it is more *amami* [for the people]." He elaborated that foreign chocolates, such as Valrhona or Godiva, are of a "different class and more expensive." Since its introduction in 1934, Para has cornered 80 percent of the market. Hila grew up on Para, having often lunched on a fifty-gram slab of Para chocolate on a roll. Twenty to thirty years ago all they had was Para, she recalled nostalgically. When David Ben-Gurion was prime minister, his wife, Paula, entertained guests with Elite chocolate.[5]

Palgui started working for Elite in 1987. He and his team develop new products using engineering, chemistry, biochemistry, thermodynamics, microbiology, and food science. They sometimes eat the chocolate straight from the machines, generally preferring bittersweet, the higher the chocolate content the better, around 70 percent. Over the years, the basic Elite milk and dark chocolates have not changed much. However, Israelis are increasingly interested in the dark version because it is thought to be healthier. Also, the growing religious market prefers pareve. Oriented to their

The Para brand of Elite decorates chocolate coins, gelt.

customers, Elite constantly runs tests and focus groups. When Elite first developed a 70 percent chocolate over a decade ago, they tested it using Lindt as a benchmark; Palgui boasted that Elite rated higher in the blind tests. The seasonal nature of chocolate in Israel recognizes the very hot summer as a low season and launches new products in the fall. Elite imports quality chocolate from the Belgian company Callebaut and the American company Cargill.

Sacred Sweets

Holy Cacao owners and chocolate makers Jo Zander and Zev Stender work from a religious perspective out of a small workshop in the Hebron Hills. They are possibly the only Israeli company that works bean to bar, meaning that they start making the chocolate with the bean. Their website boasted the appropriate blessing recited before eating chocolate and transliterates the company name into traditional Torah-style Hebrew letters. As Zander put it:

> As religious Jews we live a life in a constant state of refinement that every day should be better than the day before; and for us, chocolate making is an excellent parallel to this concept ... the next batch and all the steps in between will be even better.[6]

Diaspora Influences Both Bar and Business

Holy Cacao's founder, Zander, grew up in New Jersey. Mainstay Elite and Para flavors started in the Diaspora as well, in Riga, Latvia. Janna Gur, who grew up in Latvia, notes the similarity of Elite's bonbonnieres (chocolate boxes) and their contents to the Laima Chocolate she remembers from her childhood. Russian candy maker Eliyahu Fromenchenko

Chocolate Babkathons: New York City

Six babkas. Eight people.

Eleven babkas. Ten people.

On November 2, 2014, and then again on November 6, 2016, while New York City marathoners ran off loads of calories, a group of chocolate babka–minded foodies gathered in Clinton Hill, Brooklyn, to stage counter-marathons. The second lap in 2016 included only a couple of babka repeats since the selection had increased in the two-year interval. Just as the marathons encompassed the city, the scouts gathered loaves from the preassigned bakeries on the Upper East Side, Union Square, the East Village, Gowanus, and Williamsburg. Babkas converged by subway, car, bike, and runner. USPS delivered one from Rockland County. Full disclosure: I attended each event and sampled each babka.

Master planner Amy Rothberger trained for the competition by tracking babka bakeshops and reviews in a zaftig spreadsheet. She tracked them from articles at *Grub Street*, the *New York Times*, *Serious Eats*, *Tasting Table*, and elsewhere. Rothberger explained her obsession with what she labled Babkathons:

> *Babka is labor intensive to make yourself. In a city with so many notable babka bakeries, all purporting to be the best, a babka tasting seemed inevitable.... Babka feels special because a whole loaf is something you have to share (rather than an individual cookie, for instance), so it's sort of required to eat with friends.*[a]

(also spelled Fromchenko) fled to Latvia and founded Laima Chocolate in Riga in 1922.[7] With the Nazi rise to power, he sold Laima in 1933 and immigrated to Palestine, having explored chocolate opportunities in Palestine the year before with his partner, Yaakov Arens. They had met with Lieber (which Elite bought in 1970), which was at that time one of the very few sweets and chocolate companies in the pre-state

Only chocolate-filled babkas qualified. Undaunted by calorie intake, tasters debated the contest categories, eventually agreeing on: chocolatey-ness, gooey-ness, appearance, texture, slice-ability, and overall. Along the way, we learned more about babka, *kokosh*, *kranz*, all variations on a theme from Hungarian or Polish roots. The flatter version, *kokosh*, resembles strudel. If you shop around for babka in Israel, it would be best to ask for *kranz*. Mark's family calls this "rotten cake." The more chocolate, the more rotten, the better. Surprisingly, in Tokyo, I am told, babka is sold from closed museum cases.

Between mouthfuls people mused: "Do you think raisins are OK?" "Hmm, this seems to be barely babka." "I think this one is a waste of calories." "Look at that pretty braiding." "That one's a monster [positive]." The winning babkas were hefty, started with family recipes, and were very "rotten" with chocolate. Each year the critics hit the wall, unable to finish all the babkas. Leftovers went to friends who had never tasted babka before or were reserved for French toast.

Master chef and author Yotam Ottolenghi has spoken about food of the Jewish Diaspora in terms of "survival of the fittest." In his opinion only the best dishes from each cultural background survive in Israel. He admonishes about Polish foods, "Keep the babka."[b] Competitors in Babakthon I and II will definitely keep the babka, Yotam. We promise.[c]

Yishuv settlement. With several partners, Fromenchenko bought property in Ramat Gan and opened Elite. Production began in 1934, with distribution reaching stores in time for Passover. Fromenchenko hawked new products—such as waffle cookies covered with chocolate and sesame encased in chocolate—on the streets. As it grew, Elite located plants in then outlying areas such as Ramat Gan, Sefat, and Nazareth in order to develop Israel's economy. Poet and songwriter Jonathan Geffen captured this pioneer Israeli chocolate scene in his lyrics, "At the edge of Ramat Gan, there's a special place where you can stand and smell chocolate in the air."[8]

In those early years, Elite shipped products to Iraq and to Beirut by train. Based on Polish custom, Elite made chocolate coins in 1958 for export to the United States. In the tradition of the utopian Quaker chocolate companies of England (see chapter 9), Elite built a *beit havraah* in 1941 (a vacation retreat center) for employee use on vacation. In 1945 the company built apartments to sell to workers at special prices. It also provided a medical clinic and an orphanage in K'far Saba in the Central District of Israel.[9]

The official Elite website and other publications differ about the founding narrative from the one I learned from "Gingy" (redhead), Rabbi David Wilfond, former rabbi of the liberal synagogue in Riga. He recalled a woman known as the "Chocolate Princess," a descendant of the Laima Chocolate Factory creators. She was also an original member and leader in the Reform Synagogue of Riga. In this version, Laima was co-owned, years ago, by her family, two Jewish brothers with the family name Moiseyvich (or Moshvitz), meaning "son of Moses." They argued and their partnership dissolved. One brother made aliyah to Israel and, using the Laima chocolate recipe, started Elite. Meanwhile, with the socialization and nationalization of the company under Soviet rule, the Laima company in Riga was confiscated from the remaining Moiseyvich brother, and the chocolate recipes were altered by the new regime. After the collapse of the Soviet

Union, older folks in Riga, remembering the original taste of their beloved Laima chocolate, discovered that Elite had replicated it. Thus, Gingy says, a lot of Israel's Elite chocolate is now imported to Riga. Chocolate Princess Vera Moiseyvich reported to me that she also sees Elite in her local Riga markets.

While Elite had its roots in Riga, it prospered in Israel. Max Brenner, which since 2001 has been owned by the Strauss Group and uses its own chocolate formulas, had its start in Israel in 1996 and has now seeded chocolate throughout the Diaspora in Australia, the Philippines, Singapore, and the United States. A highlight of our trip and a must-visit shop, Chocolate by the Bald Man: Max Brenner, bears the combined names of its founders, Max Fichtman and Oded Brenner. Claiming to create a "new chocolate culture worldwide," Max Brenner tempts with its creative marketing and out-of-the-box chocolate menus for adults and for children. Supreme self-control would be required to bypass the hot chocolate options served in specially designed cups called "Hug Mugs" or "Suckao" cups, the "Choctail" cold drinks/smoothies, and other chocolate treats such as the "Aphrodisiacs" (the liquor-added drinks), the "Max I Scream" (ice cream) options, the crepes and waffles, or the "Sweet Icons" (sundaes).

For her Bat Mitzvah project in 2015, Ashira Abramowitz petitioned Strauss Group to develop a fair trade line for Passover.[10]

Old-New Chocolate

To explore the old-new chocolate of De Karina and its immigration from the Diaspora to Israel, Mark and I made a pilgrimage to the Golan Heights. Driving past numerous army installations, we saw the tiny De Karina factory at Kibbutz Ein Zivan finally emerge out of the morning fog. De Karina may be among the newest chocolate businesses in Israel. Karina Chaplinsky made aliyah from Argentina with her husband and two young children in 2002 through a program that absorbs new immigrant families in a kibbutz framework. Initially, Karina says, she cried a lot, missing her family and friends.

Having sought a change from the economic challenges in Argentina, Karina and her husband were not sure what to do once in Israel. They explored *confitura*, making jams from the local stone fruit. Seeking to provide a unique contribution, however, they soon shifted focus to her South American family business, chocolate. At first they started in her home kitchen, then expanded to the former infirmary, and then moved to the current larger factory location. Now they import high-quality chocolate from Spain and Belgium to the Golan to make the finished product, which is then trucked from the Golan to duty-free shops and stores all around the country. Because only twenty-five miles separate Ein Zivan from Damascus, the factory sits on top of bomb shelters. Local customers include United Nations officials.

While deeply rooted in her Argentinian family's chocolate history, Karina fetes her new Israeli home in the names of her products, drawing on the local mountains such as Hermon, Avital, Bental, and Gamla. A version of folded chocolate is also handmade at De Karina. Karina's grandfather, Jacob Lechtman, had worked in a chocolate company in Germany before fleeing Europe with only his immediate family after World War I. Not able to afford chocolate in the early years in Buenos Aires, he made candy. With increased financing, he slowly developed his chocolate company, Juego Real. The Lechtmans supported the Jewish community there, particularly the Conservative synagogue, Comunidad Bet-Am Medinat Israel. Karina also attended youth group there and traveled to Israel as a youngster.

The De Karina factory is inspired by her father's factory. She treasures his smudged, worn, handwritten recipes at her home, using them with some modification. Karina's father, Louis Alberto, worked by hand in his chocolate company, as she does. In Argentina, Juego Real produced seasonal items. At Easter this meant chocolate chickens, fish, rabbits, and eggs as big as eighteen pounds. At Christmas they made turonis/marzipan with dried fruits. They produced no seasonal Jewish chocolate, because there really was no local Jewish market. Karina lamented that her father did not know that she has built on his legacy.

The truffles named for the local mountains at De Karina in the Golan Heights.

Local Israeli chocolate experiences and unusual con-fections entice, whether with honey and marzipan, produced as liqueur, formed into cocoa spread, baked into *ugah kushit*, or devoured alone. Chocolate's aliyah to Israel accompanied new immigrants such as Elite's founding partners and Karina. Paralleling the growth of the state, it mirrors a heritage of determination and adaptability. From Riga, Argentina, Belgium, Switzerland, and the United States, it has transitioned from generation to generation into the Israeli palate and psyche. Today, the Holy Land chocolate trail also extends out to the Diaspora—to Europe, North America, the Far East, and Down Under.

World's Oldest Chocolate Maker in Haifa

In 2016 when Yisrael Kristal celebrated his Bar Mitzvah at the age of 113, he also celebrated a lifetime of chocolate. Kristal first established a confectionery enterprise in 1920 in Lodz. Sadly he lost his wife and two children during the Holocaust. After he survived several concentration camps, he returned to Lodz to reestablish his candy business. In 1950 he and his second wife made aliyah to Israel, where he went to work for the Palata candy factory in Haifa. Gradually he began his own business out of his home and eventually in 1952 opened his Sar and Kristal company. Specialties included mini-bottle-shaped chocolate-filled liqueurs. Not only is Kristal probably the oldest surviving chocolate maker as of this writing, he holds the Guinness World Record as the oldest living man.[a]

PART TWO

Other Religious Chocolate Revelations

Mark's Cocoa Nibs Citrus Salad

Mark created this delicious and colorful fruit salad. Though citrus was not known to pre-Columbians, the cocoa nibs harken back to the most basic form of the roasted cocoa bean of Mesoamerica.

Ingredients:

1 grapefruit, peeled (membrane removed, optional)
2 navel oranges, peeled
3 blood oranges, peeled
4 clementines, peeled
Pomegranate syrup (optional)
Several tablespoons cocoa nibs, to taste
Pistachios, roasted and chopped

Instructions:

Cut the fruit into bite-size pieces and place in a large serving bowl, preferably glass. Add the pomegranate syrup to taste.

When ready to serve, sprinkle the cocoa nibs and roasted pistachios over the fruit salad.

Quantity: 10–15 servings

Chapter Seven

Pre-Columbian Peoples Idolized Chocolate in Mesoamerica

AFTER THE LONG FLIGHT FROM NEW YORK CITY TO Mexico City, to prospect for chocolate's earliest religious heritage, my energy spiked as I meandered into an Oaxacan-based chocolate shop named Mayordomo at the airport. Inhaling the recently ground chocolate and marveling at the piles of cocoa beans, I aimed directly for several small dishes filled with a dark, thick chocolaty pudding set out on the counter, mini-spoons jutting straight up as if intended for my mouth. Perfect. My first taste of Mexico would be chocolate soufflé. I eagerly picked up the little bowl and happily, yes, greedily, stuffed a spoonful into my mouth. Within seconds I spit it out. Instead of the sweet, warm, chocolate mousse I had expected, I had bitten into a hotly spiced mole cooking sauce. I hastily replaced the little container on the display case and quickly backed out of the store. Out of the corner of my eye, I spied the attendant inserting a new mini-spoon, as she positioned the uneaten remains of my bowl for the next customer!

I had time to browse again, more cautiously, in another Mayordomo outlet at the bustling bus station in Oaxaca as we waited for our family friends, Miriam and Luis. It was close to midnight after our eight-hour bus ride. My sleep-deprived brain

111

A stone metate used for grinding cocoa beans and other local foods.

conjured doubts about the trip. Would we find anything on this chocolate trail that would fill in the mysteries of chocolate, Jews, and other religions? What kind of religious heritage of chocolate, if any, might there be in Mexico? Was this exhausting trip worth it?

Finally arriving at their home, Luis, a Mexico City native, whipped up a comforting bedtime Mexican hot chocolate—a mixture of sugar, cocoa beans, cinnamon, and almonds that had been milled for him at his favorite chocolate purveyor. That soothed the start of the investigation, and despite that first mole, Mark and I enjoyed several more delectable chocolate moments.

True, we found very little eating chocolate except at the Ferbach store next to our hotel in Mexico City; at L'Atelier du Chocolat, which only took orders; and at the Sanborns department store, which showcased truffles. Despite that deficit of eating chocolate, every restaurant and café in Mexico compensated by offering drinking chocolate. We resisted the local custom of dunking a yummy pastry or a chunky churro into each cup of hot chocolate on this pilgrimage to Mexico's chocolate center of Oaxaca, where chocolate perfumed the downtown and Christmas processions tossed brightly colored tissue—wrapped chocolate balls our way.

Chocolate for Breakfast

Multiple stalls in and around the food markets ground cacao beans to order. The larger, local *tiendas de chocolate* mills such as Soledad, Mayordomo, and Guelaguetza also sold packaged bars prickly with sugar and primitively ground chocolate—to be used mostly for drinking chocolate, mole sauce, and chocolate-covered coffee beans. Patchworked on Mina Street, the Soledad and Mayordomo companies each boast multiple storefronts, with Guelaguetza's shop just around the corner. On our first day Luis whisked us to the small town of Tiacolula and his favorite chocolate grinder, Molinos Y Chocolate, from which every few weeks he orders his custom ingredients for hot chocolate. Owner Florentine Antonio Andres filled Luis's spe-

cial request by pouring one kilo of cacao beans from the Mexican cities of Chiapas or Tabasco, two large sticks of cinnamon, and a few almonds into an annoyingly noisy electric grinder.[1] Within seconds, the warm, liquid chocolate oozed into the sugar waiting in the bowl below. Most locals use much more sugar, probably four pounds of sugar to two pounds of cacao. Florentine, who admits to drinking chocolate only a couple of times a week, mixed all of this together with his bare hands, scraping every drop into a Styrofoam container. He promised to crush the

Murals at Café Tacuba in Mexico City recall early chocolate making.

cacao with peanuts for the following week. Back at the house several hours later, we poured the still warm chocolate muck into a cookie pan, cooled it, and scored it into tablets.

At last we were contentedly supplied for a week or more of breakfast hot chocolates. Mark and I agreed that our favorite hot chocolate was homemade by Luis, with second place going to the elegant Café de Tacuba in Mexico City. Tacuba's colorful murals, memorializing the role of chocolate in Mexican and Old World culture, authenticated that delectable drink for us.

Grasshoppers and Chocolate

Sunday found us at the immaculate, orderly, and immense market called Tlacolula de Matamoros (place of abundance). We sampled strange, bright-orange fruits in the footsteps of Hernando Alonso, one of the Jews in the group that accompanied Hernán Cortés (1485–1547) in the conquest of Mexico.[2] As we tossed back flavorful *mezcal*, an alcoholic beverage made from a form of agave, I recalled how Jewish cacao traders escaped the Spanish Inquisition only to face it again in New Spain.[3] Continuing through the market's stalls we bought hand-carved gourds for chocolate drinking, measured two-foot-long sticks of cinnamon, and admired the varied designs on the chocolate stirrers known in Spanish as *molinillos*. As we stared down the market's piles of roasted grasshoppers, I mused about how Jews of the colonial period in Mexico learned chocolate-making skills from the locals and incorporated chocolate into Jewish customs.

We meandered back to Florentine's shop for the anticipated peanut-based batch of chocolate. This time Florentine not only added peanuts but he also ran the goo through the grinder several times to create a finer powder. He confessed that he paid approximately fifty to sixty pesos per kilo of cacao beans, selling the chocolate ground with sugar at 50 percent profit. To add flavor, sometimes he threw cocoa bean shells into the mix. In the busy Christmas season, Florentine needs to replace his grinding stones once a month. The Oaxacan *Posada de Cacao* (procession of cacao) would keep him especially busy. Before Christmas, the procession, representing Mary and Joseph seeking shelter, wanders from home to home singing while the carolers are refreshed with special treats of cacao.

Chocolate Heritage of Mexico

We dug into the very basic and early entwining of chocolate and religion in this region of the world to frame the later Jewish and Catholic commercial and personal use of chocolate during Mexico's colonial period.[4] Just outside Oaxaca this cacao history hovers over the expansive archeological ruins of Monte Alban, host to cultures preceding Columbus and the Spanish discovery of the New World in 1492. Cacao beans and the chocolate beverage were soul food for the people living in Central America, countries we now know as Mexico, Belize, Guatemala, Honduras, El Salvador, Nicaragua, and Costa Rica. We joke that we will die without chocolate. For the peoples at settlements such as Monte Alban, chocolate symbolized life: cacao pods represented extracted hearts and chocolate signaled blood. They depicted this notion in icons of bleeding cacao. These concepts of enlivening chocolate suffused every life transition. Traditions idolized chocolate and the cacao tree as powerful bonds between humans and gods for hundreds of years. Chocolate in cultic contexts escorted infants as well as aged, dying parents over the thresholds of life. Chocolate drinking solemnized political allegiances, noted civic agreements, and marked religious occasions. Divination rituals, human sacrifices, life-cycle offerings, and agricultural rites used cacao. Throughout these occasions cacao flowed thick and strong, sustaining the life force of the community as well as the individuals within it.[5]

Cacao's popularity and potency carried it hundreds of miles from its source. Aztec royalty in Mexico so desired cacao that to attain it they conquered the lowland of the region of Soconusco, along Mexico's border with Guatemala, transporting the beans via canoes or on the backs of porters along intricate systems of trails. Royal females prepared the cacao in formalized rituals at state banquets. The arches from ancient Mayan ruins depicted cacao alongside the god of abundance and wealth, identifying cacao with affluence, a message that the nobility and others certainly drank in.[6]

The plateau of Monte Alban whispered to us of religious tales about the cacao fruit's part in the creation of the world and how it sustained the gods. The biblical narrative focuses on the singular apple as the symbol of sin and exile; this differs greatly from the pre-Columbian elemental first food, cacao. Grown on a sacred tree, cacao was coveted among the supernatural beings and was the very substance of humanity. Before European views and mores infiltrated the area, the Mayans learned cacao stories from their *Popol Vuh*, "The Book

Generations of Chocolate Lovers

Aztec: These Native American people and cultures dominated large parts of Mesoamerica in the fourteenth, fifteenth, and sixteenth centuries, when the Spanish conquered the area. They created a significant empire in the fifteenth century and founded what became Mexico City. They learned about cacao from other peoples nearby. They spoke the Nahuatl language, which some say provides the basis for the word "chocolate," from *cacaoatl*, meaning "cacao water," or *xoco*, meaning "sour water."

Maya: Native American peoples who flourished in Mesoamerica since approximately 2000 BCE and possessed the only written language of these pre-Columbian peoples. The languages and cultures of the Maya still exist in Central America.

Mesoamerican: Area and culture of Mexico, Belize, Guatemala, El Salvador, Honduras, Nicaragua, and Costa Rica prior to the Spanish colonization that occurred in the fifteenth and sixteenth centuries.

Pre-Hispanic and pre-Columbian: The era before Europeans and European culture influenced the area and peoples, particularly before Christopher Columbus's voyages of 1492 to 1504.

of Counsel." It taught that cacao ensured a balance among the earth, sky, and underworlds.[7] In these legends the gods created humans from chocolate and maize. For them, the cacao tree was a "world tree," the first tree, the center of the universe, and the primordial source of life. These ideas were reinforced in depictions of the flower god, Ahaw Nik, who clutched a cacao tree as if it were a staff that supports life itself, as well as in images of ballplayers feeding cacao pods to a god.[8]

Gods Eat Chocolate

From the misty past of high places such as Monte Alban, these peoples would have heard and recounted the Aztec tales of the gift of cacao to humans bestowed by the Aztec god Quetzalcoatl, also called the "Feathered Serpent" or the "Gardener of Paradise." Quetzalcoatl secretly smuggled cacao beans, the food reserved exclusively for the gods, and delivered it to humans, patiently instructing them in cacao cultivation. Out of love for humans, Quetzalcoatl betrayed the other deities. Quetzalcoatl planted a cacao tree, collected its pods, toasted the beans, and then showed women how to beat it with water in gourds to produce the chocolate. When the gods saw how happy the people were, they became envious. They swore vengeance on Quetzalcoatl and banished him. To punish humans, they transformed cacao trees into thorny mesquite bushes, and Quetzalcoatl's last seeds could flourish only in remote Tabasco, in the southeast of Mexico, making cacao harder to enjoy. As a result of this gift of the godly chocolate, "the god of light, the giver of the drink of the gods, the giver of chocolate,"[9] Quetzalcoatl was adored in Mesoamerican villages at impressive gatherings. At an event in his honor, an effigy with a human body and a red-beaked bird face sat in a long, wide chamber decorated with gold, silver, jewels, and fine cloth. Forty days before the feast, a male slave, "flawless of hands and feet, without stain or blemish" was purified twice with water, dressed exactly as the god, shut up in a cage at night, served good food, and decorated with garlands. Portraying the god, the poor man sang and danced and was greeted by women and children. If he became sad or stopped performing, they forced him to drink an elixir of chocolate mixed with blood scraped from sacrificial knives. He was sacrificed at midnight as the price paid for the human enjoyment of chocolate, which should exclusively belong to the gods.[10] Thankfully our chocolate indulgences today only require sacrifices of calories and dollars.

Chocolate Is Life

In the pre-Hispanic days of Monte Alban's activity, cacao nurtured many potent and sacred moments of agriculture and fertility. Supplications for abundant maize, rain, cacao, and good weather reveled in chocolate. In a harvest ritual, gourds of chocolate and other assorted foods were used to appeal to the god Tlaloc. To wheedle rain from Cac, the cave-dwelling rain god, the moon goddess, IxChel, negotiated with him for chocolate over a large pot decorated with two depictions of cacao. In a New Year ceremony, the opossum god carried the rain god as he ate cacao. When the cacao flowers first sprouted, people offered blood from their ears and arms to the earth deities to ensure good weather for the cacao crop. The cacao harvest festival hosted by cacao plantation owners included sacrificing a dog spotted with the colors of cacao, burning incense to their idols, and presenting each of the officials the cacao fruit. To mark the end of the cacao harvest and to honor the cacao god Cacaguate, the Pipil-Nicarao peoples of Nicaragua performed a ceremony of rapturous dancing, with humans leashed to a tall pole flying around the image of the god. The planting of cacao trees deserved blessing as well. Chocolate drinking also embellished the rite of *Xochipaina*, which marked the first flowers of the season.[11] Chocolate smoothed the cycles of the agricultural year at harvest and planting.

Rituals of chocolate eased the goings and comings, the departures and returns of traveling merchants in this pre-Columbian time. Banquets extended divine protection to the merchant, which included cacao drinking songs of the gods and for the gods. Chocolate's support of the most frightful of all journeys, death, also hovered over Monte Alban's steep steps. Chocolate fed the dead, escorted the soul's travels, and promised the possibility of rebirth. It anointed the transition from one world to the next, blurring life and death and easing the sadness of mourners. Mayan funerary implements for food and drink, particularly for chocolate and maize, supplied and decorated the graves of the honored dead. Marking the portals to the underworld, cacao beans represented the bodily organs of new gods. Offerings of chocolate-filled gourds emerging from the underground are depicted at the Temple of the Owls in Yucatán. A supernatural howler monkey holding a cacao pod marched alongside the death god. An incised vessel portrayed a dead man being reborn as a cacao tree, sprouting

History of Cacao

This rich chocolate tradition dates back three millennia. Traces of a chemical component of chocolate, theobromine, have been found in ceramic vessels of Belize, and historians believe that cacao cultivation began around this time as well. The earliest iconography of cacao may be seen on a twenty-five-hundred-year-old Peruvian vessel decorated with cacao pod elements. Many more tall vases and spouted chocolate pots (air blown through the spouts foamed the chocolate) depicted cacao gods and goddesses, cacao trees, cacao pods, and the word *cacao*. Fronds and pods of cacao, emblematic of the source of the community's wealth, sprouted from the bodies of gods and humans. Jaguars were seen as protectors of cacao as they stalked their monkey prey, preventing the monkeys from eating the precious pulp of the cacao pods.[a]

from his earthly grave. The dependence on cacao in death settings may be seen from the placement of a chocolate vase next to a dead king's head.[12]

Chocolate's connection to death profoundly reflected the pre-Hispanic sense of it as a precious life force full of sacred energy. Those who lost blood were treated with chocolate. Chocolate and cacao were fed to Aztec sacrificial victims before their hearts were extracted. Birth festivities started with the purchase of chocolate and the spices often paired with it, such as pepper, cayenne, and achiote. At a Mayan banquet for a newborn, every male guest received chocolate in a *jicara*, a special gourd for drinking chocolate. Children draped in white cloths were decorated with feathers and cacao seeds. The holy water for anointing a newborn was made from "certain flowers and of cacao pounded and dissolved in virgin water."[13] A presentation of cacao would have occurred twelve days from the birth, at the time of the baby's naming. Mothers, when bathing in the river after a delivery, also offered cacao to the river to divert evil. Only young children were considered "pure" enough to serve the "*Kakaw*" drink at such occasions. Ideally, there would have been leftovers of chocolate and other foods from the feast, a good omen that the host would be blessed to offer similar plentiful feasts in the future.[14] The planting of a cacao orchard and the first fruiting of those trees commemorated the growth of a royal child. Chocolate spiced up those first days of life for the baby, the family, and the community.

Cacao and chocolate also sweetened marriage negotiations and ceremonies throughout Mesoamerican culture. In a palace scene depicted on a vase from Guatemala, matchmakers stood above a vessel of chocolate decorated with ear flower, a popular ingredient for wedding chocolate, as they haggled over the nuptial terms. Cacao beans were used as currency to pay the wedding dowry. Cacao drinking sealed traditional marriage agreements between families. At Monte Alban in the early 12th century, chocolate sealed the marriage of the Mixtec

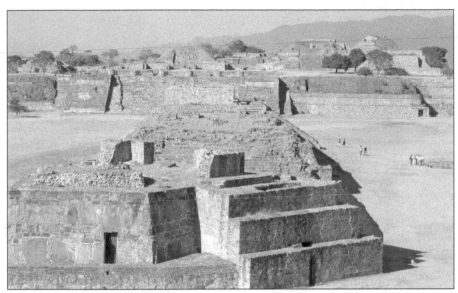

The ruins of the pre-Columbian settlement at Monte Alban, outside of Oaxaca.

ruler named 8 Deer.[15] Contemporary wedding planners might note this efficacy of chocolate in marriage celebrations.

Chocolate in Rituals Today

Today chocolate graces life-cycle occasions in Central America. A matchmaker is often paid in cacao. A gift of cacao goes from the groom's family to the bride's family via the matchmaker, and acceptance of the gift signifies approval of the match. In Yucatán, the bride and groom are feted with chocolate. At Catholic weddings and baptisms as well, the Yucatec Maya of Mexico drink chocolate. In the Kekchi Maya customs for the wedding ceremony, the groom bestows thirteen cacao beans upon the bride. In Guatemala and Mexico, drinking chocolate is served at birth ceremonies twenty days following the birth. It is also presented to godparents before and after the baptism. In Oaxaca, godparents bestow a gift of several kilos of cacao on the parents.[16]

Rituals for the dead depend on chocolate. The pastel-painted graves at the cemetery in Chichicastenango, Guatemala, often bear chocolate, candles, herbs, and sugar laid out in circular configurations. Oaxacan Day of the Dead ceremonies feature chocolate at graves, and at home altars families feast on chocolate and other festive foods. As one local commented, "In this festival, chocolate is the main drink, for the living and for the dead.... When I die, maybe the living will put out chocolate for me, because I liked it."[17] Anthropologists in the 1930s even witnessed chocolate poured into the graves of the Oaxacan dead.

Chocolate also supports the agricultural cycle. Belize villagers still appeal to the cave gods with cacao for good weather. In May, as the dry season and cacao harvest end in Comalcalco, a city within Tabasco, Mexico, the town celebrates the Fiesta de San Isidro Enrama, paying tribute to the patron of cacao, San Isidro, in a most colorful way. Cacao pods and beans are everywhere, tied to horse carts and to bicycles, and made into costumes. Cacao branches line the church steps and the pews. Necklaces of cacao beans decorate the statue of the Virgin Mary and of San Isidro. Priests bless all of these with holy water; some of the income from the local chocolate-processing plant benefits the church, so the factory is included in the blessings as well.[18]

Current Guatemalan Lenten customs connect to chocolate. During the days leading up to Easter week, they drink chocolate rather than coffee. On the Wednesday of Holy Week, the week prior to Easter, known as Semana Santa, young men customarily pilgrimage from Santiago to the coast's ancient cacao groves to gather cacao pods and cacao branches to decorate the town.[19]

I had only grazed the surface of a very deeply embedded and rich chocolate culture of the local peoples when I sought energy from that chocolate nibble at the airport in Mexico City. No wonder Carl Linnaeus's eighteenth-century classification of plants labeled cacao *Theobroma*, the "food of the gods."[20] Pre-Columbians such as those at Monte Alban revered this miraculous and elemental cacao fruit, which they understood to blend innately and inherently into the sacred essence of humanity and existence. They celebrated, perhaps better than we do, an abiding love of chocolate. This amazing fruit of the divine world was, and remains, essential to the sacred moments of human life in Mesoamerican celebrations. Jews, who arrived in this area in the seventeenth century, confronted these chocolate customs. The European clerics who followed Columbus to this region struggled with how these deep and enduring sanctities could, or should, be molded into their Catholicism. These tensions along the chocolate trail span the distance from Central America to Spain.

Mendiants

This easy-to-make confection recalls the mendicant orders of the Catholic Church and embodies the Christian chocolate connections discussed in this chapter.

Ingredients:

4 ounces dark or bittersweet chocolate, broken into pieces
¼ cup cocoa nibs, almonds, or hazelnuts
¼ cup candied ginger
¼ cup dried blueberries or raisins
¼ cup candied orange peel

Instructions:

Line a baking sheet with waxed paper. In a large heatproof bowl, set over a pan of simmering water. Stir the chocolate until melted.

Remove the chocolate from the heat. Drop tablespoonfuls of chocolate onto the prepared baking sheet, using the back of the spoon to flatten into disks. Place one of each of the four toppings onto each circle. Work a few *mendiants* at a time; they will harden as they cool. Cool on the baking sheet until hardened. Store in a cool place in a covered container.

Quantity: About 20 *mendiants*

Chapter Eight

Faith Diffused Chocolate around the World

UNDERSTANDING JEWS, RELIGION, AND CHOCOLATE required Mark and me to try the chocolate goodies (shucks) that memorialize early ties to Christianity while investigating the leads related to the chocolate appetites of sixteenth- and seventeenth-century Christian religious orders. When Catholic clergy first encountered chocolate use among the indigenous peoples in places such as Monte Alban and Central America, some became early chocolate adopters, some critics, and some salesmen. Chocolate delicacies such as the *mendiant* immortalize the mendicant (beggar) orders, those that serve the poor and rely only on donations for support—Augustinians, Carmelites, Dominicans, and Franciscans. Each nut and dried fruit in the *mendiant* treat symbolizes the color of the respective monastic robes: raisins for Dominicans, hazelnuts for Augustinians, dried figs for Franciscans, and almonds for Carmelites. We first noticed *mendiants* in Paris. Eyeing the several artful offerings in a crowded confectionary, I was intrigued by the flat, chocolate disks decorated with nuts and dried fruit. When I asked about it, the attendant muttered an indecipherable French word, which I now understand was *mendiant*. After that we saw them frequently in France and in the

The *mendiant* treat; dried fruits and nuts recall the mendicant orders of the Catholic Church.

United States as well. Though some customs associate *mendiants* with Christmas, we first saw them in the spring. In Provence, Christmas dinner customarily ends with *les treize desserts de Noël* (the thirteen desserts for Christmas), including *mendiants*.

Fishing for Easter Chocolate

Mark and I saw pre-Easter chocolate fare all over France that spring. We noted a lot of fish-shaped chocolates, which we were told are abundantly available and popular during that season in particular, though no one could explain why. I figured that Jesus and fish were associated through the miracles of the fish. Also, the Greek letters for the word for fish relate to an acrostic referring to Jesus as messiah. The French may not know the origin of the custom, but we enjoyed the miraculously yummy chocolate fish.

Geneva's Christmas Chocolate

We encountered another unique religious chocolate custom in Geneva, where December 12 every year is known as L'Escalade, or Fête de l'Escalade. Swiss chocolatiers fabricate soup pots out of chocolate and fill them with vegetables molded from marzipan. This commemorates the 1602 victory of the citizens of Geneva over the attempt of the Duke of Savoy to destroy the Reformation and reinstate Catholic order. Genevans forced the Savoyards to retreat when, according to the legend, a woman called Mére Royaume flung her hot soup cauldron out the window, killing an enemy soldier. To recall that providential triumph, the many festivities include a long-standing custom of the oldest and youngest in each family together breaking

Fish-shaped chocolate for Easter recalls Jesus.

the chocolate pot in victorious joy. A traditional song invokes these words: "God holds the victory in His hand; to Him alone our thanks we bring. May His holy name be forever blessed."[1]

Monastic Chocolate

Other chocolate delicacies with religious sources invigorated us in our travels. When we learned that many Spanish convents and monasteries specialize in chocolate and other *dulces* (sweets), we pulled on the bell of one such Toledo convent, located about forty-five miles south of Madrid, to sample their goodies.

We also sought out Barcelona's Caelum, a shop situated above what some say were Jewish ritual baths. Named for a heavenly constellation, this café features treats from convents and monasteries all over the country. The menu's "Monastic Sweet Temptations" tap into the centuries-old Catholic legacy of chocolate. In Ferrara, Italy, we devoured *pampepato*, "the bread of the pope," a spice, nut, candied-fruit concoction covered in chocolate. Known as a Christmas dainty created first at the monastery of Corpus Domini, it is baked in what the nuns describe as a skullcap shape. In a church square in Turin, Italy, we savored the distinctive *bicerin* drink, which certainly fulfilled its meaning in the local dialect as something delicious. We tried mole at dinner in Oaxaca. In the New World, the Convent of Santa Rosa in Pueblo de Los Angeles may have been home to the first mole. As the legends unravel, Sor Andrea de la Asunción, a nun, or perhaps it may have been the prioress of that Dominican convent, concocted and served a peppery sauce over turkey, adding bitter chocolate at the last minute for the visiting bishop. In another telling of the legend, some think that a nun, wishing to honor the archbishop for constructing a convent for her order, may have combined Old World with New World ingredients, including chocolate.[2] Little did Mark and I know that with these samplings, we had bitten into deeply embedded chocolate complexities and religious controversies.

Clergy Reports: Exotic New World Chocolate

Adherents of the mendicant orders, along with Jesuits and a host of others,[3] generated the first reports of cocoa beans and other New World exotica to the Old World. Some of these religious people treated chocolate's early European history with dismay, ambivalence, or disgust; others with co-optation or with passion. Informants such as Bernardin de Sahagun and Diego de Durán may have had Jewish ancestry.[4] Clerics propelled chocolate's advancement into European awareness, discourse, popularity, and economy. Some sought to squelch pre-Columbian chocolate usage, while others attempted to assimilate it into Christian religious rites. They struggled with chocolate's pagan history, worried about its exoticism, debated its theological implications, and exploited its resources. How could they allow themselves to enjoy this nourishing and tasty substance given its roots in idolatry? Would their missionizing to potential converts fail if the locals were to see chocolate in Christian settings? Could they voice their appreciation of chocolate and also root out heathen rites? How might cacao finance the church?

Not surprisingly, when Columbus and Cortés introduced the drab cocoa bean to the Spanish court, the monarchs focused instead on the glittering gold, silver, and other New World treasures. The first legal shipment of cacao arrived in Spain in 1591, while smaller, private amounts had been sent earlier. Only in 1544, when Dominicans tantalized the court with prepared chocolate presented by a Kekchi Maya delegation of

New World natives, did it slowly gain popularity.[5] From 1585 to 1630 Spain attempted to maintain a monopoly on cacao. This was preceded by written accounts of chocolate. Chocolate lover and priest Peter Martyr d'Anghera's (1457–1526) official chronicle of the New World, which characterized chocolate among the luxuries at the court of Montezuma and the highly evolved culture of Mexico, would have intrigued the reader, especially his description of chocolate "as wine, a wonderful drink, fitte for a king."[6] Confusion may have resulted from Martyr's report that sacks of cacao served as currency. Our idiom about money growing on trees turns out to be about our beloved chocolate:

> Blessed money which furnishes mankind with a sweet and nutritious beverage and protects its innocent possessors from the infernal disease of avarice, since it cannot be long hoarded nor hidden underground.[7] ... For this groweth upon trees ... drinke is made from of them for rich and noble menn.[8]

Martyr's early report of chocolate reached the Vatican, informing Pope Clement VII of its existence. Sadly, the pope, like most of the recipients of these reports, possessed neither the beans nor the equipment for making it[9] and therefore must have been baffled by it all.

Franciscan Friar Bernardino de Sahagún (1499–1590) based his writings about chocolate on interviews of local elders in Mexico.[10] Franciscan Bishop Diego de Landa of Yucatán (1524–79) witnessed a Mayan baptism that used cacao in the anointing water.[11] He also detailed Mayan processing of cacao into what he described as a butter-like grease. Born in Spain and raised in Mexico, Diego Durán (c. 1537–88) entered the Dominican Order in 1556 and then served in Oaxaca. Durán recorded chocolate's use in pre-Columbian religious rites.[12] In his report on his 1730 mission to the West Indies, Father Jean-Baptiste Labat depicted the popularity of chocolate in the New World, citing how Spaniards dunked toasted bread fingers and special biscuits into their chocolate. He also noted that the Creole population of Martinique drank *"Chicolade,"* a daily morning beverage of the New Americans.[13]

Giovanni Francesco Gemelli Careri (1651–1725), a suspected spy for the Vatican, extolled the Spanish transformation of chocolate:

> The efforts of the Spanish have raised chocolate to perfection. Today it is taken so much in the Indies that there is neither Negro nor peon who does not drink it every day and the wealthier four times per day.[14]

A critique of the foamy chocolate was penned by Jesuit José de Acosta (1539–1600) in the 1590s. He named chocolate a cultural marker that differentiated locals from the elite Spanish, describing it as a

> crazy thing prized in that land and Spanish women born in that land would die for the black chocolate ... disgusts [those] ... not of the land ... [those] who had not grown up with ... [those] could not have a taste for it.[15]

To him, it resembled feces. He also mentioned that some drank it hot, cold, or lukewarm; for medicinal purposes it could be applied as a paste.[16]

Seventeenth-century chocolate lover and English Dominican friar Thomas Gage (1597–1656) captured church ambivalence in his account. Gage defined chocolate as nutritious and noted that Spaniards drank sweet chocolate in New World public establishments called *chocolaterias* in the 1630s. His work included an account of chocolate preparation. Impressed by the popularity of chocolate in Mexico among the Spanish, he enjoyed a dinner in Veracruz at the home of a clergyman where the first course was "the Indian drink called chocolate."[17] When fleeing his post in Guatemala, he stockpiled chocolate for his journey.[18]

Chocolate Poisons Bishop

In a gossipy passage, Gage reported about colorful chocolaty incidents in Chiapas, Mexico, where the bishop warned the women to stop drinking chocolate during the Mass. The bishop condemned these disruptions of the holy ceremonies and threatened to excommunicate violators, posting warnings on the church doors against eating or drinking in church. The women protested that they could not be in church without their chocolate. They ignored the bishop and continued to drink in church, until one day the priests rudely grabbed their chocolate cups out of their hands. The husbands gallantly pulled their swords against the priests to protect their chocolate-smitten wives. The chocoholics switched allegiance to a neighborhood church where the nuns and friars were not as demanding. The bishop then mysteriously fell very ill. All of his physicians agreed that he had been poisoned. Gage thought he knew that a particular woman was responsible. She argued against grieving for the bishop. She claimed that since he had so opposed chocolate in church, the chocolate that he had drunk in his own home had disagreed with him. Thus the proverb:

> Beware of the chocolatte of Chiapa! ... that poisoning and wicked city, which truly deserves no better relation than what I have given of the simple Dons and the chocolatte-confectioning Doñas.[19]

Chocolate's popularity seeped from pre-Columbian culture and custom into the Hispanic New and Old World popular palate due, in part, to these generally positive reports from clerics, despite the real ambivalence of some church leaders.

Christians Co-opt Chocolate

Church leaders struggled with what they saw as the theological threats and opportunities presented by chocolate. Some pre-Hispanic beliefs about cacao were folded into New World Christianity in a syncretistic mix. Chocolate leaked into acceptability as it offered a "visceral link to the feel of life and religion in a past era."[20] Early on, Spanish explorer Hernán Cortés argued that pre-Hispanic religious traditions could be refashioned to serve the new rulers and religion. He insisted that Indians welcome missionaries with chocolate because this was already familiar as a customary sign of respect for Aztec priests.[21]

Chocolate could also entice respect for Christianity and Christian celebrations, as, for example, All Soul's Day, when offerings to the dead included cacao. One of twelve Franciscan friars baptizing thousands of Indians daily, Friar Toribio de Benavente (d. 1569), who was also known as Motolinia (the humble one), reported that in almost all the Indian towns mourners served chocolate to their dead kin. In 1743 Jesuits arranged a public drinking of the novel beverage in Guatemala City, a marketing technique for chocolate and Christianity at the same time.[22]

In his guide for the evangelization of the Indians of Central Mexico, Franciscan missionary Diego Valadés (c. 1533–82) fostered a Christian worldview of the centrality of chocolate. In keeping with pre-Hispanic beliefs that saw the cocoa tree as central to creation stories, his book boasts an engraving of a cacao tree at the center of his faith's arboreal realm of the heavens.[23] This veneration of the cacao tree recalled earlier celebratory offerings, the paradise of Quetzalcoatl, and the Maya creation story of the *Popol Vuh*. Valadés digested earlier chocolate pagan notions. A similar example of such co-optation may be found in the representation of the Garden of Eden centered on the cacao tree in the murals of the sixteenth-century Augustinian Monastery of the Purification (*La Purificación y San Simón*) in Malinalco, Mexico. These didactic images and beliefs presented "a world of harmony of Indians and priests in 'perfect Christianity.'"[24]

Priests themselves relied on chocolate for energy and as comfort food in the New World as well as in the Old World. In Bartolomé Marradón's 1616 *Dialogue* concerning the use of tobacco, chocolate, and other beverages, it becomes clear that chocolate had so poured into the life of Catholic priests that his Indian "character" reports that he witnessed a Spanish priest so addicted to chocolate that he interrupted the Mass to drink it while missionizing to Indians. Marradón reported:

> I once saw ... a priest saying Mass who was obliged by necessity—being exhausted—to sit on a bench and drink a *tecomate* [a deep clay cup] full of chocolate, and then God gave him the energy to complete the Mass.[25]

Likewise, in words that Gregorio Mayans y Siscar (1699–1781) dedicated to the Jesuit cardinal Álavaro Cienfuegos, "[Chocolate] introduces life-giving sap ... restores the strength and gives new breath to the spirit."[26] In 1690 a chocolate fan noted with approval:

> Preachers find much good in taking chocolate before and after preaching, taking it before relaxes and gives them better vigor for their task and after it repairs the exhausted spirits, and they ascertain that in addition it gives them ideas and fortifies the memory.[27]

Chocolate took on powerful, sacral qualities. After her family and her church superiors convinced her to enter into a worldly marriage instead of the order, the devout Carmelite novice Isabel de Jesús requested a bit of chocolate to assuage her feelings of anxiety and revive her at a cousin's wedding. Locals also drank chocolate in church, the chocolate competing with the wine and wafer as divine. Chocolate came to embody the Eucharist, building on pre-Columbian linkages between chocolate and blood. The words *chocolate, ambrosia, manna*, and *eucharist* became interchangeable. Oaxaca nuns were famous for their cinnamon- and anise-flavored chocolate. The Concepcionista nuns of Regina Coeli of Mexico City so adored their chocolate that they were called *monjas chocolateras* (chocolate nuns). With time, a Catholic cacao god adorned the Metropolitan Cathedral of the Assumption of Mary in Mexico City. Cacao beans offered at the side chapel of the cathedral enriched the priests. Unlike the bishop of Chiapas, priests permitted chocolate drinking during Mass and sold it as well.[28] Chocolate insinuated itself into the faith.

As chocolate was absorbed into Christian rite, locals soaked up Christianity into their chocolate. A tale related by the Kekchi Indians described the crucified Jesus explaining and endorsing the cacao tree, even perhaps identifying it as the tree of his crucifixion:

> Jesus came down from the tree and lay down in its shade. Then he blessed the tree that it might serve for cacao. Instantly there was cacao. He told the people ... that the cacao should serve in *cofradia* [brotherhood] in marriages and for borrowing money and maize.[29]

Those who argued for chocolate would have looked at this Kekchi tale as proof of their success in adapting chocolate into Christian rites.

Church Condemns Chocolate

For some, this transformation of chocolate into Christian ideas and customs salved the boundaries between old pagan traditions and new Christian religion. Others, however, despaired over chocolate use in long-entrenched pagan heresies, seeing it as a threat to the true faith, as some natives secretly practiced their chocolate-based pagan rites. The first bishop of Mexico, Franciscan Juan de Zumárraga (1468–1548), sought to eradicate all nonconformity, including any related chocolate use. Bartolomé Marradón's *Dialogue* ultimately condemned chocolate due to the sorcery among Indian women to avenge jealousy and to kill people.[30] A 1629 play written by Francisco Gómez de Quevedo y Santibáñez Villegas (1580–1645), *Discurso de Todos los Diablos* (A Discussion among Demons), critiqued heathen chocolate rituals that seemingly imitated Christian practice: "Chocolate-bibbers idolize the cup that they raise on high and adore and go into a trance over [it]," treating it as if it were Communion wine.[31]

Seeking to squelch such unorthodox chocolate rites, one parish priest, Baltasar Herrera, uncovered secret gatherings at the home of Francisco Pech, a Mayan noble. Covert midnight-to-dawn sessions depended on donations of thirty to fifty cacao beans from participants. A *jicara* (cup) of chocolate was passed to each participant in rank order, the art of the *puyulcha* (sacrifice) preparation having been passed down from mother to daughter. A woman named Ana Quime and occasionally her daughter, Catalina, prepared the cacao formula with ground maize and one hundred cacao beans.[32] The rite also required "four new *jicaras* ... idolators of old called it ... a sacrifice sent to the heavens."[33]

The sentencing imposed by Herrera on Pech included a flogging of fifty lashes, exile for three years, with labor at the cathedral in Mérida. Ultimately, since Herrera could not eradicate the idolatry in his area, he in turn was dismissed from his position. In another instance of uncovering these clandestine chocolate rites, one cleric climbed a supposedly abandoned Mayan temple to discover "cacao offerings and vestiges of copal burned not too long before, that was of some superstition or idolatry recently committed."[34]

Also hoping to eliminate chocolate heresies, missionizing Franciscan monks found that the local rulers of Tlanocopan were not willing to give up their gods. Two of these leaders, Tacatetl and Tanixtetl, organized secret worship following the traditional older calendar in local caverns, even when Tanixtetl's son, who had been raised by Franciscans in Mexico City, pleaded that they stop. These rites were discovered by the local *encomendero* (a recipient of a royal grant that included free labor and tribute from the Indians) Lorenzo Suárez. Though the worshippers had escaped, they left behind cultic trappings, including "food, and cacao."[35] As punishment for this transgression, Tacatetl and Tanixtetl endured public flogging and years of labor at a monastery.

In yet another such case, a man named Cristobal and his wife, Catalina, publicly professed belief in Christianity but secretly prayed to their traditional gods in Ocuituco. Their wealth included diverse objects such as a golden crucifix, rosary beads, and "twenty-eight *xicaras* which are used for serving chocolate with eleven stirring-sticks."[36] Cristobal was said to have attended confession only once in ten years. The pagan customs occurred primarily in their home, at midnight, with only a few participants, weekly and monthly. These actions ultimately led to Inquisition inquiries and sentencing to public flogging and hard labor.[37] These attempts and others sought to destroy local pre-Hispanic chocolate religious customs.

Church Debates Chocolate in the Mass, the Fast, and Communion

The ambivalence of clerics also percolated into theological questions about the drinking of chocolate by laypeople and priests during Mass, while fasting, and before Communion. Juan de Solórzano Pereira (1575–1654), a lawyer and judge in Peru whose writings helped form the basis of Spanish law in the colonies for about 150 years, expressed his view that the use of chocolate by priests prior to Communion should be banned. Chocolate challenged the ecclesiastical fast as well as the Mass, and much depended on whether chocolate was classified as a food or as drink.[38] Catholic fasts banned nourishment between midnight and the time of Holy Communion the next day and during the fast days of the Lent period, during which only one meal could be consumed. Such fasts permitted drinking to allay thirst but not to provide sustenance. In those days, bread, ground nuts, spices, or eggs were often added to liquids, including chocolate, turning them into nutritional smoothies. This complicated the questions about chocolate. Also, fasts were undertaken to lessen lascivious desires, which further challenged the permissibility of drinking chocolate. Consider the myth associated with Montezuma, who supposedly drank chocolate as an aphrodisiac before visiting his harem.[39]

While the frequent local usage of chocolate made these inquiries pressing for those in the New World, the pope and his cardinals considered these matters inconsequential and did not pay attention; they had barely heard about chocolate, much less experienced it. Perhaps for this reason as well as the deep love-hate relationship that chocolate engendered among clergy, this debate about chocolate and fasting lasted for more than one hundred years. Those who opposed taking chocolate during the fast argued that it was a food intended to nourish. As further proof, they resorted to an argument based on the Mesoamerican fast to the gods as part of the festival of Quetzalcoatl, which prohibited chocolate.[40]

Others defined chocolate as a liquid with inconsequential nutritional effects, as its essential nature, since its first use in Spain was to alleviate thirst. Further, this argument went, Christians drink wine during fasts, so chocolate drinking should be permitted.[41] It was argued that if one drank chocolate combined with water to alleviate thirst, then it should be allowed. However, if the chocolate was intended as nutriment, as when it is mixed with milk, it should not be permitted.[42] Dominicans tended to be against chocolate drinking during the fast. Finally, in 1666, the Holy Office ended the debate, determining that chocolate during Lent was to be strictly limited to that made only with water and without sugar or milk.[43] Such controversies stirred from the moment that the earliest sips of chocolate crossed the lips of observant Catholics.

Clergy Hunger for Chocolate

Despite these several theological ambivalences and controversies about chocolate, gustatory appreciation for it enrobed many members of the church in the Old World. For them, chocolate became an instrument of adulation, an offering for the greater glory of God. In Spain, monks made chocolate, drank it in secret, and hoarded their supplies and recipes. Alphonse de Richelieu (b. 1585), cardinal of Paris, was among the first there to experience chocolate, when his protégé Cardinal Mazarin brought a personal chocolate maker with him from Italy. In 1634 Mexican Jesuits were shipping chocolate to their brothers in Rome by way of Seville. At a party at his palace, thrown by the viceroy of Valencia honoring the seventh birthday of King Charles II on November 6, 1669, the winning poetry verses claimed chocolate as "manna" preparing one for heaven. For his submission to the contest, a Carmelite friar referred to chocolate as "that inspirational Ambrosia."[44]

Lorenzo Magalotti (1637–1712) imported Spain's chocolate tastes when he returned to Italy bearing a library of recipe books by Cardinal de Moncada. "Jasmine-flavored and citrus-flavored chocolate, the sharp and crackling taste of glacé chocolate, and the much softer one of chocolate flavored with frangipane enticed him."[45] For this Italian philosopher, author, diplomat, and poet, chocolate was "a holy and noble elixir of fresh life ... embellished with vanilla, orange zest, and drops of distilled jasmine, chocolate 'in *garapegra*' the Italians called it, based on the Spanish term ... iced chocolate."[46]

In 1688 Francesco Redi, court physician to the Grand Duke of Tuscany, sent twelve packets of jasmine-scented chocolate delicacies to Jesuit Father Tommaso Strozzi.[47] In 1689 a similarly precious package was sent from the Florentine palace to Jesuit Father Paolo Antonio Appiani of the Society of Jesus, conveying

> the chocolate that, in your note, you say you desire. It is contained in six packets of six different sorts, of which the amber-scented, the Spanish and the jasmine-flavoured sorts should be the best.[48]

Brillat De Savarin (1755–1826), lawyer and epicure, recalled that Madame d'Arestrel, superior of the Convent of the Visitation at Belley (France), taught him about God's part in chocolate preparation:

> When you want to have good chocolate, have it made the night before in a porcelain pot and leave it. The repose

of the night concentrates it and gives it a velvet quality which improves it greatly. The good God cannot possibly take offence at this little refinement, since he himself is everything that is most perfect.[49]

Clerics were very enamored with the New World chocolate delicacy and debated subtleties of preparation. For instance, Dominicans firmly opposed what they called the abuse of aromatic plants in the chocolate beverage from Mexico. In addition, Francesco Arisi wrote to Alessandro Litta, bishop of Cremona, warning of taking chocolate iced rather than boiling it. Benedictine tradition frowned on fancy sauces, which meant that the bishop of Imola's chef, Alberto Alvisi, did not use chocolate in a mole sauce.[50] By contrast, Ignatius Loyola's followers spread a love of chocolate, "securing a monopoly over its trade and distribution, for the 'greater glory of God and his Society.'"[51]

Such chocolate beatitudes flowed among church leaders from Spain to Italy, often insisting on good quality chocolate. Jesuit Father Roberti treated himself to a drink of what he called the "Mexican nectar" at his morning meal. He also sought inspiration from a bowl of chocolate when writing. He noted that he once procured a six-pound supply made with a secret cocoa, a gift from Count Jacopo Sanvitali. When he was in Rome, the cardinal of York had some thirty pounds of chocolate delivered to his room. When in Bologna, Father Roberti received author

Early European chocolate depicted in tiles at the Santa Catalina Bakery, Valencia.

Dr. Francesco Zanotti with a large bowl full of chocolate. Roberti details how the toothless, older man first sucked the head of froth from the top of the bowl and then dipped his *savoyard* (ladyfinger). Roberti kept the *chocolatiére* (chocolate pot) boiling and steaming so that he could replenish the bowl immediately.[52]

Church Exploits Cacao

As church chocoholic addictions increased, the economic interests of the church in the growing cacao trade boomed as well. Clergy fanned the business of chocolate along with merchants and aristocrats of the period. Evidence of this chocolate trade is seen in a lawsuit brought against a ship's captain by a Jesuit in Seville for lost containers of his chocolate. Also a shipment of five boxes of cacao and chocolate spices from Father Andrés Gonzáles, rector of the Jesuit house in Veracruz to Rome, was routed in the name of the *procurador* (delegated by the rector to handle business matters) of the Jesuit order in New Spain. Thomas Gage reported that the church hierarchy worked the chocolate route. In the Indies, clerics adopted the chocolate habit and imported the substance with them when they returned home, carrying "great wealth and gifts to the Generalls," perhaps intending to bribe the popes, cardinals, and nobles in Spain, with "some boxes of curious Chocolate" and other exotica.[53]

Religious orders, particularly Jesuits and Franciscans, were very involved in the cacao business of the New World, notably in Brazil, Paraguay, and Mexico. Between the sixteenth and eighteenth centuries they established many cacao plantations in Brazil. The local peoples were forced off their land to villages called missions, or *reductions*, where the church intended to educate them, work them, and convert them. It also imported black slaves into Brazil to aid in cacao work.[54]

In 1665 it was a Jesuit missionary who brought the first cacao cuttings from the Amazon rainforest to the Bahia and Salvador de Bahia areas of Brazil, both to satisfy the personal desire of the governor general for a reliable chocolate supply and to develop the industry. In 1674 Jesuit João Felipe Bettendorff, SJ, who had administered the Jesuit missions in Pará, traveled by canoe from Pará and transplanted cocoa seeds to Santa Lucia. That went so well that within three years the Jesuit college had more than a thousand cocoa plants. The Jesuits then distributed seeds to the locals for further cultivation. Jesuits experimented with hiring native laborers to gather cacao because they were thought to know how to find the most valuable plants and how to leave the green pods to mature for collection. Expeditions into the jungle often consisted of a mix of this skilled labor and slave labor. By 1749 slaves had systematically planted seven thousand cacao trees in lower Amazonia. This Jesuit involvement with cacao kept Europe well supplied while enhancing revenues.[55] They saw these missions as the "Jesuit Republic,"[56] part of a vision of a great Christian mission state in Brazil. As a Jesuit wrote in 1560, "If there is a paradise here on earth, it is, I would say, this Brazil."[57] Franciscans also anticipated the conversion of the entire world in order to bring about the imminent millennium. While this huge cacao endeavor was initiated and dominated by Christian orders with theological and entrepreneurial motivations, there were priests such as the Jesuit Manoel da Nóbrega in Brazil and the Dominican friar Bartolomé De Las Casas who challenged the enslavements and protested the appropriation of land during the conquest of the Americas.[58]

Similar exploits took place in Mexico, where Jesuits also ran cacao plantations and imported slaves to work on them. Again, Jesuits depended on cacao income to pay their obligations to the mother church and to sustain themselves. A 1693 letter from Jesuit priest Father Alfonso Avirrillaga to the Jesuit Provincial Father Diego de Almonacir described that the college of Chiapas had two cacao plantations, with more than seventy-five thousand trees. A third boasted twenty thousand new cacao trees. It was also equipped with a millstone, enabling processing of the cacao beans. From 1704 to 1707 the annual profit from cacao covered the costs of the college. Similar cacao plantations were located elsewhere in Mexico as well.[59] Through this perverse vision of a paradise on earth embodied in a theocratic state, whether in Brazil or Mexico, these religious orders forcibly converted and enslaved the native peoples to further their cacao revenues.

Chocolate Travels California's El Camino Real

Chocolate provided good road food as the church extended its mission to California, creating the six-hundred-mile mission trail that originated in Baja California Sur, Mexico, and ended in San Francisco. Known as the El Camino Real, or the Royal Road, it connected twenty-one Catholic missions. Excitement about cacao and chocolate journeyed there through Franciscans such as Father Junípero Serra.[60] Some forty-four of Father Serra's many letters mention chocolate, indicating its importance in the daily life of the missions. When Father Serra left Spain for his duties in the New World, he nestled chocolate in his personal belongings. One of Serra's reports about this trip complained that rationed water on the ship did not allow for chocolate drinking. When storms required them to make port at Puerto Rico and the captain reneged on his promise to feed the passengers, a local Christian mission provided sustenance in the form of chocolate: "For eighteen days we ate better than in any convent, all drinking chocolate every day."[61] And then again, when the ship returned to Puerto Rico due to storms, Serra marveled at the chocolate provided by the locals, so much that they were also supplied for the remainder of the journey.[62]

In Mexico City for his first New World position, Serra created a set of administrative guidelines for the College of San Fernando, which included chocolate usage and concerns. His rules cautioned against giving women chocolate at any of the meals in the convent, perhaps to avoid possibilities of seduction or tempting distractions. The chocolate shop (chocolatería), at the hostel on church premises held hours from 4:30 in the morning until 3:30 in the afternoon. Later, during a terrible cold spell, while founding the second mission at the Monterey Presidio, Father Serra noted "chocolate that, Thanks God, we were not lacking up to now."[63] Serra sometimes tended to the sick with chocolate allotments and also used it to motivate hard work.[64] Arguing that the port at San Blas needed to stay open for supplies and commerce, Father Serra entreated the viceroy in 1773 "not only for the corn but for the chocolate loads."[65] In addition, mission hospitality to guests was extended through chocolate. When the church determined to turn over supervision of the Baja missions to the Dominicans, Father Serra bemoaned to the padre responsible for the provisions that chocolate supplies were completely diminished at the missions. One of the first records related to chocolate in California may have been composed by Father Visitor Joseph de Echeverría, who sought to acquire chocolate and chocolate equipment, including about ten dozen hand mills. Felipe Barri, governor of Loreto, complained in 1769 that the Franciscans had stolen chocolate. When leaving Loreta to establish the mission at Velicatá, the supplies left behind for the next settlers included chocolate.[65] Chocolate traveled the route of the California missions as it had in other expeditionary ventures of the church.

Our travel trail's treats guided us to this venerable clerical tradition of chocolate. Mark and I learned that faith indeed spread chocolate into new regions of the world, into new religious contexts, and into new appreciation. As Europeans slowly acquired a taste for it, celebratory chocolate enhanced many Christian settings and unsettled others. Church leaders depended on chocolate for physical, economic, and spiritual sustenance. Catholic chocolate affirmed and adapted pre-Columbian chocolate. It proved to be much more complicated than Jewish chocolate at this time. We learned that Quakers conjured new perspectives of chocolate when our chocolate trail progressed into England.

Forgotten Cookies

The chocolate bud, or "kiss," that tops each of these cookies created quite a stir among competing chocolate makers in the late 1800s and early 1900s as unraveled in this chapter. To ensure a good result, as our friend Rabbi Marianne Luijken Gevirtz said when sharing this recipe, "Don't peek while the cookies are in the warm oven!"

Ingredients:

2 large egg whites
⅔ cup sugar
1 cup chocolate chips, cocoa nibs, or both
1 cup pecans, coarsely chopped
Pinch of salt (optional)
1 teaspoon vanilla extract
30–40 chocolate buds or kisses

Instructions:

Preheat the oven to 350°F. Line two or three baking sheets with parchment paper or aluminum foil. Beat the egg whites until foamy. Gradually add the sugar and beat until stiff. Gently fold in the chocolate chips and/or cocoa nibs, and nuts. Add the salt and vanilla. Drop teaspoonfuls onto the prepared baking sheets. Cap each cookie with a chocolate bud or kiss. Place the pans in the oven; after about 1 minute turn off the heat. Leave in the oven for several hours or overnight. Carefully peel the cookies off the paper or foil using a spatula.

Quantity: About 35 cookies

Chapter Nine

Utopian Chocolate Saved Souls

From Cadbury to Hershey

OUR QUEST FOR JEWISH AND RELIGIOUS CONNECTIONS to chocolate had us traveling to London and then another 262 miles north to the beautiful, rain-soaked town of Kendal. We were excited to pursue the description we read online about "our 1657 chocolate house, ... discover the delights of chocolate in all its different forms." When we finally arrived, we learned that while the building dates back to 1657, it had no chocolate until very recently. That was not the way it had seemed on the website. The words from Gilbert and Sullivan's comic opera *HMS Pinafore*, "Things are seldom what they seem," began to echo in our heads as we traveled a circuit of England's chocolate in Oxford, Birmingham, and the York Lake District. In Oxford, we paid homage to the site of possibly the first chocolate in England, the Grand Café. Birmingham's Cadbury, York's Rowntree, and Bristol's Fry overflowed with Quaker chocolate.

A curious blend of chocolate informed by Quaker religious utopianism, industrial paternalism, and clever tourism all folded together in the British chocolate companies of Fry, Rowntree, and Cadbury. Later, the American Hershey Company molded itself similarly. In the eighteenth and nineteenth centuries, the

Chocolate House in Kendal dates back to 1657 but only recently started selling chocolate.

then novel chocolate business offered Quakers tempting new opportunities at a time when the government of England excluded Quakers from university, prohibited their entrance into the medical, legal, or other professions, and precluded them from apprenticeships and partnerships. Pacifist Quaker views eliminated military service as a career option. Quaker support of the Temperance Movement melded well with chocolate drinking as an alternative to alcohol. The success of such Quaker chocolate businesses benefited workers and their communities. Industrial advances in chocolate-making equipment, plus improved distribution via Britain's railroad system, afforded a perfect cauldron for companies with high ideals.[1] No doubt Quaker religion influenced these British chocolate businesses, which in turn inspired Milton Hershey.

Quaker Apothecary Fry Sells Chocolate: 1759

Quaker Joseph Fry started selling drinking chocolate in Bristol in 1759. His grandfather, Zephaniah, was an early and devoted follower of George Fox, the founder of the Religious Society of Friends, the Quaker movement. As an apothecary, Fry had disguised bitter-tasting medications in chocolate. He advanced the new chocolate industry in advertisements that read, "The best sorts of chocolates made and sold wholesale and retail by Joseph Fry, Apothecary, in Small Street Bristol."[2] Using newly developing factory systems, Fry began selling "eating chocolate," or *Chocolat Délicieux à Manger*, in 1847.[3] This may have been the first widely available eating chocolate in England. Fry became the largest manufacturer of chocolate in the world of its time, having acquired the right to supply chocolate and cocoa to the Royal Navy. Though Quakers do not observe Easter, Fry saw a business opportunity in producing the first chocolate Easter egg in the United Kingdom in 1873. Having survived for 150 years, Fry was bought by another Quaker-owned chocolate company, Cadbury, in 1919.[4]

John Cadbury Opens Coffee and Tea Shop: 1824

Cadbury's story begins long before any merger with Fry. Twenty-two-year-old Quaker John Cadbury opened a coffee and tea shop in 1824 in Birmingham, where he proudly also sold cocoa: "John Cadbury is desirous of introducing to particular notice 'Cocoa Nibs' prepared by himself, an article affording a most nutritious beverage for breakfast."[5] In 1853, Cadbury obtained the royal

A hot chocolate at the site of the first coffee house in Oxford, England, opened by Jacob the Jew in the mid-seventeenth century.

privilege to supply chocolate to Queen Victoria. Cadbury imported cutting-edge Van Houten equipment from Holland in order to make its successful "Cocoa Essence," a higher-quality cocoa than had been previously available in England. John's son, Richard Cadbury, developed the first Valentine candy box, though Quakers were not observers of Valentine's Day. Between 1893 and 1899, the business grew dramatically, and the Cadbury workforce bulged from 800 to 2,600.

The Cadbury family's deep religious belief in responsibility for others led them to ameliorate dangerous and unsanitary factory conditions and workers' slum housing. Influenced by contemporary writings about garden cities and labor reform, Cadbury implemented innovative benefits to workers such as granting a half-day off on Saturdays, closing completely on legal holidays, and providing medical and dental care at the factory. Eventually the workweek was reduced to forty-eight hours and savings accounts were provided, with an initial deposit by Cadbury. In 1866, daily Bible readings created a wholesome and proper atmosphere. Revivalist hymns were introduced into the daily routine a few years later.[6] Other factory amenities included heated dressing rooms, kitchens for warm meals, gender-separate gardens, sports facilities, and swimming pools. Women workers who married were dismissed from their jobs to raise their families but received flowers and a Bible.

Beginning in 1895 Cadbury developed a model town in nearby Bournville, partly to assist employees and also to prevent developers from accessing the land. With the first homes designated for the highest-ranked employees, Cadbury added cottages with gardens for workers and others. The town was open to people of all faiths yet informed by Quaker values, so alcohol was prohibited. Cadbury built an almshouse for retired employees in 1897. Members of the Cadbury family, especially George and George Jr., were interested in education and taught in the adult school movement.[7] Young employees were dismissed early for required night school. Visiting Bournville in 1933, novelist J. B. Priestley wrote about the Cadbury family that they

> have of course long been in the class of the school of the benevolent and paternal employers.... Here in a factory run for private profit are nearly all the facilities for leading a full and happy life.[8]

Cadbury and Hershey

Milton Hershey modeled aspects of his business after Cadbury when he started out. Today, in turn, the Hershey Company holds the license for manufacturing some Cadbury chocolate products in the United States. Hershey almost bought Cadbury in 2010.

George Cadbury also exhibited a special warmth for children. At bedtime on Sunday nights, he routinely visited the youngsters hospitalized at the Birmingham Cripples Union bearing a large box of chocolates with each visit. Following World War I he took an interest in the children of Vienna, inviting some of the refugees to Bournville. Vienna's *Neue Freie Presse* called him the "Chocolate Uncle" after he sent three tons of chocolate for the Viennese waifs recovering from the stresses of war.[9] As he said, "If you can show that your life is happier by giving ... you will do more good than by preaching about it."[10] As we learned in chapter 5, the moniker "Chocolate Uncle" carried over to World War II.

In these personal and corporate actions, Cadbury reflected savvy business instincts and enlightened progressive reforms. Cadbury merged with Schweppes beverage brand in 1969, demerged in 2008, was acquired by Kraft Foods in 2010, and is now owned by Mondelēz.

Religious Rowntree Family Ventures into Chocolate: 1862

As with Fry and Cadbury, Quakerism formed a primary ingredient in Rowntree's chocolate. In 1862, Quaker Henry Isaac Rowntree purchased the Tukes' cocoa and chocolate business (founded in 1725) and was joined by his brother Joseph in 1869 in York. Mary Tuke's grandfather had been one of four thousand people jailed for their Quaker beliefs in the 1660s. The Rowntrees grew up with Bible readings after breakfast, the required memorization of a Bible verse each day, regular Society of Friends meetings at their home, openness of inquiry, and tolerance of difference at the Friends school. It was a very orderly household, with father Joseph Rowntree issuing memos about mealtimes, behavior rules, and meeting attendance. Joseph Rowntree Jr. also engaged in good works, such as tracking statistics on poverty, writing five books about temperance, and teaching adult school every Sunday morning until he was sixty years old.[11]

The Rowntree Company also extended generous benefits to its workers, including a domestic school for young women, a widow's benefit fund, and the company village with housing

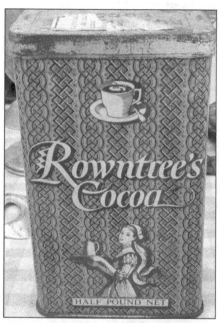

in New Earswick, near North Yorkshire, England. Joseph Rowntree's other son, Benjamin Seebohm Rowntree, conducted his own study of York's poor in 1899. Women workers who married were given a tray and a Rowntree's plaque. In 1906 the company board started a pension plan and later built gyms and schoolrooms, with compulsory classes for the youngest workers. The Joseph Rowntree Charitable Trust and Joseph Rowntree Social Services Trust were established in 1904. Veterans of World War I were given jobs, even if they could not fully accomplish the work.[12]

We found this Rowntree's Cocoa tin in Jerusalem bearing a Hebrew sales sticker.

The Rowntree's confectionery industry contributed much to the town of York as a source of employment and also as a model of social responsibility. Nestlé purchased the company in 1988.

Hershey Discovers Chocolate: 1894

Milton Hershey started his chocolate company in the Quaker state of Pennsylvania, sensing that his successful caramel company seemed to be declining and that chocolate would become more popular. His maternal grandfather was a bishop of the Reformed Mennonite Church (Anabaptist). Throughout her lifetime, his mother wore the traditional Mennonite fitted gray dress, white prayer cap, and black bonnet. However, Milton did not take to formal religion. When he was once asked about his religion, he said, "The Golden Rule."[13]

Visiting the World's Columbian Exposition of 1893 in Chicago, Hershey was enamored with the several chocolate exhibits, especially with the chocolate-making machinery displayed by J. M. Lehmann Company of Dresden, Germany. Right there he bought the equipment and had it shipped by train to Lancaster, Pennsylvania. He immediately hired chocolate makers from Baker's in Massachusetts.[14] To learn more about the business, he traveled to England to visit Cadbury, Rowntree, and Fry as well as chocolate makers in other European countries. He presciently told his cousin that he intended to concentrate more and more on making chocolate, anticipating it to be a more substantial business in the long run. In the early years Baker's and Ghirardelli of San Francisco, the second oldest chocolate company in the United States, understandably sold much more chocolate than he did. However, the earnings from the first full year of Hershey's chocolate operations (1905–6) topped one million dollars. Although the challenge of creating a milk chocolate had been accomplished by Daniel Peter and Henri Nestlé in Switzerland in 1875, Hershey experimented with his own formula for milk chocolate in the 1890s. Hershey decided not to make milk chocolate the way Europeans did. By the turn of

A chocolate set, including a chocolate pot and stirrers, displayed at the Fairfax House in York, England.

the century, he had 114 different chocolate products. Less than a century later, the 1964 World's Fair in New York featured the Hershey Company's pavilion, the third largest at the fair.[15]

The Quaker chocolate companies Hershey had visited in England, as well his own background, inspired the way he molded his philanthropic efforts. He donated generously to his wife Kitty's Catholic church and to each of the other local churches in town. Factory profits were shared with the community through the development of the town of Hershey, Pennsylvania.[16] Hershey rejected the first "cookie-cutter houses" planned by his friend, Harry Lebkicher, desiring them to be more individualized. The amenities included indoor plumbing and electricity. The town provided a bank, a department store, new schools, entertainment, a subsidized trolley, and ultimately a community theater featuring Broadway shows. Monroe Stover recalled moving to Hershey in 1911, where his family rented a house with indoor plumbing and electricity on Areba Avenue, paying only fifteen dollars a month for rent:

> It was a small house for the nine of us but it was our first
> modern home and I'll never forget it. Moving to Hershey
> was like moving to paradise.... Everybody kept chocolate
> in their cupboards.[17]

Not surprisingly the press called Milton Hershey the "Chocolate Man," describing him as a good-hearted soul. He and Kitty founded the Hershey Industrial School for poor, male orphans. As he put it, "What good is one's money unless one uses it for the good of the community and humanity in general."[18] The boys were given clothes, one hundred dollars, and help finding a job at graduation or a full scholarship to college. Sunday school attendance was required. Childless, after Kitty's early death, Hershey in 1918 transferred all of his assets and his Hershey Chocolate Company stock—essentially all of the Hershey enterprise—to the school. Several Hershey executives graduated from the school, including William Dearden, CEO and chairman of the board in the 1970s. During the Great Depression, the Hershey enterprise mounted a tremendous building project that continued to enlarge the town and also generated jobs for the community. Thus Milton Hershey's company and town prospered, unaffected by the devastating desperation elsewhere. In 1938 the Hershey Foundation endowed the short-lived Hershey Junior College, offering tuition-free higher education to all Derry Township residents (Derry Township being the governing municipality of Hershey) and all employees of the Hershey corporations.[19]

Chocolate Business: Not All It Seems to Be

Hershey, Cadbury, and the other chocolate moguls inspired by high ideals admirably sought to combat the terrible working conditions, poverty, illiteracy, and other social ills of their time. However, a closer look at these utopian chocolate companies reveals some "bloom" (discoloration) on the chocolate bar concerning ingredients, business practices, and shockingly, chocolate produced by child and slave labor. Despite the virtuous intentions of their business practices, these good people stumbled.

Adulteration of cocoa ingredients was pervasive in the nineteenth century. Cadbury and Fry each admitted to adding impurities such as starch and flour and then launched intense advertising campaigns claiming the purity of their respective products. Cadbury put Fry on the defensive, so that by 1897, Fry had been vastly diminished in the thirty-year contest between the two companies over this issue. These companies also fought over claims about the production of the first chocolate Easter eggs. Fry grabbed that distinction in 1873; Cadbury's website states that it brought out the first chocolate Easter egg in 1905.

This competitive business continued into the twentieth century. Just a few years ago British companies, Cadbury in particular, fought to gain acceptance of the use of less expensive cocoa butter substitutes such as dairy butter or vegetable oils (cocoa butter equivalents, or CBEs) in eating chocolate. This

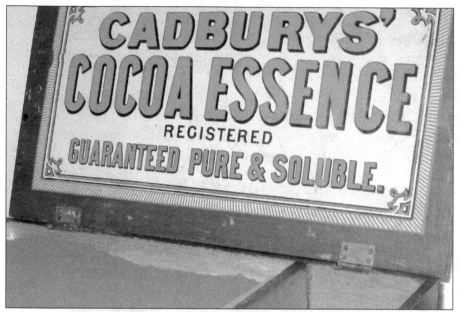

Accusations of adulterated cocoa flew between Fry's and Cadbury.

reduced the price but also affected quality and taste. Due to the advocacy of Cadbury and others, the European Court of Justice in Luxembourg ultimately settled that thirty-year controversy, determining that candy companies could diminish the amount of chocolate content by up to 5 percent yet still label it chocolate.[20] Consumers should check the packaging of those European chocolates to make sure that the chocolate is really what it seems to be (see chapter 11).

In America, Hershey was not above shenanigans in business. Milton Hershey spied on Baker's company to learn more about chocolate-processing techniques in 1900. He was sued in 1905 for copying the packaging of Daniel Peter of Europe. He initially marketed a knockoff of Baker's Bittersweet to gain a foothold in that market. Moreover, his town of Hershey was motivated not only by altruism but also to generate revenue for the company. This may explain the lack of a mayor and city council there.[21]

Mark and I sniffed out some suspicions about the vastly popular Hershey's Kisses on our visit to Pennsylvania. The town of Lititz hosts a lovely chocolate café plus a museum at the Wilbur Chocolate Factory, replete with a beautiful collection of porcelain chocolate pots. The Wilbur Chocolate Company was founded in 1865 by Henry Oscar Wilbur and Samuel Croft and was purchased by Cargill in 1992. Browsing the Wilbur chocolate treats at the museum, we noticed that at least ten years prior to Hershey's introduction of the chocolate "kiss," Wilbur had been making "Wilbur Buds." These small, conical-shaped chocolate drops, initially available only in dark chocolate when first introduced in 1894, were individually foil wrapped. It turns out that at the time a number of companies were making candy kisses in varied flavors. However, very few of these kisses, if any, were made from chocolate. The bottom of the Wilbur Bud was molded into a flower with the letters "Wilbur" in each petal. Hershey introduced his "Milk-Maid Chocolate Kiss" in 1907, with a flat, undecorated bottom, making its manufacture less expensive than that of Wilbur Buds. As the chocolate turns, in 1906 Wilbur trademarked its name of "Bud" and went to court in 1909 to stop several imitators. With time, Hershey sought to secure its Kisses from encroachment through advertisements such as

These Wilbur Buds, with their floral decorations, were made in Lititz, Pennsylvania, about ten years prior to the Hershey Kiss.

"Insist upon having the 'Genuine' Sweet Milk Chocolate Hershey's KISSES. Be Sure They Contain the Identification Tag 'Hershey's.'" The Italian Perugina chocolate company developed a kiss with epigrams inside the wrappers in 1922.

Only in 2001 could Hershey gain the trademark on "Kiss," given the prior attitude of the trademark examiners that it was a general term. Today more than sixty million Kisses, in multiple flavors and combinations, roll off the lines from at least two factories daily while Wilbur Buds may only be bought online or in Lititz.[22]

Cadbury's False Utopia: Slave Labor

Even worse than these commercial thefts and deceptions, cacao grown through slave and child labor cracked apart some of those Quaker principles. The Cadbury family had contributed to the British anti-slavery movement since at least 1893. Family members also subscribed to *The Reporter*, the publication of the Anti-Slavery Society.[23] Company founder George Cadbury belonged to the Aborigine's Protection Society from approximately 1900 to 1908.[24] In 1901 William Cadbury was told about the slave labor in cacao plantations in the West African island of São Tomé that then supplied about half of the cacao beans used by Fry and Cadbury. Those cacao harvests, some said, generated wealth comparable to that of the California Gold Rush.[25] Before beginning his journalistic investigations into the slave sources of chocolate in 1904, author Henry Woodd Nevinson contacted Cadbury company leaders to work with them in their research. They assured him they would run their own investigation. Nevinson offered to represent Cadbury in these inquiries, but its representatives wanted him to learn Portuguese first. They then selected Quaker Joseph Burtt to travel to São Tomé and to report to them about his findings. Before the journey, Burtt spent close to a year studying Portuguese.[26] Around the time that Burtt finally arrived in Africa in 1905, Nevinson was already publishing his exposé about cacao slavery in a series of articles for *Harper's Monthly Magazine* from 1905 through 1906. In 1906 it was published as a book titled *A Modern Slavery*. As Nevinson noted, slavery meant that England and America accessed chocolate and cocoa cheaply.[27] Overall, the Fry/Cadbury/Rowntree investigative process took almost a decade. Burtt's report, finally published in 1907, corroborated the Nevinson findings. Burtt concluded:

Thousands of black men and women are, against their will and often under circumstances of great cruelty, taken away every year from their homes and transported across the sea to work on unhealthy islands, from which they never return. If this is not slavery, I know of no word in the English language which correctly characterizes it.[28]

Only after a number of years, the exposé, and a lawsuit did Cadbury finally boycott Portuguese cacao.

Cadbury and the other giant reformer chocolatiers poured much good into their communities and their workers over the years. They represent a significant stage of the chocolate trail. However, the combined ingredients of the theft of the concept of Wilbur's chocolate Wilbur Buds, the use of cocoa butter substitutes in some British chocolates, the history of earlier adulterations, topped off with serious human rights violations in chocolate sourced from slave labor, leave a slightly sour aftertaste. Sadly, though well intentioned and at times very progressive, this utopian-inclined chocolate was not all it seemed.

Bicerin

This very unusual, rich, layered drink of Turin, Italy, warms us with memories of the earlier days of women drinking chocolate at the time of Mass.

Ingredients:

¾ cup whole milk or cream
3 ounces dark chocolate, finely chopped or shaved
1 cup espresso or very strong coffee
Lightly sweetened whipped cream, flavored with vanilla or
cinnamon or both, to taste

Instructions:

Warm the milk or cream slowly over low heat in a double boiler, stirring frequently, until steaming; be careful not to scorch it. Add the chopped chocolate to the steaming milk. Stir slowly over low heat, not allowing the mixture to boil. Remove from the heat.

Pour ¼ cup of the warm chocolate into each of four heatproof glasses. Using the bottom of a tablespoon held against the side of the glass to create a separate layer, pour ¼ cup of espresso into each glass. Again using a tablespoon, pour an equal layer of whipped cream over the top of each drink. The cream should be hand-whipped to a consistency just thick enough to float on top of the drink.

Quantity: 4 servings

Chapter Ten

Gods in My Chocolate

SOMEHOW GODS GOT INTO MY CHOCOLATE. MOST people would agree that chocolate is a divine delicacy. Aztec lore imagines the gods fighting over chocolate (see chapter 7), resentful about sharing it with humans. Consider the miracle of chocolate's transformation from a tiny white flower to a seed-filled, colorful pod hanging from a tree trunk to a brown bean and then into a drink or edible. No wonder botanist Linnaeus categorized chocolate as the food of the gods, *Theobroma cacao*. Religious peoples supped on this godsend; they have been chocolate traders, makers, and retailers. A godly food, miraculous in nature, enjoyed by people of faith throughout time, chocolate became a primary ingredient in passionate debates over chocolate replicas of gods in the early twenty-first century. Blasphemy or art?

Chocolate controversies surface in both commercial settings and in the arts. Chocolate figures of Hindu and Buddhist gods, along with Christianity's Jesus, cozy up together on display shelves or web pages, forging a sweetshop interfaith unity. Songwriters, authors, and sculptors seek to replenish souls and uplift spirits with chocolatey gods. Nevertheless, righteous indignation erupts at them.

The movie *Chocolat*, which was based on the 1999 book by Joanne Harris, exemplifies the tensions between the exoticism of chocolate and religious blasphemy. Vianne Rocher drifts on the sly North Wind to an uptight French Catholic town monitored by a repressed mayor and a harsh priest where people are expected to know their place. The never-married Vianne and her six-year-old daughter, Anouk, violate several rigid village norms, including not attending church. Defiantly, they open La Chocolaterie Maya chocolate shop during Lent, a period when many foreswear chocolate and other sweets. There, Vianne serves her imported, thousand-year-old Mayan recipe for hot chocolate. She feeds the community love, affection, and reconciliation through cocoa nibs, *mendiants* (see chapter 8), and nipples of Venus bonbons. Her chocolates magically restore an alienated married couple, fortify an abused wife, and reunite a grandmother estranged from her grandson. Even the mayor finally succumbs to cocoa joys in orgiastic gluttony. In the end Vianne defies the North Wind to settle permanently in her chocolate-transformed town. Just as Jesus healed, Vianne, the wandering outsider, mends the town and herself, through curative chocolate.[1]

Tom Waits's 1999 song "Chocolate Jesus" also whips up chocolate conundrums. Waits imagines that chocolate molded into a Jesus figure satisfies his soul in lieu of church attendance. Chocolate supplants the communion wafer, what he calls an "immaculate confection."[2] Since his chocolate Jesus loves him and makes him feel good, he does not need Sunday church. Several chocolate artists and chocolate producers actualized chocolate Jesuses based on Waits's words.

Similarly subversive and ostensibly sacrilegious themes about eating a Jesus formed from chocolate flow through novels. In *Chocolate Jesus*, the Reverend Willie Domingo of the Church of the Returning Vegetarian Christ instigates a mini-Armageddon by preaching against the molding of chocolate Jesuses at a local family-owned chocolate company. He intends his diatribe to divert attention from his false prediction about the end of the world. Considering this small-town chocolate Jesus, a rough character named Dude 1 timidly admits, "If I'm gonna be scarfin' up a chocolate bar,

I don't wanna be biten' off Jesus' head."[3] Writer Thomas Quinn unpacks the question of his book's title, *What Do You Do with a Chocolate Jesus?*: "Do you work your way up the legs or go right for the halo? Do you worship it? Share it with friends as at the last supper? Is it like a communion wafer that became the flesh of Christ before it hit your lips?"[4] For Quinn, Jesus chocolates elicit ridicule and disbelief.

A Trinity of Chocolate Artists

Outrage ensued when three artists—Richard Manderson in Australia, George Heslop in England, and Cosimo Cavallaro in New York City—seemingly unknown to one another, each sculpted a chocolate Jesus exhibit within an eleven-year period around the season of Holy Week. Two of them designed their pieces to denounce Easter candy consumerism. They were critiqued for their critiques. The third saw his Jesus as a gift and an offering. These "confection Christ" figures were mis-understood and denounced, as Jesus was by some in his day.[5]

Chocolate Jesus Shuts Down Gallery

"It's an all-out war on Christianity," decried Catholic League president Bill Donahue. Cardinal Egan, then archbishop of New York, called it "a sickening display."[6] These and other condemnations led to the cancellation of *My Sweet Lord*, a show created by Cosimo Cavallaro that had been scheduled for Holy Week 2007 at the Lab Gallery of the Smith Hotel in midtown Manhattan. The death threats, boycotts, protests, and national news coverage about the two-hundred-pound, life-size, nude milk chocolate figure of Jesus continued for at least six or seven months. Cavallaro was confounded by the reactions to his Jesus gift. Mostly he felt humiliated and mobbed. At the peak of the scandal, Cavallaro picked up a phone call from a stranger on her deathbed demanding that he apologize for his sin. In a conversation with me, Cavallaro speculated about the source of the intense anger: Maybe because it was Easter season? Maybe the brownness of the chocolate Jesus? Maybe the nudity of his Jesus? In retrospect he was proud that he had not become vulgar in response to the accusations and the defamation. Yet, he also admitted that subconsciously he may have sought the uproar.

Surprising support for *My Sweet Lord* came from evangelical Christian conservative David Kuo in the White House Office of Faith-Based Community Initiatives. Kuo argued, "Instead of getting all amped up over this 'art,' Christians should be spending time facing the real and very challenging Jesus found in the Gospels, and encouraging others to do the same."[7] Cavallaro was not the first to serve up a candied religious figure in New York City. It turns out that the Archdiocese of New York had handed out white chocolate Virgin Marys at an event.[8]

For Cavallaro the piece became part of a cycle of destruction and beauty. The persecuted chocolate Jesus came to recall Jesus's history, the loneliest part of the self as new life unfolds. It became a gateway to the soul through the reality of the crucifix. Cavallaro had always had positive feelings about the Eucharist and "connected that ritual of ecstasy to his own experience of chocolate."[9] The chocolate Jesus embodied both death and new life, and therefore reflected the themes of Holy Week and church traditions of religious art. As a child he longed for the crucifix over his parent's bed, yearning to taste it. He did not expect the Jesus statue to be eaten, though he admitted to nibbling bits of chocolate as he sculpted.[10]

> My intention was to celebrate this body of Christ, in a sweet, delicious, tasteful way ... using chocolate ... because it's a substance that I like. And I felt that the body of Christ, the meaning of Christ, is about the sweetness. It is as if a voice said, be of service and don't judge.[11]

Cavallaro's installations have featured ketchup, melted moz-
zarella cheese, jelly beans, and processed ham. He "looks at
something and tastes it to life," finding unexpected beauty in
destroying things. His food art manifests the battle with death
when eating, our impermanence and perishability. He wants
the art to disappear even after the effort of generating it. For
him, life is effortful yet ephemeral.[12] Like chocolate.

Trans-substantiation Art: Manderson

About thirteen years (1994) before Cavallaro's *My Sweet
Lord*, philosophy student Richard Manderson crafted his piece
titled *Trans-substantiation 2*. Manderson first dabbled in religious candy by filling mini chocolate Jesuses with red jam to sell
at a gift shop at an arts center in Canberra, Australia. To defy
the censure by some in the American press, Manderson created
a life-size Jesus using fifty-five pounds of chocolate. When
that Easter exhibit ended, he invited everyone to taste from it,
recalling the Catholic teaching known as transubstantiation
in which the communion wafer and wine become the body
and blood of Jesus. Manderson's incarnation of the chocolate
Jesus had people communing with chocolate and with each
other. He argued, "Put religion back into Easter with an edible
icon."[13] He intended his work to deepen religious experience.

Chocolate Jesus on the Cross: Heslop

Sculptor George Heslop fashioned his *Jesus on the Cross* in
2006 for a British exhibit of chocolate sculptures that included
Michelangelo's *David*, Dalí's *Venus*, and others. Heslop had
experimented with an earlier chocolate Jesus in 2004. Since the
2006 exhibit was scheduled for April and May, close to the
time of Easter, he sought a "holy theme." He intended his
life-size images of Jesus, as well as smaller versions, to rebuke
the Easter "retail opportunism" of candy companies. "There is a
chocolate overload and it's all beautifully packaged but the meaning of Easter is overlooked."[14] This piece, too, sparked polemics.

What Happened to *My Sweet Lord*?

After the Smith Hotel shut down *My Sweet Lord* in New York City, Cavallaro launched a Kickstarter campaign to mount a Jesus-melting-for-our-sins in Las Vegas but did not raise sufficient funds. Finally, he placed the sweet Jesus in a show called *Chocolate Saints ... Sweet Jesus* at the Proposition Gallery in New York. The exhibit opened on All Saint's Day, November 1, 2007, and portrayed eight small replicas of healing saints including Anthony, Augustine, Jude, Fermin, Michael, and St. Francis circling a reclining, dying Jesus.[15] Ironically, the human model for the Jesus image was at that very moment in hospice care, though Cavallaro was unaware. Cavallaro sought to expose the hypocrisy of selling saint trinkets, what he calls a "merchandising of tragedies." While the saints represent healing, their stories are "hell stories": they were beheaded, tortured, mutilated, and stigmatized. In Cavallaro's view, selling their images trades on that misery. When Cavallaro was four, his father was pronounced dead at work. His mother took their belongings and walked on her knees up the church steps pleading with St. Anthony for a miracle. His father amazingly survived. For Cavallaro the healing embodied in the *Chocolate Saints* show was personal. In this spirit Cavallaro gifted the chocolate saints to friends after the exhibit closed.

Oddly, the *Saints* exhibit did not revive the earlier controversies, even though the invitation's scratch-and-sniff feature centered on the breast of the Virgin Mary. Maybe, Cavallaro pondered, Mary is less important. Or perhaps people had been bombarded with so many images, or possibly enough time had passed.

A church in Corpus Christi wanted *My Sweet Lord*. A Canadian museum would have exhibited it. Someone in Atlanta sought to honor a black Jesus. Those did not materialize, and *My Sweet Lord* continues to repose in storage on

Twenty-Fourth Street in Manhattan. Since then Cavallaro has not produced any further work in chocolate.[16] This question remains: Will Cavallaro's chocolate Jesus be resurrected?

Lucky Buddhas

Chocolate buddhas brought Lynda Stern luck. The sign for her former shop, Bond Street Chocolate, hung camouflaged amid East Village fire escape landings. Three steps down from the pavement, her 2012/2013 Zagat-rated, mini storefront and kitchen boasted bonbons, chocolate bark, and several gold-dusted chocolate deities. Stern started making the buddhas in 1998 for a class for the nearby French Culinary Institute (now the International Culinary Institute). Then she fashioned them for a cake topper and guest gifts for a yoga teacher's wedding. She opened her store in 2008 and supplied the buddhas to Soho's gourmet food emporium Dean and Deluca. Inspired by Waits's "Chocolate Jesus," she added Jesus to her pantheon of choco-gods. The media-shy New Yorker contended with pushback from religious leaders over her "Divine Collection." Inclusion of the Hindu god of success, Ganesh, upset the leadership of the Universal Society of Hinduism.[17] Stern would not sell a chocolate Muhammad due to the Muslim prohibition against depictions of the human body. For those seeking a stunning centerpiece, Stern crafted a special-order chocolate statuette of Moses. She has said that her handmade Guittard- or Valhrona-quality "spiritual icons are treated equally in my shop with honor and respect to the religion."[18]

An original comic book penned by her friend Robbie Conrad lay open on the counter. Its characters spoof Stern's supposedly sacrilegious candy. Her cartooned childhood rabbi wags his finger at her, a former day school student. At the end, though, a vision of chocolate rapport pops up in the words "And so we see how chocolate brings everyone together."[19] Stern's multi-religious chocolate dwelled together in her shop until increased rent forced her to close her doors in April 2016. Stern's deities still coexist online.[20]

Click Here for Jesus

On the other side of the country, Lori Kessler hosts Chocolate Fantasies, an online chocolate store where she sells chocolate Jesuses also inspired by Tom Waits. Click on tabs for "Erotic Chocolate" or "Adult Candy." Search for "Religious Chocolate" to find Jesus, Mary, Crucifix Lollipops, or Ganesh, Buddha, and Tara. Jesus outsells Mary.

Born and raised in Long Beach, California, Kessler grew up helping her grandmother frost cakes in her bakery. She started selling chocolate online about two decades ago, working out of her commercial kitchen in the Seattle area. Looking to offer something unique, she supplemented the standard truffles with erotic shapes. Later, responding to requests, she added religious chocolates, reflecting her own eclectic religious background. Her father's grandmother was Swedish and Jewish. Following her Christian maternal side, she was baptized in the Lutheran Church. Now Kessler considers herself a secular humanist.

When controversy erupted over Cosimo Cavallaro's chocolate sculpture of Jesus in New York City, Kessler encouraged him. That frenzy ranked her higher in Google's search list and boosted her business, though she recalls some sincere e-mail debates with people who wanted her to stop selling the chocolate Jesus. She also produces Jewish-themed chocolates such as Bar and Bat Mitzvah lollipops and "Mazal Tov" cards. Kessler understands that the Prophet Muhammad rejected portrayals of his image and does not sell them.

Kessler uses good-quality, non-tempering chocolate and anguishes over how to keep the chocolate affordable while honoring sustainability, fair trade, organic, and kosher commitments. Such certifications for her novelty chocolate, she fears, would just make the product too expensive.[21]

Despite public outcry in portraying deities in chocolate, artisans are still at it. In Portland, Oregon, Sarah Hart has dusted chocolate icons with gold since 2005. Her assortment includes stunning hamsa amulets at Alma Chocolate. A Kickstarter campaign, initiated by Persia Tartar von Huddleston, marketed signed, numbered, limited-edition, sea-salted chocolate Jesus figures, packed with a handwritten note "from Your Own [Personal] Jesus." With sixty-three pledges, the project started in November of 2013.[22] Hershey distributes a milk chocolate cross for Easter.

The Chocolate Gods Heal

Jeanne Fleming heard a voice say, "Don't worry, the gods will take care of you ... the chocolate gods." While standing at a hotel room window in Trinidad during her son's Make-a-Wish trip, she had been worrying about seven-year-old Jordy and the cost of treating his rare cancer. That Caribbean chocolate vision launched her chocolate deity business, which indeed paid all of the hospital bills; fortunately, Jordy recovered.

Fleming designed her Belgian fair trade chocolate gods for therapeutic purposes, not to compete with other companies or for financial gain. The Chocolate Deities website explains, "Chocolate has powers to transport and inspire beyond other mere consumables."[23] She hopes to spread joy, to bring people together, to be of service, and to deepen healing. Chocolate is a side dish to her event planning for the New York City Village Halloween Parade and the nondenominational Sinterklaas (St. Nicholas, precursor of Santa Claus) Festival Day in New York's Hudson Valley.

Fleming's life reflects her varied and inclusive spirituality. She calls herself a ritualist who grew up Catholic, married a Jewish man in a Hindu ceremony in India in 1989, knows Native American traditions, and has worked with every religious group. Her website pictures forty chocolate deities and icons—categorized as Muses, Mortals, Immortals, and

Symbols—along with their stories. A handwritten greeting or prayer, plus the respective legend, accompanies each hand-painted deity when shipped. Customers have included Buddhist monks, physicians, interfaith couples, and department stores.

A bank chain in South America distributed Fleming's two-pound chocolate Mayan Calendar Wheels at branch openings.

Although some accuse her of mis-using the Hindu gods, Fleming claims that selling chocolate deities to American customers has a different cultural valence than in India. Wishes made while rubbing the ever-popular Buddha's belly on New Year's Eve are said to come true. She never portrays Shiva because he both destroys and creates; she prefers to stay on his good side. The deities may be eaten, displayed as kitchen art, or melted down to transform the shape yet retain the spirit. Fleming sees chocolate as

> intensely divine and that making chocolate is a form of prayer and eating chocolate is an offering to the body and the spirit. After flowers, chocolate is the offering most pleasing to the gods and goddesses of nearly every culture.[24]

Fleming's deities are described at the website as "prayers and wishes; food stuffs; love objects; altarpieces, spiritual chocolates, kitchen art of the highest order and yummy chocolate gifts."[25]

When asked about her favorite, Fleming hesitated and then settled on the nursing mother, Willendorf, the first chocolate god she fashioned in 2003. Modeled after the Venus of Willendorf, an artifact said to be thirty thousand years old, Willendorf is lauded on the company's website:

> We need her larger now so to feel her more.
> We make her abundance felt—a full pound of chocolate.

> Hold her, your palm-goddess, in your hands.
> Let her melt a bit, lick off the chocolate, reconnect with
>   the Earth.
> Maybe that's the way to eat her, slowly.
> Let her melt in your hand and then lick her off.
> Transform her with your body heat.[26]

Fleming also resonates to Tara, goddess of the godless, who takes everyone in, mother of all Buddhas, and does not judge; Akua'ba, goddess for pregnancy; and, Ixchel, the Mayan goddess of the moon fertility, miscarriages, and healing.

While Fleming produces a Virgin Mary and has no principled objection to fashioning a chocolate Jesus, she doesn't, since they are readily available elsewhere. She too refrains from images of the Prophet Muhammad, though she would consider crafting symbolic Muslim chocolate, maybe an inscription of a joyful Muslim idea.[27]

These chocolate purveyors and artists fashion commonality, respect, unity, cooperation, and tolerance for our chocolate palates through their gods.

Miracles in Chocolate

In a completely different religious experience with chocolate, in 2007 a worker at the Bodega Chocolate Store in Fountain Valley, California, sighted the Virgin Mary in drips that had accumulated over a weekend. Cruz Jacinto identified the choco-residue as the Virgin of Guadalupe, a likeness similar to the photo of the Virgin she kept in her pocket. To celebrate and revere this image, Cruz set up a shrine of candles and gourmet treats, which attracted pilgrims. Reassured by the chocolate visions, Cruz, who had felt overwhelmed by personal troubles and had begun to doubt God's existence, realized that "This is a sign that God exists and that my life is going to change. Just finding her has already changed me."[28] This chocolate evokes hopeful faith for Cruz and others.

Nuns Adore Chocolate

Chocolate is the holy work of the nuns of Mount Saint Mary's Abbey Trappistine Candy factory. The layout of the facility situates the chapel immediately adjacent to the main entrance, allowing the sisters to pause in devotion when entering the factory and then again when going out. They might recite a personal prayer thanking God for good chocolate and good work. Once inside the factory proper, they wash their hands as they reflect on the hand-carved wooden crucifix inscribed *Labora* (labor) and *Ora* (prayer) to honor God in the processing of the chocolate. Windowed walls in the factory and chapel connect them with nature, another important aspect of the Rule of St. Benedict. As the sisters pack chocolate squares into trays or paste labels onto boxes of almond squares or monitor the line of almond fudge, they often spontaneously pray aloud the rosary or Our Father, litanies easily recited by heart. This manifests the promise "that our Trappistine Quality Candy is made with love and prayers."[29]

In her Bavarian-tinged English, Sister Christa-Maria peppers us with questions about marketing chocolate for Father's Day, about kosher certification, and about increasing Chanukah sales. She extolls the benefits of her abbey's chocolate business, identifying something very feminine about chocolate, something specific to the taste, something about the look. It fits better with women and therefore the abbey, she thinks. It also conforms to Benedictine requirements that the labor be repetitive and meditative. The current candy business fits into a long tradition of the chocolate pursuits of earlier Cistercian (Order of Cistercians of the Strict Observance, more commonly known as Trappistine) monks in Spain, which included, for instance, their chocolate room at the monastery at Poblet (see chapter 8). The sisters generally work five hours a day, five days a week. They compress what would be comparable to a forty-hour week to accommodate their spiritual life. They mix their values into their product by using Belgian Barry

Callebaut chocolate, selecting it for its reasonable price point and because "to the best of our knowledge the company has never been cited as a company that is associated with human rights violations."[30]

Back in the 1950s Sister Damian pioneered the abbey's chocolate. She gleaned much from the instruction of John Crand, a Connecticut candy maker who donated equipment and supplies. Her handmade chocolate truffles required endless patience. At one point the sisters decided to give up the candy caramel line and stick with the chocolate, so they gave their caramel machinery to a "daughter abbey." Since there had always been chocolate, they decided chocolate would be easier—not to make them rich but to cover their costs of living.

A few years ago local food inspectors cited "the old candy house" at Saint Mary's, sequestered deep in the woods of Wrentham, Massachusetts, which had been cheaply built in 1956. A good cleaning would not do, so a committee determined to build new facilities through a "contemplative, fundraising campaign," which was successful from the start. The community transitioned from being totally silent to using oral language to help expand the business. Before the rebuild, their customers had known of the candy but not their story. They knew of the abbey but did not know the sisters. The drive started in September 2007 and finished in March 2011. Once the campaign ended, Abbess Maureen McCabe instructed the sisters to take up their quiet life again and return to the normalcy of their boundaried life. They still balance spoken words with proprietary Benedictine hand signals, including the signs for chocolate.[31]

When I inquired about chocolate Jesus molds, Mother Maureen explained in an e-mail: "As a follower of Jesus the thought of doing such a thing fills me with fear and trembling. He is worthy not only of reverence but of all adoration, worship and praise."[32] Sister Christa-Maria responded:

The answer is simple. The sisters never considered using images we hold holy and precious in our life (such as the face of Christ, the cross or praying hands) molded in chocolate for commercial purposes. Our life is sustained by Christ as the sacramental food and we feel uncomfortable diluting (profaning) this reality by selling his image for pleasure food.[33]

The sisters at Mount Saint Mary's order their chocolate with reverence for God and for people.[34]

To Eat or Not to Eat?

These chocolate deity disputes expose some of the complexities at the intersection of religiosity and food. Earlier Catholic

---

Chocolate Art

When Mark and I first saw sculpted chocolate on our chocolate trail in Europe, we were astonished at the malleability that enabled such imaginative configurations. We also cringed at the extravagance of chocolate stuck in museum cases. Since then we have seen celebratory uses of chocolate to replicate the Oscar for the annual celebration of the Academy Awards[a] or the Chanukah menorah in Denver in 2013.[b] Chocolate artist Mirco Della Vecchia captured the likeness of Pope Francis in chocolate in 2015. Since 2000 the Nikolya Museum, created by Nikolay Popov in Azerbaijan and Baku, has mounted a traveling exhibit of one hundred chocolate statues to forty cities. It portrays a history of chocolate in over one hundred pieces, some of them representing local landmark buildings such as the Government House and the Ballet Theatre.[c] Of course many chocolatiers have designed fanciful creations from chocolate for centerpieces, competitions, and cruises.

Beyond these kitschy, commemorative pieces, there are serious artists working in chocolate. The Israel Museum, Jerusalem, houses *The Chocolate Soldier* sculpture. This portrayal of a group of combat soldiers in chocolate revives an Israeli theme about fighters who melt when things heat up at the front (see chapter 6). In 1997, Vik Muniz passions had argued for and against chocolate. Deeper symbolisms and suspicions of paganism led to questions about its permissibility altogether. Here, doctrine, taste, appetite, and art comingle through religious images unforeseen by those who only drank their chocolate. Unlike wine with its symbolism in Christianity and Judaism, chocolate can now be molded into many shapes and eaten. Of course, neither Jesus nor his early followers had access to chocolate. Depictions of Jesus in clay, oils, and wood are not questioned; when it comes to a chocolate Jesus, even though not necessarily intended for eating, the chocolate medium offends some. Now, the chocolate itself is not at issue, only the forms it takes. As these chocolate

created a small series entitled *Pictures of Chocolate*, including a portrait of Sigmund Freud, fashioned using chocolate syrup. In 1998 he added *The Last Supper*.[d] In the spring of 2014, artist Anya Galaccio painted edible chocolate onto cardboard walls of an old farm building at the Gallery Jupiter Artland in Edinburgh. Forty kilo of 70 percent solid, confectioner-quality dark chocolate resulted in *Stroke*, referring to the illness, or to a touch of the hand, or to the act of brushing the chocolate onto the wall. Wall chocolate works best, Galaccio confided in an accompanying video, when tenderly applied in many layers, textures, and patterns. It becomes very meditative. Visitors to the space, which was not temperature controlled, could caress the walls, lick the chocolate, and inhale the scent. She anticipated that the piece would decay while also arousing desire, anticipation, affection, and intimacy. At the end it was thrown away. Galaccio created similar installations earlier in Vienna, London, and Japan.[e]

Also in 2014 Renzo Martens used a 3D printer to digitize scans of clay self-portraits by Congo chocolate plantation workers, members of the Congolese Plantation Workers Art League. These were exhibited at the National Museum of Art, Cardiff, in the United Kingdom and more recently at The SculptureCenter in Long Island City, Queens, New York.[f]

artists pilgrimaged along the chocolate trail, their choco-gods hit barriers, despite the deep connections that people of faith share through love of chocolate.

Meanwhile my cellophane-shrouded chocolate Jesus, a kind gift from Lori Kessler, had been staring at me from my chocolate shelf. Should I eat it or not? Is this a tempest in a chocolate pot, I wonder. I do not want to waste food, especially when it concerns good chocolate. I certainly wish to be respectful of my Christian colleagues and friends who take communion and the image of Jesus seriously. I could savor it slowly. I could display it, melt it down, or chop it up to use in baking, as Fleming advised. Admittedly my response, as that of each consumer of art or food, is flavored by my background and beliefs. When I posted a photo of my chocolate Jesus at Facebook to ask my friends if they would eat it, the comments ranged from concerns about the quality and type of the chocolate to the theological. One rabbinic colleague cautioned:

> This strikes me as somewhere on the continuum between irreverence and blasphemy.... I am fairly confident ... my other clergy colleagues would concur that this is *not* what the founder of the faith meant when he declared "*hoc est corpus meum*" (This is my body).[35]

An Episcopal priest added, "Ummm, no. We have a Host for that. Some recipes call for a bit of honey ... but not chocolate!"[36]

I mused about how these chocolate gods, whether consumed or not, could ultimately advance harmony as prayerful art and creative critiques. While I nibbled on my chocolate Jesus.

Chocolate Meditation

This chocolate meditation was written by Rabbi Michael Shefrin. He encourages practicing this with individually wrapped chocolate.

Start by breathing, get comfortable in the chair, seek stillness, and try to be present. Take a moment to really look at the package of the chocolate, notice the colors, the ingredients, the logos, the size, the weight. Pick it up. Engage all of the senses (except taste). When ready, open it slowly, listen to it, smell it. Notice the change when the chocolate scent enters the air. Consider where it comes from. Who brought it to you. If it is your custom to bless food prior to eating it, recite it or create one. Or recite the Jewish blessing for eating chocolate:

Ba-ruch a-tah a-do-noi elo-hai-nu me-lech ha-o-lam she-ha-kol ni-h'yah bi-d'va-ro. *Blessed are You, our G-d, Ruler of the Universe, by Whose word all things came to be.*[a]

Slowly put the morsel in your mouth with your eyes closed. Notice each bite slowly, or let it simply melt on your tongue. Does it stick in your teeth? Is it melty? What other elements and tastes do you notice? What are the sounds that someone else might hear? Feel the impact on your individual teeth. Swirl your tongue around in the gooey goodness. Try to activate each of your senses. Concentrate on the squishing in the mouth. Do not rush.

When there is no more tangible chocolate, stop and continue to sit for a minute to notice the aftertaste. Explore your surroundings. Are your fingers chocolatey? Perhaps you are ready for another blessing, thanking the One who brings forth chocolate from the natural world.[b]

Cayenne Kicks

Hiker Steve Rock created these healthy chunks/balls and cautions that they will "kick you down the trail a bit." As they energize you for your day, they might also awaken your conscience to the best values to use when buying chocolate.

Ingredients:

1 pound dark chocolate, chips or broken into pieces
1 cup peanuts
½ cup raisins, dates, or other dried fruit
⅛ cup coffee beans
2 teaspoons cayenne pepper, to taste
½ cup unsweetened cocoa powder
Granola, dry cereal, or oatmeal (optional)

Instructions:

Line a large baking sheet with parchment paper, aluminum foil, or waxed paper. Melt the chocolate in a large heatproof bowl set over a pan of simmering water; remove from the heat. In a food processor with the chop blade, combine the peanuts, raisins, coffee beans, and cayenne. Pulse until coarsely chopped. Stir the cocoa into the melted chocolate. Once the mixture is even and getting stiff, add the chopped nuts and fruits; keep stirring. Taste to check the spice level.

If the mixture is too moist and sticky, add more nuts, granola, or chopped cereal, or wait until firm enough to handle. (Cooling in the refrigerator will harden the mixture faster.) Roll the mixture into balls and place on the prepared baking sheet. Cool completely. Remove from the baking sheet and store in a covered container.

Quantity: Approximately 20 chunks

Chapter Eleven

The Ethics of Chocolate
Selecting the Best

> It hurt my heart deeply to think about it.... They enjoy
> something I suffered to make. I worked hard for them but
> saw no benefit. They are eating my flesh.[1]

THESE WORDS OF A YOUNG MAN RESCUED FROM
slavery on an Ivory Coast cocoa plantation reveal a sinister
side to chocolate growing and production. Chocolate stirs up
questions of basic ethics and values. Many people, faithful and
secularist alike, seek values-based lives. Chocolate is one of many
examples of this. Cocoa industry transgressions, and perhaps
those of consumers—knowingly or unknowingly—harden the
lives of destitute laborers and may also threaten the sustainability of the earth. Biblical sources teach the value of fair wages,
equitable treatment of laborers, care for the natural world, and
responsibility for others, ideas shared by many religions. This
develops into the Jewish idea known as *oshek*, oppressive labor.

People often ask me to recommend the best chocolate.
Usually they want to know which brand or type of chocolate
they should buy. My flip answer: "The one I am about to
eat." More seriously, I suggest that the best chocolate derives
from companies that develop fair business practices and from
informed consumer purchases that satisfy our chocolate crav-
ings as well as our human and religious values. Prioritizing

multiple considerations depends on a critical reading of data about formal social and health certifications, claims made at company websites, and information on product packaging. Is it possible to find a chocolate bar that matches our checklist of principles: fair labor, environmentally responsible, and nutritionally sound? Admittedly these are questions to apply to any purchase. Many factors contribute to and complicate our chocolate choices, as is evident in the review of chocolate companies in the back of this book, "A Consumer's Guide to the Ethics of Chocolate: Selecting the Best." Hopefully, the result also yields a tasty chocolate.[2] So what is the best chocolate?

The Cocoa Industry: Not Faring Well with Fair Labor

Global demand for chocolate creates a great disconnect between the standard of living of growers of cocoa beans and that of the manufacturers and consumers of luxury chocolate products. It also obscures the tragic psychological and physical danger endured by children who raise and harvest the cocoa beans needed to satiate the developed world's chocolate addictions. The complexities of chocolate ethics both reflect and surpass the challenges of tea and coffee. While coffee and tea farmers consume some form of those beverages in their own cultures, many subsistence cocoa bean workers, particularly in West Africa, never taste the final treat of either drinking or eating chocolate.[3]

Wrongs perpetrated to produce chocolate began long ago. A pre-Columbian imperial stratification of elite and underclass turned cocoa beans into an export commodity from cocoa-growing regions to areas desiring it. Tenant farmers paid obligations to lords with cocoa beans.[4] The European conquests begun by Columbus and Cortés caused cocoa to become a colonial extract product. Timothy Walker, writing about the slave labor and chocolate underpinning exports from Portuguese-dominated Brazil, noted:

> Prior to the 1880s ... at every stage of Brazilian cacao production, coerced human labor played a role in the gathering and processing of this valuable commodity ... [which] included indigenous peoples, coerced work of free blacks, mixed-race laborers and European convicts forced to emigrate to Brazil.[5]

Novelist Jorge Amado captures the shame of the Brazilian cacao business this way:

> For cacao was money, cacao was power, cacao was the whole of life; it was not merely something planted in the black and sap-giving earth: it was inside themselves. Growing within them, it cast over every heart a malignant shade, slaying all good impulses.[6]

Ironically, at about the same time that Cadbury created a utopian community for its workers in Bournville, England, it was also embroiled in a controversy over purchasing cocoa beans from slave labor plantations in São Tomé and Príncipe[7] (see chapter 9).

Chocolate makers of colonial European empires reflected both the exoticism of their black colonies and a repulsion of the indigenous populations in their products and advertising. This may still be seen in some European dainties. Chocolate-covered mounds of marshmallow (Mallomars in the United States and Krembo in Israel) are known as *mohren-köpfe* (Moor's head) in German-speaking Switzerland; *tête de nègre* (Negro head) in France; and *negerbolle* (Negro bun) or *negerkys*

Classic chocolate-covered marshmallows named Moor's king recall the colonial empire roots of European chocolate traditions.

(Negro kiss) in Denmark. For colonialists, the blackness of the chocolate manifested the conquest of the local natives.[8]

Today, over two million children work in hazardous conditions in cocoa-growing regions, according to the findings of the *2013/14 Survey Research on Child Labor in West African Cocoa Growing Areas*, compiled by Tulane University's Payson Center for the United States Department of Labor and released in 2015. It demonstrates a marked increase in the Ivory Coast and a slight decrease in Ghana since the previous study in 2008–9.[9] Ghana's Cocoa Board places tight controls on the quality of its beans related to fermentation, size, weight, and flavor, inspecting each shipment twice. Yet it requires no accountability regarding the labor that produced those cocoa beans.[10] When cocoa beans hail from West Africa—as does about two-thirds of the world's supply—the chocolate produced by major international conglomerates likely includes dangerous child labor. While attention has focused on West African chocolate sources, other areas of the world's cocoa sources still need examining for child slavery/labor.[11]

Today, farmers of cocoa in West Africa argue that the low prices of cocoa beans require labor of their own or enslaved children. The Ivory Coast and Ghanaian laws that specify that laborers be at least eighteen years old are difficult to enforce on the two million small, remote family cocoa farms. Enslaved youngsters are not paid for dangerous work harvesting cocoa pods with machetes; they are denied any personal possessions or schooling, imprisoned at night, and left untreated after beatings. In West Africa, young children living with their families may start using standard farm equipment, including machetes. Even children who are able to attend school may be instructed by teachers to weed school farm plots with those machetes.[12] Some argue that cultural differences and economic realities may explain this, though a machete-equipped child hardly seems ideal in any circumstance. As in America, children may help out on farms; however, schooling and safety are not

threatened here. When facing this child labor/slavery ingredient on our market shelf, what should we do?

It's a Complex Chocolate Business

Systemic and deep changes that eliminate poverty, child
slavery, and hazardous child labor and that welcome input
from farmers, invest in local economies, and create community
infrastructure would be desirable in all cocoa bean–growing
countries. Voluntary initiatives by chocolate companies and
industry leaders, formal third-party ethical certifications, and
direct trade arrangements seem to share similar aims in attempting to respond. The complicated economics of chocolate build
on the very inexpensive labor of farmers who primarily live in
impoverished regions. Commodity markets determine prices
of beans, promoting competition among cocoa growers to
both sell product as well as achieve best prices. Big chocolate
companies also compete to keep prices down while meeting
obligations to investors.[13] How do we select a chocolate based
on these varied considerations?

The Tulane University study for the Department of Labor
of 2015 identifies the 2001 Harkin-Engel Protocol, also known
as the Cocoa Protocol, as the framework for eliminating the
worst forms of child labor. Initially designed by Senator Tom
Harkin (D-IA) and Representative Eliot Engel (D-NY) to implement a child slave–free chocolate certification, the protocol's
signers (Guittard, World's Finest, M&M/Mars, Archer Daniels
Midland, Nestlé, Hershey, Blommer, and Barry Callebaut)
have pledged most recently to reduce the worst forms of child
labor by 70 percent by the year 2020. Harkin-Engel builds
on definitions and pledges advocated by the International
Labor Organizations Convention 182 (1999). The latter
calls for economic growth and resulting social progress for
families, free universal education, and elimination of child
slavery. However, the protocol has not been implemented, and
deadlines have repeatedly been postponed.[14] The resistance

and delays in implementing Harkin-Engel, purportedly from the signees, led the United States Congress to charge the Department of Labor with the task of eliminating the worst child labor. The Department of Labor in turn commissioned the Payson Center at Tulane University to investigate, and the resulting study identifies little progress. International chocolate organizations seek to improve the standards.

What, No More Chocolate?

Chocolate lovers went crazy in 2014 when two mega chocolate companies, Barry Callebaut and Mars, predicted a chocolate shortage by 2020. Stephen Colbert termed it a "cocoatrastrophy" and "cocoageddon" in his "Threat Down," which aired on *The Colbert Report*.[a] In 2013, the world consumed seventy thousand metric tons of cocoa, much more than it produced. Reasons for the anticipated crisis include dry weather, ebola's effect on farmers, aging trees, fungal and other diseases of the trees, coupled with increasing demand. Not only have China's and India's appetites for chocolate amplified the market, so too has the popularity of dark chocolate, which requires more cocoa bean per product. This mix has raised prices approximately 10 to 60 percent in some recent years. To counter this disaster, some scientists have launched genome projects focused on cocoa trees.[b]

This dreaded chocolate disaster contradicts the current surplus of cocoa bean product, which has caused a drop in prices.[c] This may turn out to be, according to Dr. Carla Martin, executive director of the Fine Cacao and Chocolate Institute (FCCI) and lecturer for the Harvard University course "Chocolate, Culture, and the Politics of Food," less of a chocolate shortage and more a lack of cocoa farmers.[d] When chocolate companies talk about the sustainability of cocoa beans, are they referring to sustaining farmers in the growing of the product, or are they really only concerned with amassing as many beans as possible?

World Cocoa Foundation

In the meantime, the Harkin-Engel signers have partnered, along with others, in the efforts of the World Cocoa Foundation. The foundation's website states that it represents more than 80 percent of the world market, comprises fifteen cocoa-producing countries, and includes about ninety chocolate companies. It intends to create a collective commitment to end deforestation and to empower farmers to develop strong cocoa communities and implement sustainable production. Focusing on farmer education about agronomy and business skills, it asserts to have improved the livelihoods of forty to fifty million people and at least five million small farmers.[15]

International Cocoa Initiative

Over half of the Harkin-Engel Protocol supporters also belong to an additional partnership, the International Cocoa Initiative, established in 2002. Its website describes that it fosters holistic child protections in Ghana and the Ivory Coast. In doing so they allege that they have benefited at least half a million children in about six hundred cocoa-growing communities.[16]

In-Company Initiatives

In addition to these large-scale multi-company associations, individual chocolate companies have also attempted to reduce the harsh realities of child slave labor and farmer poverty through in-company initiatives. A scan of company websites shows that a number of companies decry child labor and favor other social causes. Cadbury, a member of the World Cocoa Foundation through its parent company Mondelēz, runs its "Cocoa Partnership." Cadbury has worked with NGOs and government bodies in Ghana since 2008 to improve farmer yield by 40 percent. It contributes to the development of schools, libraries, safe water, and biodiversity and aims to assist one million farmers. The company expects this global initiative to invest $70 million, over a ten-year period, in profitable, quality cocoa to ultimately improve farmers and farms.[17] Mondelēz launched "Cocoa Life" with a third-party certifier, investing $400 million by 2022, aiding two hundred thousand farmers in several cocoa-growing regions of the world, plus training women and acting against child labor. It also claims to be the largest purchaser of chocolate certified by Fairtrade International.[18]

Another World Cocoa Foundation member and signer of Harkin-Engel, M&M/Mars, seeks a global standard for cocoa through its "Cocoa Policy." Its website notes that 40 percent of its cocoa came from certified sources in 2015 and its goal is to reach 100 percent by 2020. Collaborating with Utz, Rainforest, and Fairtrade International certifiers, it apparently connects with Ivory Coast farmers through a number of projects. Ferraro, Hershey, and Barry Callebaut have also joined in these efforts.[19]

Barry Callebaut also touts its "Cocoa Sustainability" aims for 2025 at its website. With investment of $43 million, it says that it expects to boost productivity, quality, and farmer livelihoods over the next ten years.[20]

In addition to the goals of the World Cocoa Foundation and commitment to Harkin-Engel, Hershey's website depicts its West African initiatives, including what it calls "CocoaLink," an information, education, and outreach system through farmers' cell phones.[21] Do these global organizations and company initiatives satisfy our appetite for the best chocolate?

Voluntary Pledge

Other types of volunteer initiatives also seek to address these issues. Almost sixty chocolate companies, social justice organizations, faith-based groups, labor unions, investors, and retailers signed the 2007 "Commitment to Ethical Cocoa Sourcing (CECS): Abolishing Unfair Labor Practices and Addressing Their Root Causes." The pledge encourages the chocolate industry to embrace a more ethical cocoa supply chain by providing transparency starting at the farm level; committing to sourcing exclusively from farms and cooperatives that respect these core labor standards; paying farmers a fair and adequate price for the cocoa they purchase; implementing or maintaining structural practices to ensure farmers a consistently better price; supporting the drafting and enforcement of national and international laws that prohibit human trafficking, debt bondage, and the other worst forms of child labor; committing to 100 percent fair trade–certified sourcing of cocoa; and financing the rehabilitation, reintegration, and education of children who have been exploited in cocoa agriculture. Signers include the Labor-Religion Coalition of New York State and the Unitarian Universalist Service Committee.[22] In addition Catholic Relief Services,[23] United Church of Christ,[24] and United Methodist Committee on Relief[25] respectively mount efforts to advance cocoa farmers and farming. Fair Trade Judaica, headed by its founder Ilana Schatz, brings Jewish community attention to the advantages of fair trade purchasing through education around chocolate use during the Jewish holidays of Chanukah and Passover.[26]

Social Certification: Formal Fair Trade

Several formal fair trade certification systems identified by logo on each product seek to establish a minimum price above market value and eliminate dangerous child labor/slavery. These include Fairtrade International and Fair Trade USA.[27] They aim to ensure increased gain to farmers and prohibit child labor and slavery. Certifiers suspend farmers and companies from certification for falling short on the standards. A formal fair trade certification visible on each packaged chocolate assists a customer in finding chocolate fairness for farmers and for children. However, some analysts as well as chocolatiers question the effectiveness of fair trade chocolate, since it makes up just 1 percent of the global supply. Also, the certifier's staff may not be able to reach the relevant, small, isolated farms.

Only one of these fair trade companies, Divine Chocolate, is majority owned by farmers, which advances growers even more.[28] Is the best chocolate branded with a fair trade logo?

What about Direct Trade?

Several chocolate makers prefer to sidestep the costs of a formal fair trade recognition for what is often called direct trade. Farmers benefit more, they say, from the direct contact and superior financial arrangements they bring to the interactions. These companies compensate the farmers at fair trade or better rates instead of paying a third-party certifier. They also feel assured about the absence of hazardous child labor based on their familiarity with the farms.

For instance, Massachusetts-based Equal Exchange trades directly with democratically organized small-farmer cooperatives in Dominican Republic, Ecuador, Panama, and Peru— countries generally without hazardous child labor; the company itself is a worker-owned cooperative. In addition, it coordinates an interfaith program with thirteen faith groups. Equal Exchange had been fair trade certified until 2015, ending that association in order to aid small-scale farmers rather than benefit multinationals.[29]

Noshie Bar: The name of this confection plays on the company name Askinosie and the Yiddish for snack, *nosh*.

I thought further about this when a distinctive brown package arrived in my mailbox, as company owner and founder Shawn Askinosie had promised. Askinosie Chocolate exemplifies religious ethics permeating a chocolate business. Cellophane swaddled a small "Noshie Bar," a crunchy, roasted-cocoa-nib shortbread, topped with homemade caramel, flavored with a touch of salt, and coated in dark chocolate. The Yiddish-inspired name for the bar, from *nosh*, meaning "a bite" or "a snack," hints at the Jewish family background for Askinosie's chocolate endeavor.

Shawn proudly explains that the Askinosie name links to Genesis 10:3 and the story of Noah, which later became connected with Ashkenazi Jews, that is, those descended from Central and Western Europe. Shawn's father had converted from Judaism to Christianity, raising Shawn in the Charismatic Episcopal Church, which teaches that the Holy Spirit may be available to contemporary Christians and manifest in signs, miracles, and wonders. Fourteen-year-old Shawn struggled with his faith when his father became ill and died from lung cancer. Ultimately Shawn, like his father, became a criminal defense lawyer, winning high-profile cases featured in the national media. After working two first-degree murder cases back-to-back in 1999, he needed a break. Around that time he also started baking, considering a career in the cupcake industry. He experimented with high-quality chocolate. He prayed on what to do next and eventually opened his factory. Later that summer Shawn studied chocolate's secrets and intricacies in the Amazon and became reconciled to God as a Christian.

> God gave me this idea not so that my chocolate would be God's gift to the world or that it would be financially successful, but rather an undeserved gift to me to have another chance to try something different. In faith I went about trying to do that. [I often] pray for the wisdom to do the right thing, find the right people, close the right doors, listen carefully.[30]

Shawn runs his direct trade, bean-to-bar chocolate business in Missouri with his farmers in the Philippines, Ecuador, and Tanzania. His business philosophy follows "A Stake in the Outcome," the profit-sharing management ideas of Jack Stack and Bo Burlingham. Shawn and his team know his farmers, discuss business arrangements in person, and introduce them to actual chocolate, which many of them had never seen or tasted before working with him. Shawn's religion-infused chocolate supports Askinosie's Chocolate University, a charitable endeavor enabled by income from tours of the factory. Askinosie's partnership programs with Drury University, three local schools, and Missouri Hotel (Springfield's largest homeless shelter) all benefit the neighborhood, children, and his farmers. Askinosie supports projects that feed lunch to sixteen hundred students per day in Tanzania and the Philippines. He betters the lives of the farmers and of his downtown Springfield community. Named a Forbes best small company (2016), the flavor of Askinosie's faith-based values permeates his products.[31]

Kallari Chocolate, a cooperative of 850 farmers in Ecuador, created a different model. Farmers reap 100 percent profit from the cocoa beans grown and processed in country. This business plan, based on local and organic production, yields four times the income for the farmers than fair trade would.[32]

At least a couple of companies have chosen to use third-party certifiers for their direct trade business. Such farmer support comes from Taza Chocolate's "direct trade," based in Somerville, Massachusetts. Quality Certification Services independently verifies Taza's claims about organic and direct trade.[33]

Formal fair trade certification, direct trade arrangements, and farmer ownerships and collectives each may help remediate chocolate's ethical challenges. Which of these most appeals to you as the best?

What about Single Origin Chocolate?

Some chocolate makers elect to limit cocoa beans to one region, one country, or one farm to form a single origin bar. Reasons may include the quality of the beans, accessibility, potential volume, flavor, and distance from child labor and slavery. While the industrialization of chocolate has built an expectation of a uniform taste in a multinational chocolate, the increasingly popular twenty-first-century single origin bars with a terroir, or local taste profile, entice some eaters. As Dr. Kristy Leissle of the University of Washington Bothell writes, single origin localizes the chocolate and elicits the unique flavors of a regional bean.[34] It could be a single origin bar from West Africa, though generally not. However, the United States Food and Drug Administration has no controls about single origin, and therefore there is no guarantee about the claims on a bar.[35] Dr. Carla Martin argues against the stigmatization of West African chocolate. Even with the challenges of that area's cocoa growing, many poor people in West Africa depend on that cocoa bean income.[36] Is a single origin chocolate best?

Religious Certifications: Kosher and Halal Chocolate

A religion's dietary laws may inform our chocolate intake as well. Some Jews may prioritize a kosher label; some Muslims a halal label. Generally, the kosher seal marks that the chocolate facility has been inspected by an appropriately trained rabbi to ensure that it has not been contaminated by pork products, shellfish, or their derivatives. The kosher label identifies whether the chocolate may be eaten with dairy meals or meat meals. Some producers kosher certify some of their products. Other companies kosher certify every product. Cleaning the chocolate line with water is required for the purposes of kosher certification for Passover or for switching from dairy chocolate to non-dairy chocolate. This gets tricky because water does not mix well with chocolate. Water residue in the line can ruin the chocolate. While there are some newer kosher approaches concerned with worker justice and protection of animals, this traditional certification (*hechsher*) of chocolate does not guarantee ethical standards. I asked the Orthodox Union's Rabbi Menachem Genack (CEO) and Rabbi Moshe Elefant

(COO) how they handle child slavery in their chocolate. While they do not inspect for it or inquire about it, if they find out about it, they will not provide kosher certification.[37]

Humaira Batool of the Halal Research Council in Pakistan explains that halal certification of a chocolate requires testing and analyzing the chocolate for standards defined in Islam for halal foods. This ensures that the chocolate contains no pork, pork derivatives, or liquor.[38] A Canadian Muslim halal consumer group lists permitted chocolates at its website.[39] Cadbury Australia currently lists its halal-certified candy and chocolate treats at its website, emphasizing that the gelatin in these products is certified halal. The company became enmeshed in chocolate religious conflict in England in March 2017, however, when a photo of a Cadbury halal certificate, possibly from 2014, resurfaced on Twitter and British customers attacked Cadbury for "appeasing the local Muslim population." A spokesperson for Cadbury's international conglomerate owner Mondelēz responded with this explanation of its halal-friendly, uncertified chocolate:

> In the UK our chocolate products are suitable for vegetarians and those following a halal diet, however they are not halal certified. As our chocolate products do not contain meat, the ritual of halal does not apply and in the UK carry no halal certifications of any kind. The only animal-related products we use in our British chocolate are milk and eggs.[40]

Chocolate sadly became a victim of this unfortunate backlash against Muslims. Nevertheless, the halal certification drives preferences in primarily Muslim markets. The Malaysian chocolate company Dazzle Food Sdn., which exports to Singapore, Indonesia, China, and the Middle East, claims that halal certification boosted sales 20–30 percent in the last three years. The director-general of the Malaysian Cocoa Board says: "If you don't carry the halal logo, you can't capture their market."[41] Is a halal or kosher certification a priority for your chocolate?

Social Certification: Charitable Chocolate

Some chocolate companies donate a segment of their profits to social causes. These and other admirable projects may delight our sweet tooth while contributing to worthy endeavors. A Brooklyn kosher-certified company, Rescue Chocolate, has sold, among other items, a human treat called "Don't Passover Me Bark." The chocolates are vegan and organic. All profits go to animal rescue work.[42] Another company, Endangered Species, donates 10 percent of its net receipts to protect endangered animals, habitats, and people.[43] The organic, fair trade–certified company Shaman claims that 100 percent of its sales support the Huichol Indians of the Sierra Madre mountains of Mexico. This enables the Huichol to keep their traditions alive, including their "healing and transformational shamanism."[44] Original Beans has created the Femmes de Virunga (Women of Virunga) project to advance the lives of women in North Kivu, Eastern Congo, historically a very dangerous area for women. It provides literacy and leadership courses for women, in addition to education about cacao growing.[45]

A certified Benefit Corporation status or B corporation profit entity creates benefit both socially and environmentally. It requires transparency through a benefit report. Divine Chocolate and Rescue Chocolate carry B Certification markings.[46] Does a charitable company make for a worthy chocolate?

Social Certifications: Greening Our Chocolate

Caring for the natural world is an ethical value for many faith traditions and may be expressed through our chocolate choices. For instance, Jewish ideas about not wasting that which has potential for future use resonate when considering recycling and sustainability in connection with chocolate. While coffee and tea require minor modification of the plant product through roasting the natural coffee bean or drying the tea leaf to make the infusion drink, solid chocolate as we know it, love it, and devour it today requires intense processing. Chocolate customers living in the cooler, wealthier Northern Hemisphere depend on cocoa bean imports transported long distances, often by ship, out of their equatorial homes. The end

Grenada's Green Chocolate

Mott Green did not believe in God. He believed in chocolate—specifically and uniquely, chocolate grown and made in Grenada in the only solar-powered and maybe smallest chocolate factory in the world. That belief, which then became a reality, renewed Grenada's dormant heritage chocolate industry, led to recognition by the United States State Department, and yielded awards from the London Chocolate Society.

Originally from New York, Mott, born David Friedman, had been living a simple, even monastic life in a bamboo hut in Grenada, drinking the popular local cocoa tea as he began to envision the potential for chocolate and for Grenada. He sought to improve the local cocoa bean, empower farmers, strengthen the economy, develop organic farming, and establish sustainable agriculture. He founded the Grenada Chocolate Company with two partners in 1999. From the start it was a farmer cooperative, yielding chocolate from bean to bar in three days. Green wanted to avoid any connection to the slave chocolate of West Africa; on the contrary, everyone makes an equal salary at Grenada Chocolate.

He took the name Green to express his concern for the environment. And he certainly "greened" the Grenada Chocolate Company, restraining its carbon footprint. He slept on a bare mat in the factory's employee changing room, and he built or refurbished all the equipment. The chocolate has been delivered via Fair Transport[a] cargo shipment by sailboat and cargo cyclists in the Netherlands.

Green's idealistic chocolate outlives him due to an unfortunate electric accident at the factory in 2013.[b]

product necessitates multiple energy-intensive steps, including fermentation, drying, roasting, winnowing, grinding, conching, and tempering in temperature-controlled facilities. Only then is chocolate once again shipped and delivered to your local retailer. Given the intense usage of energy in most chocolate preparation, minimal stone grinding based on techniques from Mexico could make sense.

Some companies partner with Rainforest Alliance certifier to ensure efficient farming, protect the environment, conserve the forest canopy in growing cacao, protect wildlife, and enhance sustainability.[47] It recently merged with the Utz certification system which also seeks to establish benchmarks for climate change and biodiversity conservation, advances in living wages and income stability, plus elimination of child labor and gender discrimination.[48]

Cocoa growing assists the biodiversity of the Gola Rainforest National Park in Sierra Leone. Working to enhance the quantity and quality of the forest's cocoa also improves the habitats for birds, insects, and monkeys. Conservationists there hope to export organic, fair trade cocoa beans and eventually create a "Gola Chocolate."[49]

Original Beans has developed internal environmental benchmarks for some of their chocolate lines. Like others, it uses recycled paper, prints with low-impact inks in packaging, builds green factories, and implements low-energy practices. It claims that its factory produces 25 percent less energy than standard production and that its office buildings are green. Fossil fuels in production are offset through monitored reforestation programs. Original Beans commits to "restoring our planet's most valuable forests." Enter the lot number of your chocolate bar in order to see the trees planted through that particular batch of chocolate.[50]

Food activist Michael Pollan admonishes everyone to eat local, fresh foods from the perimeters of the grocery store.[51] Consider the location of chocolate. Not only is chocolate highly processed, it is imported from great distances. Rather than importing chocolate made in Belgium, France, Switzerland, and perhaps grown in Africa, sourcing beans from Central or South America and processing them in the United States may diminish chocolate's carbon footprint. Buying

Mast Brothers Chocolate Mysteries

Several journalists unmasked Mast Brothers' chocolate endeavor. Owners and brothers Rick Mast and Michael Mast claimed to be making chocolate by hand in small batches, from cocoa bean to bar, in what they called an artisanal and craft approach since 2006 (incorporated in 2007). In 2008, the company's website and its packaging boasted, "Mast Brothers' Chocolate is handmade in Brooklyn." The Masts credited themselves with launching craft chocolate.[a] Its popularity flowed from these assertions, aided by its appealing patterned wrapper and its hipster Williamsburg, Brooklyn, location. Mast quickly became a highly touted chocolate, commercially distributed around the country and preferred by some of New York City's most prestigious restaurants.

Things soured in March 2015 when several journalists—Megan Giller at *Slate*, then later that year Scott Craig at his blog *Dallas-Food* and Sarah Maslin Nir at the *New York Times*—methodically questioned Mast's contentions.[b] Chocolate specialists doubted the sources of Mast's chocolate. It seemed unlikely that a small-batch company, crafting chocolate by hand initially in a small Brooklyn apartment, could have produced the varieties of bars with multiple types of beans from Ecuador, Madagascar, Venezuela, Trinidad, and Dominican Republic they were selling. Furthermore, the taste of the chocolate changed significantly in 2009 and had, according to several experts, deteriorated. Experts surmised that the company had likely re-melted and repackaged Valhrona's single origin chocolates at least until 2009. When members of the Manhattan Chocolate Society toured the factory in 2009, they saw bags of Valhrona on site. Further, craft chocolate generally uses only two ingredients. When the Mast ingredient list was released in 2008 and 2009, it included soy lecithin. This less expensive emulsifier and smoothening agent is often found in industrial chocolate. Small craft makers avoid it.

On several occasions in 2008, Rick Mast privately acknowledged re-melting Valhrona industrial chocolate. In December 2015, Rick Mast insisted to the New York Times that Mast re-melted Valhrona only in that first year of operation. Following those revelations, Mast could have publicly clarified what they had already told people privately, that yes, they had early on re-melted Valhrona. Instead they published two letters at their website in December of 2015 denying allegations of earlier re-melting:

> We have been open and transparent about our experimentation, techniques and recipes since day one.... Any insinuation that Mast Brothers was not, is not or will not be a bean to bar chocolate maker is incorrect and misinformed.[c]

The Mast Brothers Chocolate: A Family Cookbook (2013) claims that they "connect customers to the source. We are nothing without our farmers. In every way possible, we must pay tribute to them and share their work."[d] The company website currently purports to provide higher than fair trade compensation to its farmers. Yet both neglect to identify the country or region of origin of its beans. The consumer has no idea where those farmers are or who they are. The bars bear no certifications at all. Given the earlier misrepresentations about re-melting their chocolate, this seems suspicious. Other direct trade chocolate makers proudly introduce their farmers and origins.

Reflecting back on the controversy and her role in unmasking Mast, food writer Megan Giller says, "I am dismayed about how the controversy extended to the artisan food world in general. It undermined the perception of quality and integrity of a lot of food makers who are really doing great work."[e] Mast may have helped build appreciation for craft chocolate, and it may have created a popular brand of chocolate. Mostly, Mast's lack of transparency has diminished trust in the chocolate and food world.

"local" chocolate from Hawaii or Mexico may rectify this. How important is the locality of our chocolate?

Protecting our natural resources may also result from limited pesticide use and adulteration in the growing process. The seal from the Non-GMO Project verifies that a food has not been genetically modified. This generally applies to processed foods and applies verification standards throughout production. Long-term effects of GMOs are unknown and often accompany pesticide use. Companies such as Endangered Species, Divine, and Guittard are Non-GMO Project certified. Formal organic has been available in the United States since at least 2000. The U.S. Department of Agriculture regulates the USDA organic certification system. It also prohibits GMOs, chemical fertilizers, and antibiotics in animal or poultry feed. Some chocolate companies note that their farmers do not use chemicals, though forgo the formal certification. Some may turn to raw chocolate to help resolve these goals. While there is controversy over whether chocolate can actually be raw, since the fermentation stage temperatures cannot be controlled and generally exceed the acceptable levels for raw food, a relatively new certification, Clean Food Certified, should be noted.[52]

Many chocolate companies commit to multiple certifications or social commitments. Which are most important?

Honestly, What's in the Chocolate?

Honesty is also a shared religious value that could be honored through our chocolate purchases. Religious teachings require honesty in business dealings and prohibit fraud. Judaism prohibits misrepresentation, literally "stealing of the mind," and rejects the concept of "buyer beware," placing the responsibility for any deception on the seller. American chocolate consumers find themselves crunched between differing U.S. and European requirements for chocolate. Those purchasing from some European countries may not realize the importance of reading the label closely. For instance, I was surprised when I tasted an imported chocolate bar and spit it out, something I never do. It had an odd mouth feel. With a more careful reading of the label, I saw that it contained the unusual ingredient of dairy butterfat, a cocoa butter equivalent (CBE). Otherwise, the very politically correct company's wrapper carries fair trade, organic, and kosher certifications. I had simply missed the dairy butter on the label. Similarly, an Austrian bar branded "Shokolad/Chocolate," which I had also purchased in my neighborhood chocolate shop, contained cocoa butter but no cocoa mass, which actually makes it white chocolate. In the United States a confection such as this must be labeled "white chocolate."[53] While this Austrian company, too, meets the fair trade and organic ethical criteria, both brands confused me.

Then I learned that for several decades European Union member countries fought over the appropriate proportion of milk to cocoa in milk chocolate and also over cocoa butter equivalents. France, Germany, Italy, Belgium, Luxembourg, and the Netherlands argued against the use of CBEs as diminishing chocolate quality and taste. Initially countries using CBEs, arguing that chocolate prices would be lower, were not allowed to use the word "chocolate" to describe their products. After pressure from Britain, the European Parliament finally ruled in favor of adding no more than 5 percent CBE in 2000. This was affirmed in 2001.[54] Because American chocolate eaters have different expectations, a close reading of ingredients may be important when purchasing European products. Are there CBEs in our chocolate?

Chocolate Challenges

As our chocolate options have multiplied in the last decade, culling the best has become even more challenging. Chocolate expert and author Clay Gordon cautions that in some respects, the question of the best chocolate may be completely subjective; it is the one I like and tastes good to me. It may also be a chocolate that is, objectively, a well-made product with attention paid to a lot of details in the process. That would be a chocolate that breaks cleanly, has an even color, a glossy sheen, a smooth texture, and a real taste of chocolate.[55] Still, ethical challenges persist all along the chocolate trail.

Faced with a mélange of options when selecting chocolate, chocolate lovers could seek to improve the circumstances of millions of children and further the sustainability of the

Truth in Maccabees

Peel the gilded foil from a chocolate Maccabee to expose a secret Santa. In 2015 Jennie Rivlin Roberts, then the owner of the online Judaica shop Modern Tribe, sampled some of her inventory of milk chocolate Maccabees with her staff. They undressed a few Maccabees to discover, of all things, Santa shapes. Shocked, Rivlin Roberts called the distributor:

> They said they couldn't afford to purchase a new chocolate mold and chose, instead, to use the chocolate company's Santa mold. His question to me was, "Is this blasphemous or offensive to someone, what's the big deal?"[a]

This Santa subterfuge generated a flurry of articles in the Jewish press such as the *Forward*, *Heeb*, *Kveller*, and elsewhere. This exacerbates the annual struggle of Jewish parents and educators to counter the pervasiveness of the Christmas story with Chanukah's message of religious tolerance and freedom, in what has long been called the December Dilemma. Comments at my Facebook page featuring photos of the bare chocolate included "Doesn't look like Judah Maccabee," "Who needs chocolate soldiers?" and, the best, "Foiled again."

Dr. Jonathan Sarna, Joseph H. and Belle R. Braun Professor of American Jewish History at Brandeis University, responded to my inquiry about this meltdown in the Jewish community:

natural world. Some chocolates offer the benefits of multiple certifications; others offer fewer or none. Some companies and organizations make laudable assertions. We might follow religious dietary laws, encourage donations to charitable causes, further a healthier environment, and promote better nutrition. We may buy chocolate based on cost, package appeal, the source of cocoa beans, brand, country of processing, and taste. We can read labels, identify the certifications, check the ingredients, and research company initiatives. We could avoid

> This is a very old story that seems regularly to be rediscovered. . . . I do not really think it is misleading: The story is an interesting commentary on consumer culture in the U.S. and shows how a smart company can appeal to multiple religious audiences.[b]

In 2015 I contacted Rite Lite, the distributor of the chocolate Maccabee. They lauded the quality of their OU kosher-certified superhero:

> The chocolate shape, around which we have wrapped a foiled image of a Maccabee, is a generic shape of a medieval man. It can be, and has been, used as a foiled Santa, sorcerer, Maccabee, and other applications.[c]

On the contrary, costume experts suspect that the Jews of the time of the Maccabees and their descendants in the first century BCE probably wore tunics. The Maccabees lived long before medieval times.[d]

In 2016 I visited the Rite Lite booth at Kosherfest. The display of mounds of chocolate Maccabees thankfully highlighted a Santa-less Maccabee. Now open the chocolate Maccabee's outer coat to find a generic torpedo-shaped chocolate. Finally our Maccabees have been purified and the secret-Santa dilemma averted.

cheap chocolate. Sorting out the fluff from the informative is as hard as winnowing the shells from cocoa beans. Perhaps it is not surprising that chocolate, such an inherently complex food, fosters complexities in our shopping. Consider also:

- Gas used by some growers in the drying process of the beans may mean that ostensibly healthy, raw chocolate may be full of poly-aromatic hydrocarbons.[56]
- Beans sourced from Hawaii and Mexico may keep the carbon footprint low for North American consumers yet may not appeal to our palate because of its grittiness.
- A fair trade, organic chocolate line owned by an international food conglomerate may mean supporting other company chocolate lines that use beans from West Africa and its attendant hazardous child labor.[57]
- Support for Israeli products may conflict with dedication to fair trade and/or organic products.
- Beans from the Caribbean and Central America shipped to Switzerland for processing and then to the United States by an otherwise politically correct chocolate company may be unnecessarily carbon intense.

A consumer has little capacity to investigate the multiple claims of companies, large or small, bean to bar or not, direct trade or fair trade. Furthermore, a chocolate lover cannot discern the point at which sustainability and improvement of crops assist the farmer in advancing a better income through improved crops or only serve the chocolate industry in ensuring an expanded supply of beans or perhaps does both. Chocolate choices will be made. Which pledges do we trust? Which values do we prioritize?

The earliest chocolate lovers, Mayans and Aztecs, believed chocolate had heavenly grace. Ultimately, we may hope to approach our chocolate intake with the wisdom of the sage Rabbenu Bachya ben Asher: "See how one's eating is considered a perfect act of worship like one of the forms of the divine sacrifices."[58] We, too, might savor our chocolate with a sense of the spiritual, and full of gratitude, navigate our way to the best chocolate.

Camel's Milk in My Chocolate?

Through the years of trekking along the chocolate trail—at many chocolate shows, festivals, and boutiques in several countries—I had perfected my rhythm of tasting and, to avoid feeling sick when sated, dropping chocolate into my handy bag. At one New York Chocolate Show, I pursued the trail using that refined hand-to-mouth or hand-to-bag chocolate sampling. For the first time, however, I stopped short, arm poised, as my internal electric fence activated, just in time to avoid eating a piece of chocolate-covered bacon from a huge pile on a display tray, forbidden to me because it is not kosher.

Turning away from the pig while trying not to appear to be one, I found myself at the Al Nassma chocolate booth. This brand claims to be the "first and finest camel milk chocolate made in Dubai." That may explain why Al Nassma had run out of samples.

The company was founded in 2009 by Dubai's ruler, Sheikh Mohammed bin Rashid al-Maktoum. With a flock of three thousand camels, it aims to produce one hundred tons of premium chocolate a year, according to the *New York Daily News*. The company touts that its chocolates are produced without preservatives or chemical additives and feature a variety of Middle Eastern spices, nuts, and honey. Purportedly camel's milk has health benefits over cow's milk—less fat, more vitamin C, for example—and it allows people allergic to cow's milk to enjoy even the milkiest of milk chocolates.

After a long search, Mark and I eventually found Al Nassma chocolate for sale at the American Museum of Natural History's exhibit "On the Silk Route." We hesitated just for a second when we saw the very pricey thirteen-dollar label. Like bacon, camel's milk is also not kosher. We did buy it. And it sat in my cupboard for quite a long time.

Afterword

WITH ALL OF ITS ZIGS AND ZAGS, THIS SWATH OF chocolate's past is multifaith, multifaceted, and multinational. The many stories of religions, rituals, and the magic of cacao fashion a far-ranging trail of post-Inquisition migrations of chocolate for Catholics, Quakers, and Sephardi Jews. These mark cultural, political, economic, and religious shifts. Divine and profane meet on this trail built on tensions of escape and exploration.

Had I listened to the advice of that cultural historian, *On the Chocolate Trail* would have resulted in a dead end. Thanks to my trusty choco-dar, our many sleuthing travel adventures, the prospecting in archives and libraries, plus the assistance of many people, this slice of religious and food history is no longer under wraps.

I recently received a note from a beloved congregant who shares my love of chocolate:

> Dear Rabbi,
> When I see chocolate
> When I eat chocolate
> When I read chocolate,
> I think of you ...[1]

I hope that the stories and values in this book accompany you when you see, eat, and read about chocolate and that you are now tantalized to keep only the best chocolate in your daily diet. Blessings as you continue to explore the delights, magic, and complexities of the chocolate trail.

Additional Chocolate Recipes and Tips

Here are a few more chocolate tips and recipes that I hope you will enjoy.

TIPS

1. Raw eggs may be hazardous to your health. Use pasteurized eggs.
2. Use Dutch-processed cocoa to provide the best taste.
3. Use the best quality chocolate available, preferably fair trade and organic.
4. Do not microwave chocolate. Instead, use a large heat-proof bowl set over a pan of simmering water.
5. Try substituting matzah cake meal to transform the cake recipes, particularly the Basque Chocolate Cake and the Chocolate Pudding, into Passover options.
6. Use a *feuille guitare*, a sheet of smooth and thick plastic that makes it easy to work with melted chocolate, or a flat tray or platter that has been very lightly oiled, or parchment paper for laying out the warm chocolate goodie.

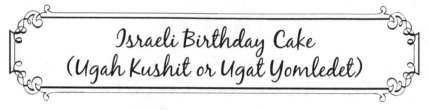

Israeli Birthday Cake (Ugah Kushit or Ugat Yomledet)

Israelis are *meshuga* for delicious chocolate cake such as this, especially at the time of birthday celebrations.

Ingredients:

CAKE:

1 cup milk
4 large eggs, lightly beaten
12 ounces butter, melted
1 teaspoon vanilla extract
3 cups flour
2 teaspoons baking powder
1 teaspoon baking soda
½ teaspoon salt
2 cups sugar
1 cup boiling water (optional: ¼ cup instant coffee for additional flavor)

¾ cup unsweetened cocoa powder

FROSTING:

½ cup whipping cream (optional: add 1 tablespoon instant coffee)
4½ ounces dark chocolate, crumbled
Sprinkles, for decoration (optional)

Instructions:

FOR THE CAKE: Preheat the oven to 320°F. Lightly grease a 10-inch springform pan or Bundt pan, or line a cake pan with parchment paper. Mix together the milk, eggs, melted butter, and vanilla. In a separate bowl, sift the flour with the baking powder, baking soda, and salt. Add the sugar and mix. Fold the milk mixture slowly into the dry ingredients. Mix the boiling water with the cocoa; stir into the batter. Pour the batter into the prepared cake pan. Bake for 40–45 minutes. Check with a toothpick to see how firm it is; bake until it is firm inside, perhaps another 20–30 minutes. Cool completely in the pan. Remove when cool.

FOR THE FROSTING: Warm the cream in a large heatproof bowl set over a pan of simmering water; do not let it boil. Add the chocolate and stir until melted. If you prefer to cover the entire the cake with frosting, double or triple the recipe. Once the frosting has cooled, apply it to the cake. Decorate with sprinkles.

Quantity: 10–15 servings

Flourless Chocolate Cake

This was the favorite childhood birthday cake of our son. Because Noam was born during Passover, I still make it annually.

Ingredients:

1 pound unsalted butter	8 large eggs
Flour, almond flour, or matzah meal for dusting the pan	1 cup plus 2 tablespoons granulated sugar
12 ounces dark chocolate	3–4 heaping tablespoons espresso powder, dissolved in 1 cup boiling water
4 ounces bitter (or unsweetened) chocolate	Confectioners' sugar, for serving
3½ ounces milk chocolate with cappuccino filling (look for Perugina or Ritter)	Whipped cream, for serving

Instructions:

Preheat the oven to 350°F. Butter and flour a 10-inch springform pan, and line the bottom with parchment paper. Set the pan on a square of heavy-duty aluminum foil, and bring the foil up around the sides of the pan. Set aside.

Combine the butter and chocolates in a large heatproof bowl set over a pan of simmering water and melt over medium heat, whisking until smooth. Transfer to a heatproof measuring cup. In the bowl of an electric mixer with the paddle attachment, beat the eggs and granulated sugar for 5 minutes at medium-high speed. With the mixer running, pour in the espresso and beat until blended; add the butter-chocolate mixture, beating until blended.

Pour the batter into the prepared pan and bake for 55 minutes. (The cake will crack around the rim.) Remove from the oven and cool on a wire rack for about 20 minutes. Cover with plastic wrap or aluminum foil, and refrigerate for at least 30 minutes. It freezes well.

Twelve to 24 hours before serving, take the cake out of the refrigerator. Remove the sides of the pan, slide a metal spatula under the parchment paper and slide the cake onto a serving plate. Sprinkle with the confectioners' sugar and/or serve with the whipped cream.

Quantity: 12–14 servings

Wacky Cake

This recipe represents another example of adaptation to chocolate shortages during wartime. Author Mary Ann Rodman writes, "I grew up thinking that this WAS chocolate cake (my mom made it as a birthday cake every year, because she refused to use packaged mixes).... It was apparently a popular holdover from World War I rationing. It's a good cake, if a little on the heavy side. We called it 'Wacky Cake.'" A contemporary version could include ground ginger or ground black pepper.

Ingredients:

CAKE:
2 ounces unsweetened chocolate
1 cup milk
1¾ cups cake flour (or almond flour or matzah cake meal)
¾ teaspoon baking soda
Pinch of salt
½ cup unsalted butter (the original recipe uses cooking oil)
1 cup sugar
1 teaspoon vanilla extract
Ground ginger or ground black pepper, to taste (optional)

ICING:
1 tablespoon unsalted butter
3 tablespoons milk
1½ cups sifted confectioners' sugar
Pinch of salt
½ teaspoon vanilla extract
Ground ginger or ground black pepper, to taste (optional)

Instructions:

FOR THE CAKE: Preheat the oven to 375°F. Lightly grease an 8-inch square cake pan. Combine the chocolate and milk in a large heatproof bowl set over a pan of simmering water for 5 minutes. Blend with a mixer. Remove from the heat and cool. Sift the flour once into a bowl. Add the baking soda and salt to the flour, then sift the dry ingredients together three more times. With an electric mixer, cream the butter and sugar. Add the butter mixture, vanilla, and chocolate mixture to the flour; beat vigorously for 1 minute. If using ginger or black pepper, add it to the batter. Pour the batter into the prepared pan. Bake for 20–25 minutes until a toothpick inserted into the center comes out clean. Cool completely in the pan.

FOR THE ICING: Heat the butter and milk in a small saucepan until melted. In a bowl, mix together the sugar and salt. Add the hot milk, stirring to blend. Add the vanilla and beat with an electric mixer on low to medium speed for 1 minute. Add the ginger or black pepper to the icing, if using. Spread on the cooled cake.

Quantity: 10 servings

 # Chocolate Matzah Brickle

This easy-to-prepare concoction works for Passover or really any time. We enjoyed combining roasted almonds, candied orange peel, cocoa nibs, and candied ginger. Thank you to our friend Ruth Belkin for this recipe.

Ingredients:

2 pounds dark chocolate, chips or broken into pieces
¼ cup vegetable oil
½–1 teaspoon vanilla extract or almond extract
1 box matzah sheets, broken into quarters
1 cup nuts, chopped
1 cup dried fruits, chopped

Instructions:

Line a large baking sheet with parchment paper or waxed paper. Melt the chocolate in a large heatproof bowl set over a pan of simmering water. Once melted, thin the chocolate with the vegetable oil; stir in the vanilla or almond extract. Coat the matzah, nuts, and dried fruits with the chocolate and spread onto the prepared baking sheet. Place the sheet in the refrigerator for at least ½ hour to cool. Once cool and hardened, remove from the pan and break into bite-size bits. Store in a closed container.

Quantity: 10 servings

Pampepato (or Panpepato)

It is said that the nuns of the Monastery of Corpus Domini in Ferrara, Italy, developed this skullcap-shaped chocolate incarnation of spice cake in the sixteenth century. This popular Christmas recipe bonds the celebration of Jesus's birth with early European chocolate. Its name may relate to its pepper ingredient or to the pope's bread. If it is difficult to locate citron and orange peel, substitute any dried fruit such as blueberries, currants, and/or ginger and sprinkle in some dark chocolate chips.

Ingredients:

CAKE:

1½ cups cake flour
1½ cups all-purpose unbleached flour (organic, stoneground preferred)
¼ teaspoon baking powder
½ teaspoon baking soda
6 tablespoons candied citron, cut into very fine dice
¾ cups plus 2 tablespoons candied orange rind, cut into very fine dice
2 small dried figs, finely minced
1¾ cups whole blanched almonds, toasted and coarsely chopped
1 cup plus 3 tablespoons water
1½ cups sugar
¼ cup ground sweet chocolate or ground sweet Mexican chocolate or chopped bittersweet chocolate
1 cup cocoa (not Dutch process)
Generous ½ teaspoon ground cloves
Generous pinch freshly ground black pepper
1 teaspoon ground cinnamon

ICING:

8 ounces bittersweet chocolate, melted

Instructions:

WORKING AHEAD: *Pampepato* must be made at least 12 hours in advance. Ideally it should ripen 3 to 4 days. Keep tightly wrapped at room temperature. It freezes very nicely (before cloaking in chocolate).

MAKING THE CAKES: Butter and flour a cookie sheet. Preheat the oven to 300°F. In a large shallow bowl, thoroughly mix the flours, baking powder, baking soda, candied fruits, figs, and nuts. In a small saucepan over medium heat, blend the water, sugar, ground chocolate, and cocoa to a cream-like consistency. Do not let it boil. Cool about 15 minutes and stir in the spices.

Make a well in the dry ingredients, filling it with the chocolate mixture. Stir with a wooden spoon to combine everything, taking care not to overmix. It will be a very sticky dough. Use a rubber spatula to make two round mounds of the dough on the cookie sheet, spacing them about 3 inches apart. Each should be no more than 6 to 7 inches in diameter. Smooth the mounds.

BAKING, MELLOWING, AND ICING: Bake the cakes approximately 1 hour or until a tester inserted in center of one comes out clean. Cool to room temperature on the sheet. Then wrap the two cakes in plastic wrap and let them ripen at room temperature 12 hours to 4 days.

Lay out a sheet of paper towels under a cake rack. Set the cakes upside down on a rack and spread an almost transparent film of melted chocolate over the bottom of each. Once it has hardened, flip the cakes over and spread a slightly thicker film over the rest of the cakes. When the chocolate hardens, rewrap the cakes and store them at room temperature.

SERVING: Slice the *pampepato* not in wedges, but like bread, across the width of the loaf, into long, ½ inch slices, using a large knife. Arrange on a platter. Serve with a sweet wine or with after-dinner coffee.

Quantity: 6–8 servings per cake

Modified from "Chocolate Christmas Spice Cake (Pampepato)," The Splendid Table, https://www.splendidtable.org/recipes/chocolate-christmas-spice-cake-pampepato.

Sacher Torte

This version of the popular Viennese torte was developed by the chef at the Neue Galerie's Cafe Sabarsky, New York City. (For more about this popular cake, see chapter 1.)

Ingredients:

CAKE:
½ cup quality semisweet chocolate chips
6 tablespoons unsalted butter, softened, plus more for brushing
All-purpose flour, for dusting
¼ cup confectioners' sugar
⅛ teaspoon ground cinnamon
4 large eggs, separated
1 large egg yolk
½ cup granulated sugar
¾ cup cake flour, sifted

RUM SYRUP AND JAM:
½ cup sugar
½ cup water
2 tablespoons dark rum or other liquor
1-1½ cups smooth apricot jam or preserves or another fruit

GLAZE:
6 ounces quality bittersweet chocolate, chopped (1 cup)
8 tablespoons (1 stick) unsalted butter

Instructions:

FOR THE CAKE: Heat the oven to 325°F. Brush a 9-inch round cake pan with butter and dust with flour. Line a baking sheet with parchment paper. In a double boiler or a medium bowl set over a saucepan of simmering water, or in a microwave, heat the chocolate chips until just melted. Remove from the heat and stir until smooth.

In a large bowl, using a hand-held mixer, beat the butter with the confectioners' sugar and cinnamon until pale and creamy, about 2 minutes. Add the egg yolks, one at a time, beating after each addition until smooth. Add the melted chocolate and beat until just combined.

In another large bowl, using clean beaters, beat the egg whites at medium speed until slightly thickened and foamy, about 2 minutes. Gradually add the granulated sugar, and beat until the whites hold a soft peak. Using a rubber spatula, stir one-third of the beaten egg whites into the yolk mixture to lighten it. Gently fold this mixture into the remaining egg whites just until smooth. Fold in the flour.

Using an offset spatula, spread the batter in the prepared pan. Transfer to the oven and bake until a toothpick inserted into the middle comes out clean, 35 to 45 minutes. Remove the cake from the oven and carefully flip it onto the prepared baking sheet. Let the cake cool for about 20 minutes.

FOR THE RUM SYRUP: In a small saucepan, combine the sugar with the water and cook over medium heat, stirring occasionally, until the sugar dissolves. Stir in the rum, remove from the heat, and let cool.

Generously brush the cake all over with some of the rum syrup; reserve the remaining syrup. Cover the cake with plastic wrap and refrigerate overnight.

Cut the cake horizontally in half. Brush each cut side generously with the rum syrup. Spread ½ cup of the jam evenly over the bottom of the cake. Set the other half on top. Spread the remaining 1 cup of jam evenly over the top and sides of the cake. Refrigerate until set, about 2 hours.

FOR THE GLAZE: In a double boiler or a medium bowl set over a saucepan of simmering water, or in a microwave, heat the chocolate with the butter until just melted. Remove from the heat, stir until smooth, and let cool slightly. Remove the cake from the refrigerator.

Pour the glaze over the top and sides of the cake, then spread it evenly all over the cake. Refrigerate the cake until the glaze is set, 5 to 10 minutes, before serving. Serve with a side of whipped cream as in Vienna.

Quantity: 12 servings

Modified from http://www.seriouseats.com/recipes/2012/01/sachertorte-viennese-chocolate-cake-apricot-recipe.html

Devil's Food Cake

Ingredients:

CAKE:

½ cup milk (not nonfat)
1 tablespoon distilled white vinegar
4 ounces semisweet chocolate, chopped
1 stick unsalted butter, cut into pieces
1 cup water
2 cups all-purpose flour
1 teaspoon baking soda
½ teaspoon salt
2 cups sugar
2 large eggs
1 teaspoon vanilla
1 teaspoon espresso powder or instant coffee
(Instead of milk and vinegar, substitute ½ cup mayonnaise

FROSTING:

1½ cups sugar
1 cup heavy cream
4 ounces unsweetened chocolate, chopped
1 stick unsalted butter, cut into pieces
1 teaspoon vanilla

Instructions:

FOR THE CAKE: Preheat oven to 350°F. Butter two 8-inch round cake pans with 2-inch-high sides and dust with flour, knocking out excess.

Stir together milk and vinegar and set aside to "sour" (mixture will curdle). Dissolve instant coffee or espresso powder into the warmed water. Melt chocolate and butter with coffee/espresso in a large metal bowl set over a saucepan of simmering water, whisking until smooth. Cool slightly. Sift together flour, baking soda, and salt. Beat the sugar into the chocolate mixture with an electric mixer. Add the eggs, one at a time, beating well after each addition, then beat in the vanilla. Add the flour mixture and beat on low speed just until combined. Add the soured milk and beat on high speed for 2 minutes.

Divide the batter evenly between the cake pans. Bake in the middle of the oven until the tops of the layers spring back when touched lightly and the edges have just started to pull away from the sides of the pans, about 35–45 minutes. Cool the layers in the pans on wire racks for 5 minutes. Run a thin knife around the edges of the pans, then invert the layers onto the racks to cool completely.

FOR THE FROSTING: Bring the sugar and cream to a boil in a heavy saucepan, stirring constantly, and simmer 10 minutes. Remove from heat, and add the chocolate, butter, and vanilla, stirring until smooth. Transfer to a bowl and cool to room temperature, stirring occasionally. Chill the frosting, stirring frequently, until thickened and spreadable.

ASSEMBLE THE CAKE: Brush any loose crumbs from the layers, and put 1 layer upside down on a serving plate. Spread with about 1 cup of frosting. Place the other layer on top, right side up. Frost the top and sides of the cake with the remaining frosting.

Quantity: 8 servings

 ## Curaçao's Hot Chocolate

The three-hundred-year-old Jewish community of Curaçao customarily drinks this hot chocolate at the circumcision of a newborn baby boy.

Ingredients:

1 12 ounce can evaporated milk
12 ounces brewed coffee
3½ tablespoons cocoa
4 tablespoons sugar (or to taste)
Dash of salt
1 teaspoon vanilla
1 egg

Instructions:

Place coffee, cocoa, sugar, salt, and vanilla in a saucepan, mix well, and bring to a boil, stirring constantly. Remove from heat and add evaporated milk and cool to drinking temperature. Beat the egg well, add some of the cocoa mixture to the egg, then combine all. To spice it up add a dash of pepper, cardamom pods, orange rind, additional vanilla, espresso, or cinnamon.

Quantity: 4 servings

Modified from Sisterhood Board of Mikvé Israel-Emanuel, *Recipes from the Jewish Kitchens of Curaçao* (Drukkerij Print Express N.V., 1982).

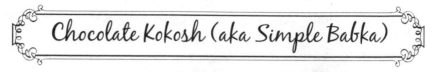

Chocolate Kokosh (aka Simple Babka)

Chocolate kokosh, a simple, flat version of babka, bakes quickly and tastes delicious.

Ingredients:

DOUGH:
1 packet (2 ¼ teaspoons) instant dry yeast or active dry yeast
1 teaspoon granulated sugar
¼ cup warm water, about 110–115°
¼ cup granulated sugar
2 eggs
2 teaspoons vanilla extract
⅓ cup orange or lemon juice (optional lemon zest)
1 ½ sticks (6 oz.) butter, softened
3 cups packed all purpose flour
¼ teaspoon salt
Canola or vegetable oil, or butter for spreading
1 egg mixed with 1 teaspoon sugar, for brushing

FILLING:
1 stick butter, melted and slightly cooled
1 cup cocoa powder
2 ¼ cups granulated sugar
2 teaspoons vanilla extract
Pinch salt
3 egg whites
Chocolate chips, optional

Instructions:

FOR THE DOUGH: In the bowl of your mixer with paddle attachment, mix yeast with teaspoon of sugar. Pour warm water on top and let mixture foam for 5–10 minutes. Combine the dough ingredients and add yeast. Knead on medium speed for a couple of minutes. Or beat briefly and then knead by hand. If dough is too sticky, add a bit more flour.

FOR THE FILLING: In a medium bowl, mix cocoa powder with melted butter. Add in rest of filling ingredients and stir until combined and mostly smooth.

ASSEMBLY: Preheat oven to 350 F. Line 2 baking sheets with parchment paper. Flour the work surface and rolling pin. Divide dough into 2–4 balls, depending on number of logs desired. Roll out first piece of dough into rectangle about ⅛ inch thickness. Spread a light coating of oil or melted butter on top of dough. Then, spread a layer of chocolate filling over dough, leaving about an inch of dough bare on all the edges. Roll up dough from shorter side, flattening the dough slightly between each roll. Brush top of log generously with the beaten egg and sugar mix. Repeat process with rest of dough. Lay seam down onto the prepared pan and prick with fork along the top. Experiment with the layering; one calzone type roll works as well. Bake for about 30–35 minutes (depending on size of loaf) or until tops and bottoms are a deep golden brown. Depending on the oven, rotate the pan midway. Serve warm or room temperature.

Suggestion: The filling makes a delicious gluten-free cookie. Drop teaspoonfuls onto prepared cookie pan and bake 8–10 minutes.

Quantity: 2–4 loaves

Modified from Truffles and Trends https://www.trufflesandtrends.com /home/2017/3/15/better-than-babka-kokosh-cake-with-video and Food52 https://www.leahkoenig.com/articles?lightbox=dataItem-j0v8liyg.

Three-Course Savory Chocolate Dinner

Concoct the chocolate bean soup, chocolate vinaigrette, chocolate mole, and a favorite chocolate dessert for a celebratory chocolate-in-each-course dinner. Thank you to Rabbi Shaul Osadchey, who first created the black bean soup and the vinaigrette with his caterer for a chocolate Shabbat dinner at Congregation Beth Tzedec in Calgary.

Chocolate Black Bean Soup

Ingredients:

PART 1:

½ cup canola oil
1 cup carrot, finely diced
1 cup celery, finely diced
3 cups onion, finely diced
½ cup red pepper, finely diced
¼ cup garlic, finely diced
¼ cup jalapeno, seeded and finely diced
1 chipotle pepper, seeded and finely diced
2 teaspoons oregano
2 teaspoons cumin
2 teaspoons coriander
1 teaspoon ground cinnamon
5 bay leaves

PART 2:

10 cups black beans, presoaked or canned, drained and rinsed
½ cup tomato paste
½ cup vinegar
4 cups vegetable or chicken stock
1 cup dark chocolate, chopped
Sugar/honey to taste
Salt & pepper to taste

Instructions:

Sauté part 1 ingredients until translucent. Add part 2 ingredients and stir consistently until slow boil.

Quantity: 20 servings

Chocolate Vinaigrette Dressing

Ingredients:

9 ounces dark chocolate, chopped
4 cups vinegar
⅔ cup canola oil
3½ tablespoons honey
Salt & pepper to taste

Instructions:

Melt dark chocolate in double boiler. Add the rest of the ingredients and whisk to blend.

Chocolate Mole

Our friend Shana introduced us to this delicious mole; she advised adding more sugar and chocolate, so we have. The mole makes a great topping for chicken, fish, or enchiladas.

Ingredients:

2 tablespoons vegetable oil
½ white onion, diced
4 cloves garlic, minced
1 teaspoon salt
1 teaspoon sugar
2 dried pasilla peppers, stemmed, toasted in a dry skillet
2 dried ancho peppers, stemmed, toasted in a dry skillet
1 cup unhulled sesame seeds, toasted in a dry skillet
1 slice bread (use gluten free if desired)
⅓ cup cocoa nibs (or ¼ cup cocoa powder), plus one bar of dark
    chocolate
1 tablespoon oregano, preferably Mexican oregano
1 teaspoon cumin
1 teaspoon allspice
½ teaspoon cinnamon
4 cups clear vegetable broth (or part bean-cooking liquid)

Instructions:

Heat the oil in a medium saucepan. Add the onion, garlic, salt, and sugar, and cook until the onion has softened, about 2 minutes. Tear up and add the toasted pasilla and ancho peppers, the sesame seeds, and the bread. Add the cocoa nibs, cumin, allspice, cinnamon, and vegetable broth, and bring to a simmer. Cook for about 20 minutes. Puree, then return to the pot, taste, and adjust seasoning. Add broth as needed to produce a fairly thick but saucy consistency. It could also be plated with the mole underneath the entrée.

To serve, thin the mole a little with broth (or water) to a saucy consistency, and make sure it is piping hot. Ladle a generous amount over each plate. Top with a few rings of white onion and a scattering of cotija, if desired, and serve immediately.

Quantity: 8+ servings

Modified from "Enchiladas de Mole with Mushrooms and Zucchini," Herbivoracious, http://herbivoracious.com/2013/03/enchiladas-de-mole-recipe.html.

Red Chile Bizcochitos (Little Cookies)

Thank you to Hannah Gross for this recipe for Christmas cookies customary in Mexico and known as the New Mexico state cookie. They can be shaped to celebrate other local customs, including the Day of the Dead.

Ingredients:

¼ cup unsweetened cocoa powder
3 cups flour
1½ teaspoons baking powder
½ teaspoon salt
¾ cup sugar
1 teaspoon ground cinnamon
1¼ cups butter
¼–½ teaspoon ground dried red chipotle chile, to taste
¼ teaspoon vanilla extract
1¼ teaspoons aniseed
1 large egg
6 ounces dark chocolate, broken into pieces

Instructions:

Preheat the oven to 400°F. Sift together the cocoa powder, flour, baking powder, and salt into a medium bowl and set aside. Combine ¼ cup of the sugar with the cinnamon in a small bowl and set aside. Put the butter, ground chile, and the remaining ½ cup sugar into the bowl of a standing mixer fitted with the paddle attachment, and beat on medium speed until fluffy, about 1 minute. Add the vanilla, aniseed, and egg and beat, stopping the mixer once or twice to scrape down the sides of the bowl with a rubber spatula, until well mixed, about 1 minute. Reduce the speed to low, then gradually add the flour mixture, scraping the sides of the bowl as needed, and beat until the dough begins to gather into a ball and comes cleanly away from the sides of the bowl, about 2 minutes. Transfer the dough to a lightly floured surface and divide in half. Shape each half into a smooth ball. Cover with a clean dish towel and set aside to rest for 15–20 minutes.

Roll out half of the dough on a lightly floured surface or between sheets of parchment paper to a thickness of about ⅛ inch. Form into desired shapes with a cookie cutter (Day of the Dead or other special occasion cookie cutter shapes may be found online), and arrange 1 inch apart on ungreased cookie sheets. Bake until golden, about 10 minutes. Transfer the cookies to a wire rack and sprinkle lightly with the reserved cinnamon-sugar mixture while still warm. Repeat the process with the remaining half of dough. Cool completely.

Line a baking sheet with parchment paper or waxed paper. Melt the chocolate in a large heatproof bowl set over a pan of simmering water, stirring until smooth. Dip the cookies halfway into the melted chocolate and place on the prepared baking sheet to cool, or place the cookies on the prepared baking sheet and drizzle the chocolate on top of the cookies with a fork. The chocolate will harden as it cools.

Quantity: 3–5 dozen, depending on the size of the cookie cutter

Chocolate Charoset Truffles Ⓥ ⒼⒻ

This is a great combination of chocolate and *charoset*, the Passover fruit concoction representing the building of granaries by the Hebrew slaves.

Ingredients:

3 pounds dark or bittersweet chocolate, broken into pieces
¼ cup pistachios
¼ cup pecans
⅛ cup almonds
⅛ cup pine nuts
½ tart apple
¼ navel orange, with rind
A few drops of sweet white wine
A few drops of honey
Pinch of fresh or ground ginger (or to taste)
Pinch of ground cinnamon (or to taste)

Instructions:

Line a large baking sheet with parchment paper or waxed paper. Grind the nuts, apples, and orange separately in a food processor. The nuts should be as close to a powder as possible without becoming "butter." Combine the nuts, apple, orange, wine, honey, ginger, and cinnamon in a bowl, mixing well. The *charoset* filling should have a smooth, thick texture. Roll the *charoset* into 1-inch balls. Melt the chocolate in a large heatproof bowl set over a pan of simmering water; remove from the heat. Using two forks, dip the balls into the melted chocolate and place on the prepared baking sheet; refrigerate until the chocolate has set.

Quantity: 24 truffles

Timeline of Chocolate and Religion

1275   Jacobus de Vorgine, archbishop of Genoa, writes the *Golden Legend* story of St. Nicholas's coins.

1492   Jews are expelled from Spain, which leads them to new lands and new business opportunities including trading cacao.

1496   Jews are expelled from Portugal.

1502   Europeans first encounter chocolate in the New World when Columbus and his crew sight cacao beans in a canoe off the coast of Honduras.

1528   Cortés brings chocolate-making equipment to Spain.

1544   Dominicans present drinking chocolate to the Spanish court through the presentation of the Kekchi Maya delegation.

1571   The Inquisition is formally established in New Spain, endangering Jews who fled from Spain to the New World.

1580   Spain annexes Portugal, causing many conversos living in Portugal to return to Spain.

c. 1600–1650	Some Jews in New Spain amass wealth as traders of cacao. Inquisition records document Jewish chocolate usage and trade.
1641	Chocolate arrives in St. Augustine, Florida, during a voyage (ending in a shipwreck) that had been bound for Spain.
1650	Jacob the Jew opens the first coffeehouse, which also serves chocolate, in Oxford, England.
1655	Don Esteban Gammarra is assured that the Jews of Amsterdam are expert chocolate makers.
1663	Emanuel Soares de Rinero, a Jew, is granted the first permit to fabricate chocolate in Brabant, Belgium.
1664	Louis XIV dictates that all of the property in the Caribbean belongs to the French crown. Jewish cocoa farmer Benjamin d'Acosta de Andrade loses his factories and plantations.
1685	Jews are expelled from the French colonies, ending their chocolate trade in Martinique.
1701	The first known business record of the import of chocolate in New York by a Jew.
1725	Abraham d'Andrade, a Jew, is arrested for making chocolate in the city of Bayonne, France.
1752	Obadiah Brown builds an early water mill for chocolate grinding in Providence, Rhode Island.
1761	Chocolate makers of Bayonne, France, found a guild to exclude Jews from making or selling chocolate.
1763	Caffè al Bicerin is founded and named for the specialty drink of Turin.

1772	Aaron Lopez buys chocolate from Joseph Pinto for Passover in Newport, Rhode Island.
1772	First recorded sale of Baker's chocolate.
1779–1781	Rebecca Gomez makes and advertises chocolate in New York City.
1824	John Cadbury opens his coffee, tea, and cocoa business.
1847	Many identify Fry & Sons with the first eating chocolate in Bristol, England.
1876	Daniel Peter created the first commercial milk chocolate in Switzerland.
1894	Wilbur Chocolate makes Wilbur Buds, preceding Hershey's Kisses by over ten years.
1934	Elite launches Para chocolate line.
1940s	Stephen Klein, founder of Barton's Bonbonniere, provides immigration assistance and jobs to refugees of the Holocaust.
1940s	Pietro Ferrero develops Nutella.
1948	Chocolate Pilot, Uncle Wiggly Wings, Gail S. Halvorsen drops chocolate over Berlin.
1950s	Chocolate spread becomes a popular, cost-effective accompaniment to meals in Israel, especially for soldiers in the army.
1978	The Klein family sells Barton's.
1990s	Rolf Bloch, CEO of the Swiss chocolate company Camille Bloch and president of the Swiss Federation of Jewish Communities, leads the effort to bring to light Swiss injustices to Jews during the Holocaust.
2001	"CBE [cocoa butter equivalent] wars" in European Union end.

A Consumer's Guide to the Ethics of Chocolate

Selecting the Best

PEOPLE OFTEN ASK ME TO RECOMMEND MY FAVORITE chocolate or what I consider to be the best chocolate. As detailed in chapter 11, I would say that the best chocolate derives from companies that are guided by our humane and religious values. The following list of some chocolate brands helps inform consumers about chocolate buying. It reviews a sampling of chocolate companies and the claims made at their respective websites regarding categories of charity, eco-practices, worker justice, and quality of ingredients. This brings together information that helps you decide which is the best. If you wish to add to this list, please contact me at www.onthechocolatetrail.org.[1]

Al Nassma

Umm Nahad, Al Ain Road, Exit 26, PO Box 11-75-84, Dubai, UAE
www.al-nassma.com

QUALITY: Local food. No preservatives. No artificial flavors.

GENERAL NOTES: Uses camel milk, bourbon vanilla, and acacia honey. Not kosher and not hallal-certified: contains camel milk.

Alter Eco

2339 Third Street, Suite 70, San Francisco, CA 94107
415-701-1212 | www.alterecofoods.com

CHARITY: Certified B Corporation.

ECO-PRACTICES: Certified Carbon Neutral Product and uses compostable packaging.

WORKER JUSTICE: Fair Trade USA–certified. Works with farmer co-operatives.

QUALITY: USDA Organic–certified; contains no soy emulsifiers or artificial flavors. Single-origin cacao beans from Peruvian Amazon or the Ecuador coast. Non-GMO Project Verified.

GENERAL NOTES: Also sells other fair trade products such as sugar, rice, and quinoa. Named France's #1 fair trade brand; awarded the best organic or fair trade product line at the International Chocolate Salon. Recipient of the Acterra Award for sustainability. Chocolate is processed in Switzerland. No kosher certification.

Askinosie Chocolate

514 E. Commercial, Springfield, MO 65803
417-862-9900 | www.askinosie.com

CHARITY: Chocolate University teaches local children about social entrepreneurship, direct trade, and sustainability; builds wells in Africa; 100 percent of proceeds from chocolate tours support Chocolate University educational projects for local children. The company supports lunch programs for children in Tanzania and Philippines, communities where it sources chocolate. A Product of Change sells their products in America to support local PTAs and schools.

ECO-PRACTICES: Reuses cocoa bean bag strings in chocolate wrappings.

WORKER JUSTICE: Direct trade with farmers through "stake in outcome"; 10 percent of net profits go to the farmers and pays above fair trade. Financial transparency at the factory and in the fields.

QUALITY: Unofficially organic; uses certified organic sugar. Single-origin bean-to-bar chocolate from Ecuador, the Philippines, and Tanzania. No additives.

GENERAL NOTES: Use online "Choc-o-lot" system to trace the story of the cocoa beans in your bar. Some products certified kosher by Vaad Hakashruth.

Barry-Callebaut

Westpark, Pfingstweidstrasse 60, 8005 Zurich, Switzerland
+41-43-204-0404 | www.barry-callebaut.com

CHARITY: Its Cocoa Horizons Foundation furthers sustainability, entrepreneurial farming, productivity, and community development.

ECO-PRACTICES: By 2025 intends to be carbon- and forest-positive. Its Belgium facility will be green energy and will only use sustainable ingredients. Supports Biolands program.

WORKER JUSTICE: Signed onto Harkin-Engel Cocoa Protocol 2001; partner in the International Cocoa Initiative and member of World Cocoa Foundation. Pledges to eradicate child labor from the supply chain and to lift five hundred thousand farmers from poverty by 2025. Includes some fair trade products.

GENERAL NOTES: Claims to be the world's largest cocoa and chocolate manufacturer; produces couverture for manufacturers and consumers. Some lines are organic. Avoids GMO ingredients. Some kosher options. First multinational company to be granted a global kosher certificate in the 1970s.

Barton's Candy

1035 Mill Road, Allentown, PA 18106
610-366-1606 | www.bartonscandy.com

GENERAL NOTES: See Miss Chocolate (www.misschocolate.com/passover.html) for Passover fundraising featuring Barton's Kosher for Passover products. Items are certified kosher dairy or pareve by the Orthodox Union.

Blommer

600 West Kinzie Street, Chicago, IL 60654

800-621-1606 | www.blommer.com

CHARITY: Provides tools and training for local farmers. Utilizes the Farmer Field School method.

ECO-PRACTICES: Offers Rainforest Alliance–certified products.

WORKER JUSTICE: Signed Harkin-Engel Cocoa Protocol; supports and partners with Cocoa Livelihoods program. Member of the World Cocoa Foundation. Offers Fair Trade USA, Fairtrade International, and Utz certifications.

QUALITY: Offers USDA Organic–certified.

GENERAL NOTES: Fourth-generation family owned. Claims to be North America's largest cocoa bean processor for couverture.

Cadbury

Linden Road, Bournville B30 2LU, Birmingham, England
+44-121-458-2000 | www.cadbury.co.uk

CHARITY: Cadbury Foundation donates to charities in UK and Ireland since 1935.

WORKER JUSTICE: Dairy Milk and hot chocolate lines are fair trade in some countries. Launched Cadbury Cocoa Partnership, which uses 70 percent of funds to invest in small farms, primarily in Ghana.

QUALITY: Uses some CBEs.

GENERAL NOTES: Owned by Mondelēz, which also owns Green & Black's.

Camille Bloch

Grand-Rue, CH-2608, Courtelary, Switzerland
+41-(0)32-945-1200 | www.camillebloch.ch/en

WORKER JUSTICE: Partners with Sourcetrust to further transparency and to invest in farmers and communities in Ghana.

GENERAL NOTES: Third-generation family owned. Kosher and kosher for Passover. Confectionary.

Dagoba Organic Chocolate

1105 Benson Way, Ashland, OR 97520
866-608-6944 | www.dagobachocolate.com

ECO-PRACTICES: Recyclable packaging and Rainforest Alliance–certified.

WORKER JUSTICE: Cocoa beans from farmer co-operative in Tanzania, a specific farm in Dominican Republic, and a community of farms in Peru.

QUALITY: USDA Organic–certified.

GENERAL NOTES: Owned by Hershey since 2006. Only the hot chocolate is certified kosher by Orthodox Union.

Dandelion

740 Valencia Street, San Francisco, CA 94110
415-349-0942 | www.dandelionchocolate.com

WORKER JUSTICE: Sources directly from farms in Dominican Republic, Ecuador, Guatemala, Liberia, Madagascar, Papua New Guinea, Tanzania, and Trinidad.

GENERAL NOTES: Small-batch, craft chocolate. Provides annual sourcing report, inspired by Taza Chocolate. Cultivates a direct relationship with a very small network of cacao growers.

Divine

804 East Street SE, Washington, DC 20003
202-332-8913 | www.divinechocolate.com

CHARITY: Certified B Corporation.

WORKER JUSTICE: Fairtrade International/Fair Trade USA–certified and co-owned by farmer co-operative called Kuapa Kokoo, with over sixty-five thousand members, in Ghana. Supports initiatives for women's empowerment in the cocoa industry.

QUALITY: Unofficially organic. Uses some soy lecithin. One product uses dairy butter. Non-GMO Project Verified.

GENERAL NOTES: Makes fair trade kosher coins for Chanukah gelt. Certified kosher by Triangle-K.

El Ceibo

Av. Juan Pablo II No. 2560, El Alto, La Paz, Bolivia
703-745-7945 (U.S.) | www.elceibo.org

WORKER JUSTICE: Fairtrade International/Fair Trade USA–certified cacao beans grown and manufactured by the farmers of El Ceibo farmer co-operative in Bolivia.

QUALITY: USDA Organic–certified and Biosuisse–certified.

GENERAL NOTES: Developed in consultation with Chloé Doutre-Roussel.

Elite/Max Brenner

841 Broadway, New York, NY 10011
646-467-8803 | www.maxbrenner.com

Owned by Strauss Group since 2001. Chocolate sold in shops is certified kosher dairy by Bet–Shemesh Rabbinate. Max Brenner is mostly confectionary.

Endangered Species

5846 W. 73rd Street, Indianapolis, IN 46278
800-293-0160 | www.chocolatebar.com

CHARITY: Donates 10 percent of profit to fund species and habitat conservation. Reports at website.

ECO-PRACTICES: Contributions support Rainforest Trust and Wildlife Conservation Network.

WORKER JUSTICE: Fair Trade America using West African cacao.

QUALITY: Non-GMO Project Verified. Unofficially organic.

GENERAL NOTES: Certified gluten-free and kosher dairy by Orthodox Union.

Equal Exchange

50 United Drive, West Bridgewater, MA 02379
774-776-7400 | www.equalexchange.co-op/products/chocolate

ECO-PRACTICES: Green America–certified.

WORKER JUSTICE: Worker-owned company; direct trade with small-scale farmer co-operatives in Dominican Republic (Conacado), Ecuador, Panama, Paraguay, and Peru (Cacvra).

QUALITY: USDA Organic–certified.

GENERAL NOTES: Founded in 1986. Kosher: hot chocolate, baking cocoa, and spicy hot chocolate certified by Orthodox Union. Bars and minis kosher and kosher for Passover certified by Rabbi Abraham Hochwald, Germany.

Fruition

(Retail) 17 Tinker Street, Woodstock, NY 12498
845-657-6717 | www.tastefruition.com

WORKER JUSTICE: Cocoa beans come from fair trade and organic sources in Peru, Ecuador, Dominican Republic, Costa Rica, and Bolivia.

GENERAL NOTES: Small-batch bean-to-bar chocolate workshop created by Bryan Graham.

Ghirardelli

1111 139th Avenue, San Leandro, CA 94578
800-877-9338 | www.ghirardelli.com

WORKER JUSTICE: Part of Lindt-Sprüngli Cocoa Farming Program.

GENERAL NOTES: All products to be non-GMO by 2018.

Gnosis Chocolate

Brooklyn, NY
877-446-6747 | www.gnosischocolate.com

ECO-PRACTICES: Certified Forest Stewardship Council. Certified by Green America.

QUALITY: California Certified Organic Farmers; cocoa beans from Bali, Ecuador, Madagascar, and Peru; certified raw; certified by Vegan Action.

GENERAL NOTES: Certified kosher by Earth Kosher.

Godiva

800-946-3482 | www.godiva.com

CHARITY: Lady Godiva Annual Awards to further health care, child welfare, and animal protection.

WORKER JUSTICE: Member of World Cocoa Foundation and Cocoa Horizons Foundation.

GENERAL NOTES: Certified kosher by Orthodox Union. Mostly confectionary.

Green & Black's

20 Constitution Boulevard, South Shelton, CT 06484
888-682-5770 | www.greenandblacks.com

WORKER JUSTICE: Fairtrade International–certified (the organic line). All cocoa beans are sourced through Cocoa Life.

QUALITY: California Certified Organic Farmers (CCOF) certification.

GENERAL NOTES: Founded by Craig Sams and Jo Fairley in London, 1991. Bought by Cadbury and now owned by Mondelēz.

Grenada Chocolate

www.grenadachocolate.com

ECO-PRACTICES: Much of equipment is solar powered; chocolate is transported by sailboat.

WORKER JUSTICE: Farmer and worker co-operative harvests and makes chocolate in Grenada.

QUALITY: CERES organic and environmental certified.

GENERAL NOTES: Claim to be the original tree-to-bar co-operative.

Guittard

10 Guittard Road, Burlingame, CA 94010
800-468-2462 | www.guittard.com

ECO-PRACTICES: Forest Stewardship Council–certified packaging; Heirloom Cacao Preservation Initiative member; offers Rainforest Alliance Certification.

WORKER JUSTICE: Signer of Harkin-Engel Cocoa Protocol. Member of World Cocoa Foundation, Cocoa of Excellence Program, International Cocoa Initiative. Fair Trade USA–certified.

QUALITY: Non-GMO.

NOTES: Couverture including for See's Chocolate.

Hawaiian Vintage

1050 Bishop Street #162, Honolulu, HI 96813
808-735-8494 | www.hawaiianchocolate.com

QUALITY: Not organic; local cocoa beans.

GENERAL NOTES: Claims to have created first new variety of cocoa in eighty years. Only available online.

Hershey's

100 Chrystal A Drive, Hershey, PA, 17033-0810
800-468-1714 | www.hersheys.com

WORKER JUSTICE: Signer of Harkin-Engel Cocoa Protocol 2001. Member of the World Cocoa Foundation. Committed to 100 percent certified cocoa by 2020.

QUALITY: No artificial flavors, preservatives, sweeteners. Uses soy lecithin.

GENERAL NOTES: Also owns Dagoba and Scharffen Berger. Many products certified kosher by Orthodox Union.

Jacques Torres

350 Hudson Street, New York, NY 10014
929-337-8856 | www.mrchocolate.com

QUALITY: No preservatives, no artificial flavorings, no essential oils.

GENERAL NOTES: Some products are certified (OK) dairy kosher.

Lindt & Sprüngli

Seestrasse 204, CH 8802 Kilchberg, Switzerland
+41-44-716-22-33 | www.chocolate.lindt.com

CHARITY: Lindt Cocoa Foundation.
WORKER JUSTICE: Lindt-Sprüngli Cocoa Farming Program.
GENERAL NOTES: Owns Ghirardelli, Russell Stover, and Whitman's.

Kallari

www.facebook.com/pg/Kallari-Chocolate-68963262649
/about/?ref=page_internal

WORKER JUSTICE: Farmer co-operative.
QUALITY: Uses Nacional cacao, a local cocoa bean that is grown and
manufactured by indigenous Kichwa farmers in Ecuador.

Lake Champlain Chocolates

750 Pine Street, Burlington, VT 05401
800-465-5909 | www.lakechamplainchocolates.com

CHARITY: Underwrites Family Support Scholarship.
WORKER JUSTICE: Fair for Life–certified for organic bars. Member
of the World Cocoa Foundation. Cocoa powder is Fair Trade USA–
certified.
QUALITY: USDA Organic–certified. Uses local products for honey,
butter, maple syrup.
GENERAL NOTES: Certified kosher by Star-D and Star-K Kosher.
Associated with direct trade company, Bandana Chocolate.

Madécasse

630 Flushing Avenue, Brooklyn, NY 11206
917-382-2020 | www.madecasse.com

ECO-PRACTICES: Mostly grown and produced in Madagascar.
WORKER JUSTICE: Direct Trade certified by Quality Certification
Services. Future reports to be posted.
QUALITY: Two bars are USDA certified organic. The rest use
certified organic cocoa, though not labeled.

Madelaine

9603 Beach Channel Drive, Rockaway Beach, NY 11693
718-945-1500 | www.madelainechocolate.com

QUALITY: Kosher-certified by Orthodox Union. Foil-wrapped novelty
chocolate.

Malie Kai

PO Box 1146, Honolulu, HI 96807
808-599-8600 | www.maliekai.com

WORKER JUSTICE: Uses no child or forced labor.

QUALITY: Single origin, small batch. Uses soy lecithin. Local beans
from North Shore of Oahu. No GMOs. No certifications.

M&M/Mars

6885 Elm Street, McLean, Virginia 22101-6031
703-821-4900 | www.mars.com/global/home

CHARITY: Built seventeen Cocoa Development Centers in Ivory Coast
and planning Cocoa Village Clinics in Soubré. Mars Center for
Cocoa Science in Bahia, Brazil, opened in 1982.

ECO-PRACTICES: Works with Rainforest Alliance. Started the Cacao
Genome Project in 2008.

WORKER JUSTICE: Works with Utz and Fairtrade International.

GENERAL NOTES: By 2020, 100 percent cocoa to be certified.
Primarily confectionary business.

Mast Brothers

111 N. 3rd Street, Brooklyn, NY 11249
718-388-2644 | www.mastbrothers.com

GENERAL NOTES: Sources beans from around the world and
claims to pay more than fair trade minimums. See the sidebar in
chapter 11.

Nestlé

Avenue Nestlé 55, 1800 Vevey, Switzerland
+41-21-924-1111 | www.nestle.com

ECO-PRACTICES: By 2030 zero environmental impact.

WORKER JUSTICE: Signer of Harkin-Engel Protocol 2001. Member
of International Cocoa Initiative. The Fair Labor Association audits
some of their West African cocoa bean sources. Seventy farmer co-
ops. Working to monitor and remediate hazardous child labor.

GENERAL NOTES: Primarily confectionary.

Newman's Own Organics

www.newmansown.com/food/type/chocolate

CHARITY: All profits after taxes go to Newman's Own Foundation.

ECO-PRACTICES: Rainforest Alliance–certified.

WORKER JUSTICE: Uses no forced labor.

QUALITY: USDA Organic–certified.

GENERAL NOTES: Family owned. Certified kosher by Orthodox
Union.

Omanhene

5441 S. 9th Street, Milwaukee, WI 53221
414-744-8780 | www.omanhene.com

WORKER JUSTICE: Claims to be "beyond fair trade."

QUALITY: Single-sourced from and processed in Ghana since 1991.

GENERAL NOTES: The name Omanhene in the Twi language of
Ghana means the "Paramount Chief." Kosher hot chocolate.

Original Beans

Keizersgracht 452 1016 GD Amsterdam, Netherlands
503-692-3323 ext. 10 (U.S.) | www.originalbeans.com

ECO-PRACTICES: FairWild-certified. Seeks heritage cocoa beans. Over one million trees planted since 2008. For each purchased chocolate bar, a cocoa or shade tree is planted in the rainforest. Lot numbers track trees and bars. Climate-positive by independent study.
WORKER JUSTICE: Member of Direct Cacao and believes in direct trade.

Patric

6601 Stephens Station Road, Suite 109, Columbia, MO 65202
573-814-7520 | www.patric-chocolate.com

ECO-PRACTICES: Uses Forest Stewardship Council and Green-Seal–certified products; recycles all possible materials, and ships via UPS Carbon Neutral program.
WORKER JUSTICE: Pays at least fair trade or higher.
GENERAL NOTES: Described as American craft, making chocolate from scratch—from the cocoa bean. Made by Alan McClure.

Rescue Chocolate

Brooklyn, NY
347-875-0078 | www.rescuechocolate.com

CHARITY: 100 percent net profits donated to animal rescue organizations.
WORKER JUSTICE: Uses Guittard fairly traded chocolate.
QUALITY: Organic via Guittard.
GENERAL NOTES: Earth Kosher via Tumbador's Brooklyn factory.

Rogue

Three Rivers, Massachusetts
www.roguechocolatier.com

WORKER JUSTICE: Single-origin chocolate bars from farms in Peru, Dominican Republic, Ecuador, Trinidad, Tobago, and Honduras; pays more than fair trade.

GENERAL NOTES: Made by Colin Gasko. Small, authentic bean-to-bar manufactory. Available online.

Sunspire

The Hain Celestial Group, Inc., 4600 Sleepytime Drive, Boulder, CO 80301
800-434-4246 | www.sunspire.com

CHARITY: Supports ECHOES alliance of the World Cocoa Foundation.

WORKER JUSTICE: Fair Trade USA–certified. Member of the World Cocoa Foundation.

QUALITY: USDA Organic–certified. Kosher-certified by Orthodox Union.

Taza

561 Windsor Street, Somerville, MA 02143-4192
617-623-0804 (office) | 617-284-2232 (store) | www.tazachocolate.com

ECO-PRACTICES: Stoneground chocolate.

WORKER JUSTICE: Direct Trade certified by Quality Certification Services. Reports at website.

QUALITY: USDA Organic–certified. Non-GMO Project Verified.

GENERAL NOTES: Certified kosher pareve by Orthodox Union.

TCHO

3100 San Pablo Avenue, Berkeley, CA 94702
844-877-8246 | www.tcho.com

WORKER JUSTICE: Sources beans directly from Ecuador, Ghana, Madagascar, and Peru.

GENERAL NOTES: Calls itself a "New American" chocolate maker. Certified by Earth Kosher.

Theo

3400 Phinney Avenue, N. Seattle, WA 98103
206-632-5100 | www.theochocolate.com

WORKER JUSTICE: Fair for Life–certified.

QUALITY: USDA Organic–certified. Non-GMO Project Verified. Demeter Certified Biodynamic.

GENERAL NOTES: Claims to be the first organic, fair trade–certified, bean-to-bar factory in the United States. Certified kosher by Square-K.

Valrhona

222 Water Street, Brooklyn, NY 11201
718-522-7001 | www.valrhona-chocolate.com

ECO-PRACTICES: Intends to cut its environmental impact in half by 2025.

WORKER JUSTICE: Works on reducing waste. Some lines are Fairtrade International–certified. Member of the World Cocoa Foundation. No child or forced labor through its Responsible Purchasing Charter.

QUALITY: Some USDA Organic–certified.

GENERAL NOTES: Some lines are certified kosher by Triangle-K. Multinational French company.

Vosges

2950 North Oakley Ave., Chicago, IL 60618
773-388-5560 | www.vosgeschocolate.com

CHARITY: Supports several social initiatives.

ECO-PRACTICES: They advance their "Green Purchasing Oath." Planting new areas with cacao trees.

QUALITY: Uses Valhrona, Felchin, and others; some are fair trade and organic.

GENERAL NOTES: Wild Ophelia is a fair trade, non-GMO chocolate "sister" line.

Zotter

8333 Riegersburg, Bergl 56, Austria
+43-3152-5554 | www.zotter.at/en/

ECO-PRACTICES: Factory is 60 percent self-sufficient.

WORKER JUSTICE: Fairtrade Austria–certified.

QUALITY: Organic certification from Austria.

GENERAL NOTES: Recipient of awards for corporate responsibility. Has a second shop in Shanghai.

Chocolate Museums and Tours around the World

CREATE YOUR OWN CHOCOLATE TRAIL OF MUSEUMS and factory tours using this list. Before you visit, I encourage you to check each website listed or call for additional details on hours, availability, and fees. Some of the museums are company owned and discount prices on products. Generally all give samples. Some charge admission. For other chocolate experiences as you travel, you may wish to search for chocolate shows and festivals that happen all over the world, including Ashland (Oregon), Bayonne (France), Bruges (Belgium), New York, Paris, Seattle (Washington), Tokyo, and Turin (Italy). For instance, New York features Chocolate Expos in several venues each year. The Big Chocolate Show, inaugurated in 2016 in New York, has expanded to include events in New York and Miami. Some resorts also feature chocolate-learning experiences, such as the Cotton Tree Lodge in Belize.

CHOCOLATE TRAVELING TIPS

Here are some suggestions when buying chocolate while traveling:

1. When visiting shops, inquire about local specialties, the staff favorites, and whether samples are available. Check out local markets for their offerings in addition to specialty stores.
2. Carry an insulated bag or two, especially in hot climates, for purchases and samples.
3. Keep a supply of small plastic bags and a marking pen to store each acquisition separately, and mark to identify store, location, and date.
4. Alternatively, take a photo to provide a visual record, date/time stamp, and location.
5. Keep a journal of what you have tasted, where, your experiences, and any other thoughts.

BRAZIL

Chocolate Caseiro Prawer
Avenida das Hortênsias, 4100
Gramado-RS Rio Grande do Sul,
   Brazil
CEP: 95670-000
www.prawer.com.br

CANADA

The Chocolate Museum
73 Milltown Blvd.
St. Stephen, NB E3L 1G5
New Brunswick, Canada
www.chocolatemuseum.ca

Le Musée du Chocolat
634 rue Saint-Jean, G1R 1P8
Quebec, Canada
www.ericochocolatier.com

Le Musée du Chocolat de la Confiserie Bromont
679 rue Shefford Bromont, J2L 1C2
Quebec, Canada
www.lemuseeduchocolatdelacon-fiseriebromont.com

CUBA

Museo del Chocolate
Mercaderes Street and Amargura
Havana, Cuba
www.lahabana.com/guide
/museo-del-chocolate

EUROPE

Chocolate Museum Heindl
Willendorfer Gasse 2-8
1230
Vienna, Austria
www.schokomuseum.at

Choco Story
Wijnzakstraat 2 (Sint-Jansplein) 8000
Bruges, Belgium
www.choco-story.be

Roose's Chocolate World
Havenstraat 1 8000
Bruges, Belgium
www.chocolate-world.be

Choco-Story
Rue de la Tete d'Or 9-11
1000
Brussels, Belgium
www.choco-story-brussels.be

Planète Chocolat
Rue du Lombard 24
1000
Brussels, Belgium
www.planetechocolat.com

Temple du Chocolat Côte d'Or
Brusselsesteenweg 450
B-1500 Halle
Brussels, Belgium
www.cotedor.be/home/temple

Le Musée du Chocolat Jacques
Rue de l'industrie 16
B-4700
Eupen, Belgium
www.chocojacques.be/fr/musee

Choco Story Praha
Celetná 10 (Staré msto)
110 00
Prague, Czech Republic
www.choco-story-praha.cz

Cadbury World
Linden Road
Bournville, B30 1JR
Birmingham, England
www.cadburyworld.co.uk

Chocolate Museum
187 Ferndale Road
SW9 8BA
London, England
www.thechocolatemuseum.co.uk

York's Chocolate Story
King's Square
YO1, 7LD
York, England
www.yorkschocolatestory.com

Choco-Musée Puyodebat
Rue Argenterie
64100
Bayonne, France
www.chocolats-puyodebat.com

Chocolaterie de Beussent Lachelle
66 Route de Desvres
62170
Beussent, France
www.choco-france.com

Planèt Musée du Chocolat
14 Avenue Beaurivage
64200
Biarritz, France
www.planetemuseeduchocolat.com

Michel Cluizel's Chocolatrium Musée
Route de Conches
27240
Damville, France
www.cluizel.com

Musée Les Secrets du Chocolat
Rue du Pont du Péage
67118
Geispolsheim, France
www.musee-du-chocolat.com

Le Paradis du Chocolat Musée
Rue Jacques de Saint-Georges
38260
La Côte-Saint-André, France
www.paradis-chocolat.fr

Chocolaterie du Drakkar et Musée du Chocolat
ZA Bayeux Intercom
14400 Nonant
Normandy, France
www.chocolateriedrakkar.com/musee

Le Musée du Chocolat
Z.A.E.S. du Moulin Rouge
24120
Terrasson-Lavilledieu, France
www.bovetti.com

Imhoff Schokoladen Museum
Am Schokoladenmuseum 1a
50678
Cologne, North Rhine-Westphalia, Germany
www.schokoladenmuseum.de

Halloren Schokoladenmuseum
Delitzscher Strasse 70
06112
Halle, Germany
www.halloren.de/wisl_s-cms/extern
   /schokoladenmuseum.php.html

Csokoládé Múzeum
1162 Budapest Bekecs Street 22
Budapest, Hungary
www.csokolade-muzeum.hu

Museo del Cioccolato Antica Norba
Via Capo dell' Acqua, 20
04010
Norma, Italy
www.museodelcioccolato.com

La Casa del Cioccolato Perugina
Viale San Sisto 207/C
Perugia, Italy
www.perugina.com/it
   /casa-del-cioccolato/la-casa

Laima Chocolate Museum
Miera Street 22
1001
Riga, Latvia
www.laimasokoladesmuzejs.lv

Museo del Chocolate
Avd. De la Estación 16
24700
Astorga, León, Spain
www.aytoastorga.es/turismo-y-ocio
   /MUCHA/index.html

Museu de la Xocolata
Carrer Comerç 36
08003
Barcelona, Spain
www.museuxocolata.cat

Chocolate Comes Artesano
Calle Sant Josep, 29
46410
Sueca (Valencia), Spain
www.chocolatescomes.com

Chocolates Clavileño Museo del Chocolate
Calle de Colón 187
03570
Villajoyosa, Alicante, Spain
www.chocolatesclavileno.com/

Valor Chocolate Museum
Pianista Gonzalo Soriano, 13
03570
Villajoyosa, Alicante, Spain
www.valor.es

Maison Cailler Chocolate Factory
Rue Jules Bellet 7
1636
Broc, Switzerland
www.cailler.ch

Shokoland
via Rompada 36
6987
Caslano, Switzerland
www.alprose.ch

Maestrani Chocolarium
Toggenburgerstrasse 41
9230
Flawil, Switzerland
www.chocolarium.ch

Swiss Chocolate Train
The train travels to Montreaux on the Swiss Riviera, to Gruyères Cheese Factory, to Broc and the Cailler-Nestlé Chocolate Factory.
traintickets.myswitzerland.com/european-trains/chocolate-train/how-to-book.html

ISRAEL

De Karina
Kibbutz Ein Zivan
Golan Heights
www.de-karina.co.il

Galita Chocolate Farm
Kibbutz Degania Bet or Kibbutz Tzuba
www.galita.co.il

NEW ZEALAND

Silky Oak Chocolate Company Museum and Factory Tours
1131 Links Road, Hastings
Hawkes Bay, New Zealand
www.silkyoakchocs.co.nz

UNITED STATES

Askinosie Chocolate
514 E. Commercial
Springfield, MO 65803
www.askinosie.com

Candy Americana Museum
45 North Broad Street
Lititz, PA 17543
www.wilburbuds.com

Chocolatrium Michel Cluizel
53 Cooper Road
575 Route 73 North
West Berlin, NJ 08091
www.cluizel.us

Choco-Story New York
Jacques Torres
350 Hudson Street
New York, NY 10014
www.mrchocolate.com

Dandelion Chocolate
740 Valencia Street
San Francisco, CA 94110
www.dandelionchocolate.com

Ethel M. Chocolates Factory Tour
2 Cactus Garden Drive
Henderson, NV 89014
www.ethelm.com

Hershey's Chocolate World
101 Chocolate World Way
Hershey, PA 17033
www.hersheys.com/chocolateworld

Hershey Story Museum
63 West Chocolate Avenue
Hershey, PA 17033
www.hersheystory.org

Lake Champlain Chocolates Factory Tour
750 Pine Street
Burlington, VT 05401
www.lakechamplainchocolates.com

Mast Brothers Chocolate
111 N. 3rd Street
Brooklyn, NY 11249
www.mastbrothers.com

Taza Chocolate
561 Windsor Street
Somerville, MA 02143
www.tazachocolate.com

Theo Chocolate
3400 Phinney Avenue N.
Seattle, WA 98103
www.theochocolate.com

World of Chocolate Museum
11701 International Drive #400
Orlando, FL 32821
www.wocorlando.com

Notes

PREFACE

1. Rabbi Lynne Goldsmith, e-mail to author, April 14, 2014.
2. Rabbi Amy Perlin, March 16, 2015.
3. Izak Prins, "Chocolate and Politics," *Jerusalem Post*, March 1, 1957.
4. Earlier versions appeared as: "From Prins to Prinz: The Mysteries of the Chocolate Trail," *Jewish Journal*, September 21, 2013, accessed June 5, 2017, http://jewishjournal.com/culture/food/121734/from-prins-to-prinz-the-mysteries-of-the-chocolate-trail/; "From Prins to Prinz: The Mysteries of the Chocolate Trail," *Jerusalem Post*, May 15, 2014, accessed May 28, 2017, www.jpost.com/In-Jerusalem/Arts-And-Culture/From-Prins-to-Prinz-The-mysteries-of-the-chocolate-trail-352346.

INTRODUCTION

1. Clay Gordon, "Serious Chocolate: First Three, Now Ten Genetically Different Kinds of Cacao," *Serious Eats*, accessed May 28, 2017, http://sweets.seriouseats.com/2008/10/cacao-by-any-other-name-does-it-taste-just-as.html.
2. Clay Gordon, e-mail and interview with the author, April 19–May 4, 2017.
3. Abraham Cresques, known as the "map Jew" or the "compass Jew," drew the Catalan map, perhaps the most famous and comprehensive image of the then known world. See Meyer Kayserling, *Christopher Columbus and the Participation of Jews in Spanish and Portuguese Discoveries* (New York: Longman's Green, 1894), 5–6, 13, 48, 113.
4. Eli Rosenblatt, "Christopher Columbus: Jew?" *The Jewish Daily Forward*, February 8, 2008, accessed November 22, 2011, www.forward.com/articles/12638/#ixzz1eYODaj86.
5. Louis Evan Grivetti and Howard-Yana Shapiro, eds., *Chocolate: History, Culture and Heritage* (Hoboken, NJ: John Wiley & Sons, 2009), 927.

CHAPTER 1: DID JEWS INTRODUCE CHOCOLATE TO FRANCE?

1. Sophie D. and Michael D. Coe, *The True History of Chocolate* (London: Thames & Hudson, 1996), 155–56; Susan J. Terrio, *Crafting the Culture of French Chocolate* (Berkeley: University of California Press, 2000), 72ff.

2. Jonathan I. Israel, *European Jewry in the Age of Mercantilism 1550–1750* (Oxford: Clarendon Press, 1989), 66; Grivetti and Shapiro, eds. *Chocolate*, 923. More about coffeehouses may be found in the following sources: Norma Aubertin-Potter and Alyx Bennet, *Oxford Coffee Houses 1651–1800* (Oxford: Hampden Press, 1987), 13; Ellis Markman, *The Coffee House: A Cultural History* (London: Weidenfeld and Nicolson, 2004), 30. The excitement of coffeehouse culture and its cultural generativity may be seen in the work of Steve Johnson, *Where Good Ideas Come From: The Natural History of Innovation* (New York: Riverhead Books, 2010).

3. Jonathan Irvine Israel, *Diasporas within Diasporas: Jews, Crypto-Jews and the World Maritime Empires (1540–1740)* (Leiden, the Netherlands: Brill Publishers, 2002), 440.

4. Frédéric Duhart, *Le Chocolat au Pays Basque* (Donastia, Spain: Elkar Éditions, 2006), 22.

5. Ralph G. Bennett, "The Sephardic Path to North America," accessed 2006, www.sefarad.org/publication/lm/030/bennett.html.

6. Gérard Nahon, "The Portuguese Nation of Saint-Esprit-lès Bayonne: The American Dimension," in *The Jews and Expansion of Europe to the West 1450–1800*, ed. Paolo Bernardini and Norman Fiering (New York: Berghahn Books, 2001), 257; Mordechai Arbell, "Jewish Settlements in the French Colonies in the Caribbean (Martinique, Guadeloupe, Haiti, Cayenne) and the 'Black Code,'" in *The Jews and Expansion of Europe*, 292.

7. Tirtsah Levie Bernfeld, *Poverty and Welfare among the Portuguese Jews in Early Modern Amsterdam* (Oxford: Littman Library of Jewish Civilization, 2012), 197, 447.

8. Elliott Horowitz, "Coffee, Coffeehouses and the Nocturnal Rituals of Early Modern Jewry," *Association for Jewish Studies Review* 14 (1989): 42.

9. Hanne Trautner Kromann, *The History of Jews in Denmark*, Jewish Gen Scandinavia—SIG (Scandinavia Special Interest Group), accessed 2007, www.jewishgen.org/scandinavia/history.htm.

10. Christian Teubner, *The Chocolate Bible* (New York: Penguin Books, 1997), 71.

11. "Cocoa in France," The Worldwide Gourmet, accessed 2006, www.theworldwidegourmet.com/products/articles/cocoa-in-france.

12. Israel, *Diasporas within Diasporas*, 22, 27, 132, 247, 253; William Gervase Clarence-Smith, *Cocoa and Chocolate 1765–1914* (New York: Routledge, 2000), 94.

13. Gerard Nahon, "The Sephardim of France," in *The Sephardi Heritage: Essays on the History and Cultural Contribution of the Jews of Spain and Portugal*, ed. R. D. Barnett and W. M. Schwab (New York: Ktav Publishing House, Inc., 1971), 51.

14. Esther Benbassa, *The Jews of France: A History from Antiquity to the Present*, trans. M. B. DeBevoise (Princeton, NJ: Princeton University Press, 1999), 52.

15. Jonathan Irvine Israel, *Dutch Primacy in World Trade 1585–1740* (Oxford, UK: Clarendon Press, 1989), 261; Israel, *Diasporas within Diasporas*, 268; Fernand Braudel, *Civilization and Capitalism, 15th–18th Century*, vol. 1, *The Structures of Everyday Life: The Limits of the Possible*, trans. Sian Reynolds (New York: Harper and Row, 1979), 249; Clarence-Smith, *Cocoa and Chocolate 1765–1914*, 107.

16. Eugenio Piñero, "The Cacao Economy of the Eighteenth Century Province of Caracas and the Spanish Cacao Market," in *The Atlantic Staple Trade: The Economics of Trade*, vol. 2 of *An Expanding World: The European Impact on World History 1450–1800*, ed. Susan Socolow (London: Variorum, 1996), 501. A Jamaican Jew, Isaac Nunes, had contact with a brother living in Bayonne; Stephen Alexander Fortune, *Merchants and Jews: The Struggle for British West Indian Commerce 1650–1750*, Center for Latin American Studies Book (Gainesville: University of Florida Press, 1984), 133.

17. Duhart, *Le Chocolat au Pays Basque*, 20.

18. Clarence-Smith, *Cocoa and Chocolate*, 67.

19. The shop was run by Monsieur Lemoine, and the review was written by Grimod de la Reynère in *L'Almanach des Gourmands*, quoted in Nathalie Bailleux, et al., eds., *The Book of Chocolate* (Paris: Flammarion, 1995), 101.

20. Mort Rosenblum, *Chocolate: A Bittersweet Saga* (New York: North Point Press, 2005), 12. Terrio, *Crafting the Culture*, 73; and Antony Wild, *The East India Company Book of Chocolate* (London: Harper Collins, 1995), 13.

21. Zvi Avneri, "Bayonne," *Encyclopaedia Judaica*, 2nd ed. ed. Fred Skolnik (Detroit, MI: Macmillan Reference USA / Keter Publishing House, 2007), 3, 231.

22. Joan Nathan, *Quiches, Kugels and Couscous: My Search for Jewish Cooking in France* (New York: Alfred A. Knopf, 2010), 320.

23. Duhart, *Le Chocolat au Pays Basque*, 20.

24. Terrio, *Crafting the Culture*, 66ff., 77.

25. Ibid., 78; Anne Benard-Oukhemanou, *La Communaute Juive de Bayonne au XIXe Siecle* (Ann Arbor: University of Michigan Press, 2001), 100, 114.

26. Ibid., 78–79.

The Rabbi's Chocolate Diaries

a. Hayyim Joseph David Azulai, *The Diaries of Rabbi Ha'im Yosef David Azulai: The Good Journey*, trans. Benjamin Cymerman (Northvale, NJ: Jason Aronson, 1996).

b. Ibid., p. 125: "5516/1755 25 Teveth from Nice to Cuneo. Over snowy mountains, very hard trip…. Mercifully, I had some raw chocolate, and I ate about a litre!"

c. Ibid., p. 246: "5538/1777–8 Amsterdam Iyar 6. Next morning, an hour before mid-day, I went to the circumcision [of the son of S. Moses ben Isaac Israel Soasso] where I found all the Parnessim, his friends. They made me stay for the meal which consisted of … and various sweetmeats. I did not wash hands for eating the bread but only ate some sweetmeats and chocolate."

d. Ibid., p. 102: "5537/1776 Shevat 21, Trieste, Italy. Meeting with leaders of the council. But the first and prime force in everything was S. Marco who sent me a large vessel full of coffee and chocolate.…"

e. Ibid. Further diary entries about chocolate:

   p. 45: "5534/1774, Iyar 20, just before Shavuot, Livorno, Italy. And they brought me gifts: S. Leon, coffee and chocolate."

   p. 152: "5537/1776 Montpellier, France. Thursday. I went to the synagogue established by the deceased Melinde and his widow supports the synagogue. They conduct themselves according to the rites of the Four Congregations [Carpentras, Avignon, Lisle and Cavaillon]. After prayers I drank chocolate with the said widow together with some of the Yehidim."

   p. 174: "5538/Heshvan 16 1778, France. Later I went to drink chocolate with S. Samuel Astruc; then I went to dine at the home of…. "

   p. 178: "5538/Kislev New Moon 1777, Sunday, *Vayetse*…. In the morning I drank chocolate at the home of S. Judah and Haim bar-Mordecai who are called by the name of Lange."

   p. 194: "5538/Teveth 6 5538 1777, Monday. I drank chocolate with Solomon Ravel."

   p. 205: "5538/1777–8 Teveth 27, Amsterdam. The eve of Monday; we found in the village of Dragehave a Jewish householder living there with his family. On each holy Sabbath a minyan came there to pray and they had a Sefer Torah. We stayed there some three hours and they regaled us with chocolate and other delicacies."

p. 234: "5538/1777–8 Amsterdam, Adar 27. Thursday I went to visit some gentiles with S. ibn Dana: Britano, Pibelsman, Carlo Vernandi. They did me much honor, especially Pibelsman who gave me two pounds of home-made chocolate."

An earlier version appeared as "Rabbi Diaries: Chocolate Drinking in Eighteenth Century," *Jewish Journal*, March 1, 2017, accessed June 5, 2017, http://jewishjournal.com/culture/food/215799 /rabbi-diaries-chocolate-drinking-eighteenth-century/.

Complexities of Jewish Identity

a. Richard L. Kagan and Philip D. Morgan, eds., *Atlantic Diasporas: Jews, Conversos, and Crypto-Jews in the Age of Mercantilism 1500–1800* (Baltimore, MD: Johns Hopkins University Press, 2009), viii–ix, 4–5, 24.

b. Seymour B. Liebman, *The Jews in New Spain: Faith, Flame and Inquisition* (Florida: University of Miami Press, 1970), 152; Jorge Cañizares-Esguerra and Erik R. Seeman, *The Atlantic in Global History 1500–2000* (NJ: Prentice Hall, 2007), 40.

CHAPTER 2: THE INQUISITION: CHOCOLATE OUTED JEWS AND DIVIDED CHRISTIANS

1. Label at the Barcelona Museu de la Xocolata, www.pastisseria.com/en/ PortadaMuseu.

2. Marcy Norton, *Sacred Gifts, Profane Pleasures: A History of Tobacco and Chocolate in the Atlantic World* (Ithaca, NY: Cornell University Press, 2010), 142.

3. Haim Beinart, "The Records of the Inquisition: A Source of Jewish and Converso History," *Proceedings of the Israel Academy of Sciences and Humanities* 2, no. 11 (1967): 213; Stanley M. Hordes, "The Inquisition as Economic and Political Agent," *The Americas* 39, no. 1 (July 1982): 29.

4. Francesca Trivellato, "Sephardic Merchants in the Early Modern Atlantic and Beyond: Toward a Comparative Historical Approach to Business Cooperation," in *Atlantic Diasporas*, 120.

5. Arnold Wiznitzer, "Crypto-Jews in Mexico in the 17th Century," *Proceedings of the American Jewish Historical Society* 51 (June 1962): 264–66. Hordes, "The Inquisition," 119.

6. Martha Few, *Women Who Live Evil Lives: Gender, Religion, and the Politics of Power in Colonial Guatemala: 1650-1750* (Austin: University of Texas Press, 2002), 28–29, 32, 53–55, 64; Marcy Norton, *Sacred Gifts, Profane Pleasures*, 138.

7. Robert J. Ferry, *The Colonial Elite of Early Caracas: Formation and Crisis 1567–1767* (Los Angeles: University of California Press, 1989), 48, 62; Robert J. Ferry, "Don't Drink the Chocolate: Domestic Slavery and the Exigencies of Fasting for Crypto-Jews in Seventeenth-Century Mexico,"

Nuevo Mundo Mundos Neuvos, 2005, accessed November 2011,
http://nuevomundo.revues.org/934; Robert Ferry, "Trading Cacao: A
View from Veracruz: 1629–1645," *Nuevo Mundo Mundos Neuvos*,
2006, accessed November, 2011, http://nuevomundo.revues.org/1430;
Stanley M. Hordes, *The Crypto-Jewish Community of New Spain,
1620–1649: A Collective Biography* (Ann Arbor, MI: Dissertation Services,
1980 / Dissertation, Tulane University, May 1980), 68, 71, 81, 83.

8. Stanley M. Hordes, e-mail message to author, December 28, 2010.

9. Stanley M. Hordes, *To the End of the Earth: A History of the Crypto-
Jews of New Mexico* (New York: Columbia University Press, 2005),
42, 53–54, 83–84, 92, 109; Ferry, *Trading Cacao*, 16–17; Hordes,
Crypto-Jewish Community, 71; Liebman, *New Spain*, 317, 327.

10. Norton, *Sacred Gifts*, 179.

11. Ferry, *Trading Cacao,* 52; Hordes, *End of the Earth*, 81.

12. Ferry, *Trading Cacao*, 25ff., 41, 57, 63.

13. David M. Gitlitz and Linda Kay Davidson, *A Drizzle of Honey: The Lives
and Recipes of Spain's Secret Jews* (New York: St Martin's Griffin: 1999),
106; David Gitlitz, *Secrecy and Deceit: The Religion of the Crypto-Jews*
(Philadelphia, PA: Jewish Publication Society; Albuquerque: University of
New Mexico Press, 1996), 57, 355; Liebman, *New Spain*, 47, 79, 258.
Between Juan Méndez de Villaviciosa and Ana Suarez, arranged by
another merchant, the bride's mother, and the bride's grandmother,
from Inquisition testimony (October 24, 1642).

14. Ferry, *Trading Cacao*, 8–9.

15. "Process or Trial of Gabriel de Granada, Mexico 1642," *Publication of
the American Jewish Historical Society* 7 (1899): 93, 95.

16. Liebman, *New Spain*, 47, 83, 84; Gitlitz, *Drizzle of Honey*, 44.

17. Gitlitz, *Secrecy and Deceit*, 356, 358.

18. Gitlitz, *Drizzle of Honey*, 103.

19. Ferry, *Trading Cacao*, 9.

20. Gitlitz, *Secrecy and Deceit*, 364, as reported by Isabel Rodriguez and
Juan Pacheco de León from approximately 1650.

21. Ferry, *Trading Cacao*, 13.

22. Gitlitz, *Secrecy and Deceit*, 398–99.

23. Ferry, *Trading Cacao*, 14.

24. Ferry, "Don't Drink," 12.

25. Gitlitz, *Secrecy and Deceit*, 397.

26. Ibid., 398.

27. Ferry, "Don't Drink," 11.

28. Ferry, *Trading Cacao*, 12.

29. Ibid., 5, 14, 15.

30. Ibid; Liebman, *New Spain*, 2–4, 10, 15, 203.

31. Hordes, *End of the Earth*, 60.

The Inquisition

a. Liebman, *New Spain*, 16, 33.

b. Arnold Wiznitzer, "Crypto-Jews in Mexico in the 16th Century," *The American Jewish Historical Quarterly* 51 (1962): 175–76.

c. Richard Greenleaf, *Zumárraga and the Mexican Inquisition, 1536–1543*, Academy of American Franciscan History Monograph Series, vol. 4 (Washington, DC: Academy of American Franciscan History, 1961), 89.

d. Hordes, "The Inquisition," 26, 28, 36.

e. Liebman, *New Spain*, 24, 28, 168–69.

f. Coe, *True History*, 138–9.

Cacao in Central America

a. J. H. Elliott, *Empires of the Atlantic World: Britain and Spain in America 1492–1830* (New Haven, CT: Yale University Press, 2006); Ferry, "Trading Cacao", 21. Louisa Schell Hoberman, "Merchants in 17th Century Mexico City," *Hispanic American Historical Review* 57 (August 1977): 21, 25–29, 91, 111, 206–7.

CHAPTER 3: JEWS DIP INTO CHOCOLATE IN THE AMERICAN COLONIAL PERIOD

Chocolate Pudding

a. Esther Levy, *The Jewish Cookery Book, on Principles of Economy, adapted for Jewish Housekeepers with the addition of many useful medicinal recipes and other valuable information related to housekeeping and domestic management* (Philadelphia, PA: W. S. Turner, 1871), 94. This is the first known American Jewish cookbook.

Detailed charts of chocolate shipping and production information may be found at the website for *On the Chocolate Trail* at www.jews-onthechocolatetrail.org/booksupplement/.

1. Jacob R. Marcus, *The Colonial American Jew, 1492–1776* (Detroit, MI: Wayne State University Press, 1970), 673.

2. Anthony M. Sammarco, *The Baker Chocolate Factory: A Sweet History* (Charleston, SC: History Press, 2009). Baker's predecessor, John Hannon's chocolate grinding on the Neponset River since 1765, was preceded by many. Indeed, Sephardi Isaac Navarro in Maryland was grinding in 1748.

3. Elvira N. Solis, "Note on Isaac Gomez and Lewis Moses Gomez from an Old Family Record," *Publications of the American Jewish Historical*

Society (1893–1961): 1903; vol. 11, *American Jewish Historical Society Journal*, 140, 142.

4. Malcolm Stern, *First American Jewish Families: 600 Genealogies, 1654–1977* (Cincinnati, OH: American Jewish Archives; Waltham, MA: American Jewish Historical Society, 1978), 185.

5. James Gay, "Chocolate Production and Uses in 17th and 18th Century North America," in Grivetti and Shapiro, *Chocolate*, 283, 285, 289; "Franklin's Print Shop," accessed November, 2011, www.history.org /history/teaching/enewsletter/volume9/jan11/featurearticle.cfm.

6. James Gay, interview with the author, February 2008, Williamsburg, Virginia. However, the earliest written and archaeological records for chocolate north of Mexico date to the eighth century and consist of the following:

   • First report: Eighth-century chocolate usage connects Mesoamericans to the Southwest United States over one thousand years ago. Chocolate residue has been identified in shallow clay bowls at a settlement of the ancestral Pueblo peoples at Alkali Ridge of southeastern Utah. See Dorothy K. Washburn, William N. Washburn, and Petia A. Shipkova, "Cacao Consumption During the 8th century at Alkali Ridge, Southeastern Utah," *Journal of Archaeological Science* 40, no. 4 (April 2013): 2007–13. Chocolate in clay cylinders found north of Central Mexico, in Chaco Canyon, New Mexico, dates back to about 1000 CE. Patricia L. Crown, and W. Jeffrey Hurst, "Evidence of Cacao Use in the Prehispanic American Southwest," *Proceedings of the National Academy of Sciences* 106 (7): 2110–3, accessed March 2, 2017, www.pnas.org /content/106/7/2110.full.pdf.

   • Second report: A manuscript dated September 29, 1641 reports the plight of a ship named the *Nuestra Señora del Rosario y el Carmen* traveling the Bahamas Channel to Spain. Caught in a hurricane, the captain tossed much of the cargo in order to save the ship. However, he elected not to throw the valuable chocolate/cocoa beans overboard. After the storm passed, the ship finally landed at St. Augustine, Florida. Conversos were among the settlers of St. Augustine, Florida, in 1565 and may have enjoyed these first tastes of the shipwrecked cocoa. See Saul S. Friedman, *Jews and the American Slave Trade* (New Brunswick, NJ: Transaction Publishers, 1998), 103. The drenched cargo included thirty-two crates of chocolate and nine chocolate grinding stones. Ultimately, the chocolate was auctioned off to locals and then distributed to a long list of men and boys. See Beatriz Cabezon and Louis Evan, "Paleography and the St. Augustine Chocolate Saga," in Grivetti and Shapiro, *Chocolate*, 669–98.

   • Third report: A lovely chocolate cup, Rochester Museum item 875/99, manufactured sometime between 1655 and 1675 in Delft, the Netherlands, used by Native Americans perhaps as decoration, was found in the Hudson Valley. Peter G. Rose, "Dutch Cacao Trade in New Netherland During the 17th and 18th Centuries," in Grivetti and Shapiro, *Chocolate*, 379. Also, e-mail correspondence with George R. Hamell, collections manager, Rock Foundation Collection, Rochester Museum, August 4, 2009: "The present cup on loan to the Museum of the City of New York and another similar cup from a contemporary archeological site were probably acquired at Fort Orange–Beverwijck [Albany], which the Seneca and Iroquois [Haudenosaunee] frequented for trade. There are also references to visits to trade and to attend councils at New Amsterdam. It is also possible the cups and other Euroamerican ceramics known from Seneca and the lower Iroquois [Haudenosaunee] archeological village sites were directly acquired from Euroamerican colonists on the lower Mohawk Valley or in the Hudson Valley, or indirectly from native or Euroamerican traders traveling through Seneca and Iroquois [Haudenosaunee] communities during the seventeenth century."

- Fourth report: The diary of Massachusetts Bay mint-master John Hull records that in the winter of 1667–68 "our ship *Providence* ... cast away on the French shore ... carrying ... cocoa." Gay, "Chocolate Production," in Grivetti and Shapiro, *Chocolate*, 281.

- Fifth report: In 1670 the city of Boston granted permission to Dorothy Jones and Jane Barnard to open a "Coffee and Chucaletto" house. Ibid.

- Sixth report: British customs records show cocoa arriving in America in 1682: "1682 ... Jamaica ... to ... Boston." Ibid.

7. Celia D. Shapiro, "Nation of Nowhere: Jewish Role in Colonial American Chocolate," in Grivetti and Shapiro, *Chocolate*, 59.

8. Marquez was endenizened in New York, October 16, 1695, and made a freeman on September 17, 1697. See Stern, *First American Jewish Families*, 185; Liber 30 of Conveyances Registers Office Borough of Manhattan, New York City, "An Account of his Majesty's Revenue of the Province of New York," P255/Box#19, American Jewish Historical Society (AJHS), New York.

9. Leo Hershkowitz, "Some Aspects of the New York Jewish Merchant and Community, 1654–1820," *American Jewish Historical Quarterly* 66, nos. 1–4 (September 1976–June 1977): 25.

10. Oppenheim Collection, 255/18/4, American Jewish Historical Society, New York.

11. Marcus, *The Colonial American Jew*, 2:1486n16; 2:1494n38; Celia D. Shapiro, "Nation of Nowhere," 58; Hershkowitz, "Aspects," 22; correspondence Daniel Gomez to Aaron Lopez, Microfilm 597, New York, June 19, 1753, American Jewish Archives (AJA), Cincinnati, OH; Daniel Gomez Ledger, Microfilm 597, AJA, Cincinnati, OH.

12. Virginia Barnett and Jan K. Gilliam, *Food in the Eighteenth Century Chesapeake* (Williamsburg, VA: Colonial Williamsburg Foundation Library, 1991), 71, 74.

13. The first coffeehouse in England was founded in Oxford by Jacob the Jew (see chap. 1); Mary R. M. Goodwin, *The Coffeehouses of the 17th and 18th Centuries* (Williamsburg, VA: Colonial Williamsburg Foundation Library, Research Report Series, 1956).

14. Gay, "Chocolate Production," in Grivetti and Shapiro, *Chocolate*, 285. An entry in the daybook of Josiah DuBois 1807–1820 notes that the town of New Paltz paid for half a pound of chocolate "for relief of John A. Freer and family ... A family of color" on September 15, 1819, and again on October 19, 1819.

15. *The Providence Gazette and Country Journal*, March 25, 1775, 4.

16. Mary R. M. Goodwin, "Christmas in Colonial Virginia," in *Library Research Report Series* (Williamsburg, VA: Colonial Williamsburg Foundation, 1955), xxix.

17. Ibid., xxxii.

18. *Essex Gazette*, January 11, 1774, 94.

19. "Report of the Committee of Commerce and Manufactures on the Memorials of Sundry Manufacturers of Chocolate, February, 8, 1797," *Early American Imprints, Series I*, Rockefeller Library, Williamsburg, VA.

20. To learn about chocolate preparation in the colonial period, see the website for *On the Chocolate Trail* at www.onthechocolatetrail.org.

21. *The Boston News-Letter*, July 2, 1772, 2.

22. John Scharffenberger and Robert Steinberg, *The Essence of Chocolate* (New York: Hyperion, 2006), 55. In England in the latter part of the eighteenth century, chocolate drop confections modeled after a treat from Naples were known similarly as *diavolino* or *diablotin*. See Peter Brown, *Pleasures of the Table: Fairfax House—Ritual and Display in the European Dining Room 1600–1900* (York, UK: York Civic Trust, 1997), 79.

23. *A New England Weekly Journal*, November 25, 1728.

24. *Boston Gazette*, May 18, 1761.

25. Gerald W. R. Ward, "Silver Chocolate Pots of Colonial Boston," in Grivetti and Shapiro, *Chocolate*, 144.

26. Grivetti and Shapiro, *Chocolate*, 893.

27. "[1702] Monday, October 26 From thence to Billericay. Visited languishing Mr. Sam Whiting, I gave him 2 Balls of Chockalett and a pound of Figgs, which very kindly accepted....

   "[1707] March 31 Visited Mr. Gibbs, presented him with a pound of Chockalett and 3 of Cousin Moodey's sermons....

"[1707] I gave Mr. Stoddard for Madam Stoddard two half pounds of Chockolat, instead of Commencement Cake and a Thesis." Thomas M. Halsey, *The Diary of Samuel Sewall 1674–1729* (New York: Farrar, Straus and Giroux, 1973), 476, 563, 570.

28. "I go to Mr. Belcher's where I drink warm chockelat and no beer; find myself much refresh'd by it after great Sweating to day, and yesterday.... October 20, 1697 I wait on the Lieutenant Governour at Dorchester and there meet with Mr. Torry, breakfast together on venison and chockalatte." Ibid., 626, 380.

29. Rose, "Dutch Cacao Trade," in Grivetti and Shapiro, *Chocolate*, 379.

30. *Boston Evening-Post*, December 14, 1747, 2.

31. Edith B. Gelles, ed., *The Letters of Abigail Franks 1733–1748* (New Haven, CT: Yale University Press, 2004), 146–4.

32. Hershkowitz, "Aspects," 14.

33. Jonathan Sarna, "Jews in British America," in Bernardini and Fiering, *Jews and the Expansion of Europe to the West*, 524–25.

34. Gelles, *Letters of Abigail Franks*, 143.

35. David de Sola Pool, "The Mill Street Synagogue (1730–1817) of the Congregation Shearith Israel," pamphlet 930, AJHS, New York, 34, 36, 40.

36. David de Sola Pool and Tamar de Sola Pool, *An Old Faith in the New World: Portrait of Shearith Israel 1654–1954* (New York: Columbia University Press, 1955), 525.

37. Pool, "*Mill Street Synagogue*," 23, 40.

38. Willem Klooster, "Jews in Suriname and Curaçao," in Bernardini and Fiering, *Jews and the Expansion of Europe to the West*, 354.

39. Daniel Gomez Account Book, Microfilm 597, AJA, Cincinnati, OH; Oppenheim Collection of Daniel Gomez Shipping Notes, 255/18/2 AJHS, New York.

40. Daniel Gomez Account Book, Microfilm 597, AJA, Cincinnati, OH.

41. *New York Gazette, or The Weekly Post Boy* (February 5 and 12, 1759), in Oppenheim Collection, Daniel Gomez File/Box 4, AJHS, New York.

42. Lee M. Friedman, *Early American Jews* (Cambridge, MA: Harvard University Press, 1934), 75ff.

43. *New Jersey Journal*, September 3, 17, 19, and 24, 1788, 4.

44. *Mercantile Advertiser*, July 20, 1799, and August 1, 1799.

45. *The National Advocate*, March 15, 1815–June 26, 1815.

46. Gelles, *Letters of Abigail Franks*, 128 n8.

47. A couple of decades later, in 1790, Levy Solomons of Albany opened a chocolate factory to serve his Dutch customers. "Items Relating to the Solomons Family, New York," *Publication of the American Historical Society* 27 (1920): 376.

48. *New York Gazette and Weekly Mercury*, January 25, 1779, 2.

49. *Royal Gazette*, December 2, 1780, 3.

50. *New York Gazette and Weekly Mercury*, February 12, 1781, 4.

51. *New York Gazette and Weekly Mercury*, March 12, 1781, 4.

52. Friedman, *Early American Jews,* 75–76.

53. Bruce Macmillan Bigelow, *The Commerce of Rhode Island with the West Indies Before the American Revolution,* parts 1 and 2 (PhD diss., Brown University, 1930), 2:4.

54. Marcus, *The Colonial American Jew,* 2:649; 2:628.

55. Stanley F. Chyet, *A Merchant of Eminence: The Story of Aaron Lopez* (PhD diss., Hebrew Union College–Jewish Institute of Religion, 1960), 191.

56. Marcus, *The Colonial American Jew,* 2:642.

57. Sarna, "The Jews in British America," in Bernadini and Fiering, *Jews and the Expansion of Europe to the West,* 527.

58. Bruce Macmillian Bigelow, "Colonial Merchant of Newport," *New England Quarterly* 4, no. 4 (October, 1931): 776.

59. Marcus, *The Colonial American Jew,* 2:673.

60. Stanley F. Chyet, *Lopez of Newport* (Detroit, MI: Wayne State University Press, 1970), 28.

61. MS 231 Folder 1/9, AJA, Cincinnati, OH; Lopez Letterbook 640, February 21, 1781, 66, NHS, Newport, Rhode Island.

62. Aaron Lopez Account Book, 720/322, NHS, Newport, RI.

63. Aaron Lopez Store Blotter, 667 20 April 1770, Newport Historical Society, Newport, Rhode Island.

64. Lopez Account Book, 736 14 April 1772, Newport Historical Society, Newport, Rhode Island.

65. Chyet, Lopez of Newport, 160. On a voyage from London that began in May of 1750, George Fisher described that because of the small allotment of food allowed by the captain, "myself and most of my family subsisted almost entirely on Coffee, Tea and chocolate, wherewith we were well provided." See *William & Mary Quarterly Historical Magazine,* series 1, vol. 17, no. 1 (July 1908): 133.

66. James B. Hedges, *The Browns of Providence Plantations: Colonial Years* (Cambridge, MA: Harvard University Press, 1952), 8–9.

67. MSS Book 650 Lopez Collection 1780–8, NHS, Newport, RI.

68. From the *Memorandum Book O 554,* Lopez Collection, 119, NHS, Newport, RI.

69. On June 16, 1773, John Baker of Boston charged James Baker 1 pound, 2 shillings, 6 pence for "one days work at your Chocolate Mill." Miller "Calendar," 5.

70. For nearly a century, 1725–1807, the American slave trade was quite connected with Rhode Island. Rhode Island merchants controlled between 60 and 80 percent of the American slave traffic. However, according to Bert Lippincott, librarian and genealogist at Newport Historical Society, only 1 percent of Lopez's trade dealt in slaves (interview with the author, September 10, 2009). See Saul S. Freidman, *Jews and the American Slave Trade* (New Brunswick, NJ: Transaction Publishers, 1998), 121. In Newport, the census of 1730 showed a population of 4,640 people plus 649 slaves, according to Weeden, *Rhode Island*, 192.

    Prince Updike is not listed as a member of free Negro households in the 1774 town census, which suggests that he may not have been free during the time of his chocolate manufacturing activities.

    According to Keith Stokes of the Newport Chamber of Commerce, in an e-mail message to author, September 2009: "Enslaved Africans and Mulattos (African and Indian mix) comprised nearly 20 percent of the entire Newport population by 1770. For the most part, slaves were trained to work within urban seaport economies, i.e., sail lofts, rope works, fish processing, rum making and spermaceti candles, etc. Many of these slaves were apprenticed and trained as artisans. Slaves in the households of Lopez, Rivera, and other Newport Jews were given Jewish names including Sara, Moses, Rebecca, etc. These close work, home, and religious relationships would create unique bonds between master and slave. When a five-year-old enslaved African boy drowned in Newport Harbor, Aaron Lopez funded the proper burial and marker. By 1780, the Free African Union Society was formed at Newport, a first of its kind in the Americas where former slaves organized and chartered a self-help organization with the Rhode Island General Assembly."

71. Eli Faber, *A Time for Planting: The First Migration 1654–1820*, vol. 1, *The Jewish People in America* (Baltimore, MD: Johns Hopkins University Press, 1992), 136.

72. For further information about Prince Updike, see *Spinner's Book* 715/36, NHS, Newport, RI.

73. Regarding Abraham or Abram Casey, see *Spinner's Book* 715/37, 40, NHS, Newport, RI. The *Rhode Island Newspaper* reports Abraham Casey's death in the September 25, 1844 issue. Regarding Cornelius Casey, see *Memorandum Book O*, Lopez Collection, 142, NHS, Newport, RI.

    In an 1805 list of occupations, the *Book of Occupations* by George H. Richardson, NHS, Newport, RI, Casey is recorded as a chimney sweep. These later references suggest that Abraham must have been rather young when he was grinding chocolate for Lopez. We do not know whether Cornelius was his father, his brother, or even related.

Jews Retailed Chocolate before Baker's

a. Bruce Miller, "A Calendar of Walter Baker & Company, Inc., and Its Times," General Foods Corporation, 1940, Rockefeller Library, Williamsburg, VA.

b. *Boston Gazette and Country Journal*, July 14, 1760, 4.

c. *New York Gazette*, May 11, 1761, supplement 2.

d. *New York Gazette and Country Journal*, December 2, 1760, 2; *New York Mercury*, January 26, 1761, 4.

e. Special Collections 4477, AJA, Cincinnati, OH. In 1763 Nathan Hart did the same in an advertisement in *The Newport Mercury*, June 27, 1763, 4.

f. September 24, 1760, AJA, Cincinnati, OH; and Jacob Rader Marcus, *The Jew in the American World: A Source Book* (Detroit, MI: Wayne State University Press, 1996), 54.

g. Jacob Rader Marcus, *American Jewry: Documents Eighteenth Century* (Cincinnati, OH: Hebrew Union College Press, 1959), 350. Also, Special Collection 11496, AJA, Cincinnati, OH. Others in the retail business included:

[1773] Benjamin Levy, the first Jew to settle permanently in Baltimore, who ran the largest ad in the *Maryland Journal and Advertiser* for his chocolate and snuff business. *Paving Our Way: Early Maryland Jewish Life 1632–1845: A Living History Resource Kit*, presented by the Jewish Museum of Maryland, accessed 2006, www.jhsm.org /html/documents/PavingOurWay1.3.07.pdf.

[1770s] Abraham Wagg, who married Rachel Gomez, daughter of Mordecai and Rebecca on July 4, 1770, engaged in the business of wholesale grocer and chocolate manufacturer. Abraham G. Duker, "Emerging Culture Patterns in American Jewish Life: The Psycho Social Approach to the Study of Jewish Life in America," *Publications of the American Jewish Historical Society* 39 (September 1949–June 1950): 1–4.

[1770s] Benjamin Lyon and Isaac Werden in Canada competed for business, including chocolate sales. Jacob Rader Marcus, *Early American Jewry: The Jews of New York, England and Canada 1649–1794* (Philadelphia, PA: Jewish Publication Society, 1951), 236.

[1808] Jacob Philipson advertised chocolate and sugar in the *Missouri Gazette* when he announced the opening of his new store opposite the post office.

Business Advertisements from the *Missouri Gazette* 1808, AJA, Cincinnati, OH.

What Did Alexander Hamilton Drink?

a. "Extract from Thomas Jefferson to John Adams, Paris, November 27, 1785, Jefferson Quotes & Family Letters," Jefferson Monticello, accessed March 2, 2017, http://tjrs.monticello.org/letter/1789.

b. "Askos," Jefferson Monticello, accessed March 2, 2017, www.monticello.org/site/house-and-gardens/askos.

c. "John Adams to Abigail Adams 2d, Decr 12, 1779," The Adams Papers, Massachusetts Historical Society, accessed March 2, 2017, www.masshist.org/digitaladams/archive/diary. "I will enquire whether it is the Superiour Quality of the Cocoa Nut, or any other Ingredient which they intermix with it, or a better Art of making it, which renders it so much superiour to any other."

d. "Diary of John Adams, Volume 4, 1779 December 10 Fryday," Massachusetts Historical Society, accessed May 26, 2017, www.masshist.org/publications/apde2/view?id=ADMS-01-04-02-0002-0009.

e. "Diary of John Adams, Volume 4, 1779 December 22. Wednesday," Massachusetts Historical Society, accessed May 16, 2017, www.masshist.org/publications/apde2/view?id=ADMS-01-04-02-0002-0020.

f. "Abigail Adams to John Quincy Adams, 6 September 1785," *National Archives: Founders Online*, accessed May 23, 2017, https://founders.archives.gov/documents/Adams/04-06-02-0107.

g. Nicholas Cresswell, *The Journal of Nicholas Cresswell, 1774–1777* (Port Washington, NY: Kennikat, 1968), 27–28.

h. Stephen A. McLeod, *Dining with the Washingtons: Historic Recipes, Entertainment and Hospitality from Mount Vernon* (Chapel Hill: University of North Carolina Press, 2011); "Mount Vernon Historical Chocolate Making," The Chocolate Tourist, accessed March 2, 2017, www.youtube.com/watch?v=fVxNcPZU_nw.

i. Thomas J. McGuire, *Stop the Revolution: America in the Summer of Independence and the Conference for Peace* (Canada: Stackpole Books, 2011), 10, https://books.google.com/books?id=OsNi7Byog6kC&pg=PA211&dq=stop+the+revolution+mcguire&hl=en&sa=X&ved=0ahUKEwiuxuiXuZDUAhVM7SYKHSWxAKEQ6AEIKDAA#v=onepage&q=chocolate&f=false.

j. Christina Regelski, "'A Glass of Wine ... Is Always Ready': Beverages on Virginia Plantations, 1730–1799," *Madison Historical Review* 10, article 4, 2014, accessed May 26, 2017, http://commons.lib.jmu.edu/cgi/viewcontent.cgi?article=1012&context=mhr.

k. Amanda Lange, "Chocolate Preparation and Serving Vessels in Early North America," in Grivetti and Shapiro, *Chocolate*, 137.

l. Ibid.

m. Joy Santlofer, *Food City: Four Centuries of Food-Making in New York* (New York: W. W. Norton, 2016), 37.

n. Alexander Hamilton, *Hamilton's Itinerarium, Being a Narrative of a Journey from Annapolis, Maryland through Delaware, Pennsylvania, New York, New Jersey, Connecticut, Rhode Island, Massachusetts and New Hampshire from May to September, 1744*, ed. Albert Bushnell Hart, accessed March 2, 2017, https://cdn.loc.gov/service/gdc /lhbtn/02374/02374.pdf.

o. Douglas A. Irwin, "The Aftermath of Hamilton's 'Report on Manufactures,'" accessed May 26, 2017, https://www.dartmouth. edu/~dirwin/docs/ham.pdf.

p. An earlier version appeared as "What Did Hamilton Drink?" *Huffington Post*, July 25, 2016, accessed June 5, 2017, www.huffingtonpost.com/rabbi-deborah-r-prinz/what-did-hamilton-drink_b_11077402.html.

Colonial Chocolate Recipes

a. Hannah Glasse, *The Art of Cookery Made Plain and Easy, 1796 Edition* (New York: United States Historical Research Service, 1994), 341.

Jews Traded Cacao from Philadelphia

a. Maxwell Whiteman and Edwin Wolf, *The History of the Jews of Philadelphia from Colonial Times to the Age of Jackson*, 2nd ed. (Philadelphia, PA: Jewish Publication Society of America, 1957), 339, citing *Poulson's American Daily Advertiser* record of December 8, 1801.

Jewish Estate Inventories: Personal Chocolate Usage

a. Leo Hershkowitz, "Original Inventories of Early American Jews (1682–1763)," *American Jewish History*, 90n3 (September 2002): 283, 300–301, 307–8, 318–19, 409, 419, 425, 440–42. Aaron Lopez Estate Inventory, Death Notices, 1783, MS 231/1/4, AJA, Cincinnati, OH.

Jewish Chocolate Grinders Working for Aaron Lopez

a. Lopez Memorandum Book 459/491, NHS, Newport, RI; Lopez Memorandum Book R/118/318, NHS, Newport, RI; Lopez Memorandum Book 463/ 215, NHS, Newport, RI; Lopez Memorandum Book 716/327, NHS, Newport, RI.

CHAPTER 4: CHANUKAH AND CHRISTMAS CHOCOLATE MELT INTO GELT

1. Marvin Tameanko, "The Original Chanukah Gelt," American Numismatic Association, accessed March 2, 2009, http://theshekel.org /articles_chanukah_gelt_4.html.

2. Tina Wasserman, "Who Invented Chanukah Gelt?" *Reform Judaism*, Winter 2005, accessed March 2, 2009, http://reformjudaismmag.org /Articles/index.cfm?id=1081.

3. Amy Klein, "In Search of Chanukah Gelt," *Jewish Journal*, November 29, 2007; Mark Mietkiewicz, "Gelt Is Good: Net Clarifies Old Traditions, New Customs," *Jewish News Weekly of Northern California*, November 15, 2002; Yisrael Rice, "Why the Gelt?" Chabad Lubavitch, accessed March 2, 2009, www.chabad.org/holidays/chanukah/article_cdo /aid/103084/jewish/Why-the-Gelt.html; Eliezer Segal, *Holidays, History and Halakah* (New York: Jason Aronson, 2000), 87; "From Gelt to Gifts," an online column about the holidays, accessed March 2, 2009, acs.ucalgary.ca/~elsegal/Shokel/961121_Geltl.html.

4. "History of Chocolate," Chocoladefabriken Lindt & Sprüngli AG, Lindt Chocomania, accessed December 2006, www.lindt.com /1222/1228/1254/1255.asp; Sophie D. Coe, *America's First Cuisines* (Austin: University of Texas, 1994), 102–3.

5. Wasserman, "Who Invented Chanukah Gelt?"; Jenna Joselit, *The Wonders of America: Reinventing Jewish Culture 1880–1950* (New York: Hill and Wang, 1996), 233ff; Yehuda Shiff and Dani Dor, eds., *Israel 50* (Israel: Elite, 1997), issued in celebration of the sixty-fifth anniversary of Elite.

6. "Chocolate Coins," accessed December 2010, www.youtube.com /watch?v=g8HvhJ5Os6w&feature=related.

7. "Feast of St. Nicholas," Fish Eaters, accessed March 2, 2009, www.fisheaters.com/customsadvent3.html.

Finding Good Gelt

a. Francine Segan, interview with the author, November 10, 2014.

b. "Guilt Free Gelt," Fair Trade Judaica, accessed March 6, 2017, http://fairtradejudaica.org/make-a-difference/fair-trade-jewish-holidays /fair-trade-your-chanukah/original-guilt-free-gelt/; "Spinning the Dreidel for Fair Trade Chocolate Gelt," Hazon, accessed March 6, 2017, https://hazon.org/jewish-food-movement/holidays/hanukah /spinning-the-dreidel-for-fair-trade-chocolate-gelt/.

c. Earlier versions appeared as: "The Ethics of Hanukkah Gelt," *Lilith*, November 25, 2015, accessed June 5, 2017, http://lilith.org/blog/2015 /11/the-ethics-of-hanukkah-gelt/; "How Fair Trade Gelt Embodies Hanukkah's Themes," *Reform Judaism*, accessed June 5, 2017, www.reformjudaism.org/blog/2015/12/11 /how-fair-trade-gelt-embodies-hanukkahs-message;

"Chocolatiers Raising the Bar When It Comes to Hanukkah Gelt," *Jewish Telegraphic Agency*, accessed June 5, 2017, www.jta. org/2014/12/11/life-religion/chocolatiers-raising-the-bar-when-it-comes-to-hanukkah-gelt; "December Dilemmas Melt into Chocolate," *Reform Judaism*, accessed June 5, 2017, www.reformjudaism.org /blog/2014/12/18/december-dilemmas-melt-chocolate; "Chocolate from Chanukah's Gelt," *Jewish Journal*, November 30, 2014, accessed

June 5, 2017, http://jewishjournal.com/cover_story/147606 /chocolate-from-chanukahs-gelt/; "Getting Good Chocolate Gelt," *Forward*, November 25, 2013, accessed June 5, 2017, http://forward.com/food/188273/getting-good-chocolate-gelt/.

CHAPTER 5: CHOCOLATE REVIVES REFUGEES, SURVIVORS, AND IMMIGRANTS

1. Lisa Hoffman and Charles Atkins, "Elsa Hoffman's Gift—a Thanksgiving Story," November 24, 2005, accessed July 2011, www.charlesatkins.com/chocolate_thanksgiving.htm.

2. Gil Marks, *Encyclopedia of Jewish Food* (Hoboken, NJ: John Wiley & Sons, 2010), 171–72.

3. See information about some business controversies and questions related to Tootsie Rolls at the "Candy Professor," accessed April 2010, http://candyprofessor.com.

4. Steve Almond, *Candyfreak: A Journey through the Chocolate Underbelly of America* (Chapel Hill, NC: Algonquin Books, 2004), 140.

5. "World's Finest Chocolate," accessed July 2011, www.worldsfinestchocolate.com.

6. Devan Sipher, "A Family Tree Just Covered in Chocolate," *New York Times*, December 25, 2011, MB3, accessed December 25, 2011, www.nytimes.com/2011/12/25/nyregion/jomart-chocolates-in-brooklyn-stays-in-the-family.html.

7. "Koppers Chocolate," accessed July 2011, www.kopperschocolate.com /main.html.

8. James Stevenson, "Talk of the Town: Chocolates," *New Yorker*, February 1966, 29. http://archives.newyorker.com/?i=1966-02-19#, 30.

9. Ellen Miller, *The Window Shop: Safe Harbor for Refugees* (Bloomington, IN: iUniverse, 2007); Joan Nathan, *The Jewish Holiday Kitchen* (New York: Schocken Books, 1988); "The Window Shop," accessed 2009, www.harvardsquare.com/History/Glimpses/The-Window-Shop.aspx.

10. Ernest Weil, interview with the author, September 9, 2007. Ernest Weil, *Love to Bake: Pastry Cookbook 40 Years of Fantasia Confections' Best 1948–1988* (San Francisco: Ernest Weil, 2006).

11. "Business and the Holocaust," accessed July 2011, www.stockmaven.com /medrepcN.htm.

12. Nick Bryant, "The Secret History of the Nazi Mascot," BBC News, August 21, 2007, accessed July 2011, http://news.bbc.co.uk/2/hi/ europe/6945847.stm.

13. WW2 Talk, May 9, 2005, accessed July 2011, www.ww2talk.com /forum/news-articles/5343-death-chocolate.html; Paul Reynolds, "Nazis'

Exploding Chocolate Plans," BBC News, September 4, 2005, http://news.bbc.co.uk/2/hi/uk_news/politics/4204980.stm.

14. Maureen Dowd, "Hitler's Talking Dogs," *New York Times*, July 13, 2011, A27.

15. Haim Gouri, *The Chocolate Deal*, trans. Seymour Simckes (New York: Holt, Rinehart and Winston, 1968), 132.

16. "Liberators' Testimonies," accessed July 2011, www.remember.org /liberators.html. Deprivation back home led to creative versions of cakes such as the "World War II (Vegan) Chocolate Cake," accessed July 2011, http://yummyplants.com/vegan-recipe/wwii-vegan-chocolate-cake. See the recipe on page 192.

17. "Chocolate in the 20th and 21st Centuries," Cadbury, accessed December 29, 2011, www.cadbury.co.uk/cadburyandchocolate /historyofchocolate/Pages/chocolate20th21st.aspx.

18. "Ration D Bars," Hershey Community Archives, accessed July 2011, www.hersheyarchives.org/essay/details.aspx?EssayId=26.

19. Hoffman and Atkins, "Elsa Hoffman's Gift."

20. Harry Herder, "Liberation of Buchenwald," Holocaust Cybrary: Remembering the Stories of the Survivors, accessed July 2012, www.remember.org/witness/herder.html.

21. Theo Richmond, *Konin: One Man's Quest for a Vanished Jewish Community* (London: Vintage Books, 1996), quoted in "The Liberation of Mauthausen, May 5, 1945," Scrapbookpages Blog, accessed June 2011, http://furtherglory.wordpress.com/2010/05/07 /the-liberation-of-mauthausen-may-5-1945.

22. "Berlin Airlift," accessed November 2011, www.spiritoffreedom.org /airlift.html.

23. Gail S. Halvorsen, *The Berlin Candy Bomber* (Bountiful, UT: Horizon Publishers, 1990), 101, 104–5, 109, 113–23.

24. Michael O. Tunnell, *Candy Bomber: The Story of the Berlin Airlift's Chocolate Uncle* (Watertown, MA: Charlesbridge Publishing, 2010), 62, 67.

25. Margot Theis Raven, *Mercedes and the Chocolate Pilot: A True Story of the Berlin Airlift and the Candy That Dropped from the Sky* (MI: Sleeping Bear Press, 2002), 22, 137.

26. Gregg J. Rickman, *Swiss Banks and Jewish Souls* (New York: Transaction Publishers, 1999), 141.

27. Tom Bower, *Nazi Gold: The Full Story of the Fifty-Year Swiss-Nazi Conspiracy to Steal Billions from Europe's Jews and Holocaust Survivors* (New York: HarperCollins Publishers, 1997), 41ff., 303–4; Brigitte Sion, *Anti-Semitism: Knowing It Better, Fighting It Better* (Geneva: CICAD, 2002), 59–60.

28. Bower, *Nazi Gold*, 295.

29. Dr. Brigitte Sion, interview with the author, March 4, 2011.

30. Brigitte Sion, e-mail message to author, March 6, 2011.

31. Ibid.; Lawrence Grossman and David Singer, "Switzerland," *American Jewish Year Book* (New York: American Jewish Committee, 2002), 303.

32. Morris Freedman, "Orthodox Sweets for Heterodox New York: The Story of Bartons," *Commentary Magazine* (May 1952): 474.

33. A. Leib Scheinbaum, *The Klein Family Edition, the World That was America 1900–1945: Transmitting the Torah Legacy to America*, (The Living Memorial: A Project of the Hebrew Academy of Cleveland and Shaar Press, 2004), 417.

34. Freedman, "Orthodox Sweets," 473.

35. Ibid.

36. Ibid.

37. Freedman, "Orthodox Sweets," 473, 476–7, 478, 480.

38. Jeffrey Ariel Yoskowitz, "Creating a Kosher America: The Orthodox Union's Program to Reclaim Kashrut, 1945–65" (honors thesis, Department of History, Brown University, 2007); Yoskowitz, "A Seder Different from All Other Seders," *The Atlantic*, April 8, 2009, accessed April 2009, www.theatlantic.com/life/archive/2009/04/a-seder-different-from-all-other-seders/7340/; Yoskowitz, "The Kosher Chocolate Wars," *The Atlantic*, April 15, 2009, accessed April 2009, www.theatlantic.com/life/archive/2009/04/the-kosher-chocolate-wars/13045.

Chocolate Smuggles Jewelry

a. Geoff Edgers, "How the Fonz Takes Care of a Plant Smuggled Out of Nazi Germany," *Washington Post*, March 12, 2016, www.washingtonpost.com/entertainment/how-the-fonz-takes-care-of-a-plant-smuggled-out-of-nazi-germany/2016/03/11/2f77f9a0-db06-11e5-925f-1d10062cc82d_story.html?utm_term=.53831e64b71e.

b. Earlier versions appeared as: "Escaping Danzig with Help from a Box of Chocolate," *Reform Judaism*, accessed June 5, 2017, www.reformjudaism.org/blog/2016/09/01/escaping-danzig-help-box-chocolate; "A Chocolate Escape from Danzig 1939," *Jewish Journal*, July 26, 2016, accessed June 5, 2017, http://jewishjournal.com/news/los_angeles/community/187703/a-chocolate-escape-from-danzig-1939/.

Childhood Chocolate Losses

a. "Albert and Maja Einstein chocolate cups," Leo Baeck Institute, The Edythe Griffinger Art Catalog, accessed May 25, 2017, https://www.lbi.org/artcatalog/record/4547927.

b. "Hear It, Draw It, Remember It," accessed March 7, 2017, www.indiegogo.com/projects/hear-it-draw-it-remember-it-forever#/; Bob Pool, "For Jewish Child, Dreams of Chocolate Fueled Escape from

Nazis," *Los Angeles Times*, July 21, 2013, http://articles.latimes.com
/2013/jul/21/local/la-me-chocolate-nazis-20130722; Leon Prochnik,
interview with the author, December 2, 2016.

c. Colleen Annek, "Woman Reunited with Child She Helped in
Concentration Camp after 70 Years," *San Francisco Globe*, December
16, 2015, http://sfglobe.com/2015/12/15/woman-reunited-with-child-
she-helped-in-concentration-camp-after-70-years/; "What Makes Us
Human," interview with Francine Christophe," September 11, 2015,
www.youtube.com/watch?v=gXGfngjmwLA.

Chocolate Recovery

a. Estee Farber, interview with the author, October 2016.

b. Ibid.

c. Earlier versions appeared as: "Chocolate Survival: Holocaust and
Hurricane," *Jewish Journal*, November 28, 2016, accessed June 5,
2017, http://jewishjournal.com/hollywood/212913/chocolate-survival-
holocaust-and-hurricane/; "Chocolate Revives: Hurricane and the
Holocaust," *Jewish Week*, November 22, 2106, accessed June 5, 2017,
www.jwfoodandwine.com/article/2016/11/22
/chocolate-revives-hurricane-and-holocaust.

What Makes Chocolate Kosher for Passover?

a. David Golinkin, "A Responsum Regarding the Custom of Abstaining
from Eating *Qitniyot* on Passover," personal website of Benjamin
Mordechai Ben Baruch, 1988, accessed March 12, 2017,
http://home.earthlink. net/~bbenbaruch/qitniyot-kitniyot.htm; Nathan
Jeffay, "Pesach Kitniyot Rebels Roil Rabbis as Some Ashkenazim
Follow New, Permissive Ruling," *Forward*, April 1, 2009,
www.forward.com/ articles/104483; Eli J. Mansour, "Eating Rice on
Pesach," Daily Halacha, accessed March 12, 2017,
www.dailyhalacha.com/displayRead.asp?readID=537; "The Year's
Reformer: Efrat Rabbi Tilts against Passover Food Restriction for
Ashkenazi Jews," Matzav.com, April 15, 2011, http://matzav.com
/this-years-reformer-efrat-rabbi-tilts-against-passover-food-restrictions-
for-ashkenazi-jews; Liza Schoenfein, "Conservative Movement
Overturns 800-Year-Old Passover Ban on Rice and Legumes," *Forward*,
April 14, 2016, http://forward.com/culture/food/338525
/conservative-movement-overturns-800-year-old-passover-ban-on-rice-
and-legum/.

b. Abraham Regelson, ed., *Hagadah of Passover* (New York: Shulsinger
Bros., 1944).

c. *Survey Research on Child Labor in West African Cocoa Growing Area*,
Payson Center for International Development, July 30, 2015, accessed
May 28, 2017, www.payson.tulane.edu/projects
/survey-research-child-labor-west-african-cocoa-growing-areas.

d. Ilana Schatz, e-mail to author, March 12, 2015; "The Rabbinical Assembly Pesach Guide," Rabbinical Assembly, accessed March 7, 2017, www.rabbinicalassembly.org/pesah-guide-5776.pdf.; "Next Year—Fair Trade Kosher for Passover Chocolate," Fair Trade Judaica, accessed March, 12, 2017, http://fairtradejudaica.org /make-a-difference/become-a-fair-trade-advocate/ next-year-fair-trade-kosher-for-passover-chocolate/.

e. "Next Year—Fair Trade Kosher for Passover Chocolate," Fair Trade Judaica, accessed May 28, 2017, http://fairtradejudaica.org /make-a-difference/become-a-fair-trade-advocate /next-year-fair-trade-kosher-for-passover-chocolate/.

f. Deborah Prinz, "A Haggadah for a Socially Responsible Chocolate Seder," accessed March 7, 2015, http://onthechocolatetrail.org /booksupplement/haggadah/.

g. Earlier versions appeared as: "Chocolate at Passover? Not So Fast!" *Forward*, April 5, 2017, accessed May 23, 2017, http://forward.com /food/368254/chocolate-at-passover-not-so-fast/; "Chocolate Causes for Passover: Season of Freedom," *Huffington Post*, March 18, 2015, accessed June 5, 2017, www.huffingtonpost.com/rabbi-deborah-r-prinz /chocolate-causes-for-pass_b_6887814.html; "Finding the Afikoman May Be Easier: The Best Chocolate for Passover," *Reform Judaism*, March 2014, accessed June 5, 2017, www.reformjudaism.org /finding-afikoman-may-be-easier-best-chocolate-passover.

CHAPTER 6: ISRAELIS: *MESHUGA* FOR CHOCOLATE

1. Shoshana Brickman, "Land of Milk, Honey ... and Chocolate," *Inbal Magazine*, 2008; "100 Tons of Chocolate Swiped from Israeli Factory," *Columbus Dispatch*, February 28, 2008.

2. Brinkers, a Dutch company that originally manufactured margarine, claims to have created the first chocolate spread in 1948; accessed April 2011, www.brinkers.com/thecompany/history/index.html.

3. "The Chocolate Soldier," accessed April 2011, http://en.wikipedia.org /wiki/Chocolate_Soldier_%28disambiguation%29; Jay Hurvitz, e-mail to author, April 23, 2011.

> Come, chocolate soldier
> Come to me to the outpost
> Sit and rest, have no fear
> And you'll return to your dust (ashes)
> The chef serves meat to the master chef
> The master chef serves meat to the cannons
> All people are brothers under the flowers
> The cannons roar, the children cry
> Come, chocolate soldier ...

My brother was brave, he fell on his watch
The rooms of his heart are now open to the grass and the dew
My brother had blood, but that blood has been used up
Even the general's orders won't bring him back
Left, right, right and left, the battalion marches and sings
Life is clumsy, death is short
The entire battalion marches behind the rear of the master sergeant
The master sergeant also goes the way of all flesh

(TRANSLATED BY JAY HURVITZ)

4. The Vered Hagalil chocolate company, now owned by Unilever, could not compete with Elite, though it is still available (Janna Gur, interview with the author, February 27, 2011).

5. Shiff and Dor, *Israel 50*.

6. Amihai Zippor, "Full of Beans," *Jerusalem Post*, March 2, 2010, accessed December 21, 2011, www.holycacaochocolate.com/Press.html.

7. "Elite," accessed July 22, 2012, www.strauss-group.com/en/Menultem-AboutUs/history/1930; Bernhard Press, *The Murder of the Jews in Latvia: 1941–1945* (Evanston, IL: Northwestern University Press, 2000), 20.

8. "The Smell of Chocolate," accessed June 2009, www.shiron.net/artist?type=lyrics&lang=1&prfid=342&wrkid=7401.

The Smell of Chocolate

Besof Ramat-Gan yesh makom meyuchad,
Sham efshar la'amod ulehariach shokolad.
Yesh sham bayit gavoha gavoha
Bli chalonot, im shalosh arubot
Ushloshim mechonot yom valayla ovdot
Veshiv'im poalim im sinar ukfafot
Mechinim shokolad bechol hatzurot.

Chorus:
Shokolad katan veshokolad gadol (sho-ko-ko-)
Shokolad yakar veshokolad bezol
Shokolad egozim veshokolad stam
La'ashirim, ulechulam
Vehareyach bechinam ...
vechol ha'ezrachim (tu-tu-tu-tu ...)
Otzrim umerichim (mmm ...)
Otzrim hayeladim sheratzim bashchuna
Otzer ha'otobus me'ever lapina
Hachatulim mafsikim livroach mehaklavim
Vehashotrim omdim leyad haganavim
Kulam mabitim el ha'arubot
Ule'at le'at, ha'af shelahem
Mitmaleh bereyach shel shokolad.

Chorus:
Shokolad katan veshokolad gadol....
Besof Ramat-Gan yesh makom meyuchad,
Sham efshar la'amod ulehariach shokolad.

At the edge of Ramat Gan there's a special place
Where you can stand and smell chocolate in the air
There's a big tall house
With three chimneys and no windows
And thirty machines inside working all day and night
Seventy workers in aprons and mitts
Making chocolate of every kind.

Chorus:
Small chocolate, big chocolate (*sho-ko-ko-*)
Expensive chocolate, cheap chocolate
Chocolate with nuts and plain
For the rich people, and for us all
And the smell is free
so all the citizens
Stop to sniff the air (mmm ...)
The kids stop running in the streets
The bus stops at the corner
The dogs stop chasing the cats
Even the policemen stand near the thieves
Everyone gazes up at the chimneys
And their noses slowly fill
With the sweet smell of chocolate

Chorus:
Small chocolate, big chocolate ...
There is a special place at Ramat Gan where it is possible to stand
and smell chocolate.

9. Shiff and Dor, *Israel 50.*

10. "Israeli chocolate company, Elite, should sell slave-free, fair trade
chocolate for Passover," Change.org, accessed March 8, 2017,
www.change.org/p/ofra-strauss-israeli-chocolate-company-elite-will-sell-
slave-free-fair-trade-chocolate-for-passover.

Chocolate Babkathons: New York City

a. Amy Rothberger, e-mail message to author, November, 2, 2016.

b. "The Organic Epicure Jerusalem Culinary Star Yotam Ottolenghi Hams
It Up at JCCSF," *JWeekly*, October 31, 2014, accessed May, 17, 2017,
www.jweekly.com/2014/10/31/the-organic-epicure-jerusalem-culinary-
star-yotam-ottelenghi-hams-it-up-at/.

c. For details of winners, bakeries, and a sampling of recipes, see earlier versions: "Happy Babka-ka/Chocolate Babka for Chanukah," *Jewish Journal*, December 22, 2016, accessed May 28, 2017, http://jewishjournal.com/culture/religion/213270/happy-babka-ka-chocolate-babka-for-chanukah/; "Babka Love Affair: Valentine's Day," *Huffington Post*, January 20, 2015, accessed June 5, 2017, www.huffingtonpost.com/rabbi-deborah-r-prinz/babka-love-affair-valenti_b_6502710.html; "Babka Love Is Blind, in This Taste Test," *Jewish Week*, December 16, 2014, accessed June 5, 2017, www.jwfoodandwine.com/article/2014/12/16/babka-love-blind-taste-test; "10 Very Best Babkas for Valentine's Day," *Forward*, February 11, 2014, accessed May 28, 2017, http/:forward. com:food:362879:10-very-best-chocolate-babkas-for-valentines-day.

World's Oldest Chocolate Maker in Haifa

a. Richard Gonzales, "World's Oldest Man Celebrates His Bar Mitzvah 100 Years Late," WNYC Radio, October 6, 2016, www.npr.org /sections/thetwo-way/2016/10/06/496938817/world-s-oldest-living-man-celebrates-his-bar-mitzvah-100-years-late; "Yisrael Kristal," Wikipedia, accessed March 8, 2017, https://en.wikipedia.org/wiki/Yisrael_Kristal.

CHAPTER 7: PRE-COLUMBIAN PEOPLES IDOLIZED CHOCOLATE IN MESOAMERICA

1. View this at *Jews on the Chocolate Trail*, www.jews-onthechocolatetrail. org/2009/01/chocolate-in-mexico.
2. Liebman, *New Spain*, 19–20.
3. Wiznitzer, "Crypto Jews in Mexico in the 16th Century," 168–9; Wiznitzer, "Crypto-Jews in Mexico in the 17th Century," 262. See chapter 2.
4. Liebman, *New Spain*, 151; Hoberman, "Merchants," 27.
5. Lisa J. LeCount, "Like Water for Chocolate: Feasting and Political Ritual among the Late Classic Maya at Xunantunich, Belize," *American Anthropologist* 103, no. 4 (2001): 947–48.
6. Patricia A. McAnany and Satoru Murata, "America's First Connoisseurs of Chocolate," *Food & Foodways* 15 (2007): 5, 14, 20.
7. Meredith L. Dreiss and Sharon Edgar Greenhill, *Chocolate: Pathways to the Gods* (Tucson: University of Arizona Press, 2008), 4, 9.
8. LeCount, "Like Water," 948; McAnany and Murata, "America's First Connoisseurs," 20, 24–25, 27, 49. This concept of "world trees," a motif in Mesoamerican myth and art, recalls the four directions and connects the earth with the heavens.
9. Ana M. de Benítez, *Cocina Prehispanica* (Evanston, IL: Adler's Foreign Books, 1977), 113–20, based on the Codex Borgia, a Mesoamerican

ritual and divinatory manuscript, written before the Spanish conquest of Mexico, in southern or western Puebla.

10. Fray Diego Durán, *Book of the Gods and Rites and the Ancient Calendar*, trans. and ed. Fernando Horcasitas and Doris Heyden (Norman, OK: University of Oklahoma Press, 1971), 130–32, 156–200.

11. Coe and Coe, *True History*, 44; Durán, *Book of the Gods*, 155–58, 215; Dreiss and Greenhill, *Chocolate*, 35, 44, 58; Dennis Tedlock, *2000 Years of Mayan Literature* (Los Angeles: University of California Press, 2010), 34–35.

12. Michael Coe and Rex Koontz, *The Maya* (London: Thames and Hudson, 2005), 42, 57, 218; Dreiss and Greenhill, *Chocolate*, 21, 27; Norton, *Sacred Gifts*, 24, 27, 29–30.

13. Meredith L. Dreiss and Sharon Edgar Greenhill, *Chocolate: Pathways to the Gods* (Tucson: University of Arizona Press, 2008), 66.

14. Sophie D. Coe, *America's First Cuisines* (Austin: University of Texas, 1994), 77–80; Coe and Koontz, *Maya*, 49, 173; Dreiss and Greenhill, *Chocolate*, 66–67, 69; Norton, *Sacred Gifts*, 35.

15. Tedlock, *2000 Years*, 35, 64, 66.

16. Cameron L. McNeil, "Traditional Cacao Use in Modern Mesoamerica," in *Chocolate in Mesoamerica: A Cultural History of Cacao*, ed. Cameron L. McNeil (Gainesville: University Press of Florida, 2009), 361, 363.

17. Seth Kugel, "Frugal Summer: Highs and Lows," *The New York Times Frugal Traveler Blog*, September 19, 2010, accessed, July 2011, http://frugaltraveler.blogs.nytimes.com/2010/09/14/frugal-summer-highs-and-lows; Dreiss and Greenhill, *Chocolate*, 76; McNeil, "Traditional Cacao Use," in McNeil, *Chocolate in Mesoamerica*, 363.

18. Dreiss and Greenhill, *Chocolate*, 42, 59.

19. McNeil, "Traditional Cacao Use," in McNeil, *Chocolate in Mesoamerica*, 357; Dreiss and Greenhill, *Chocolate*, 52.

20. Grivetti and Shapiro, *Chocolate*, 105.

History of Cacao

a. Coe and Coe, *True History*, 39; Coe and Koontz, *Maya*, 99, 174–75; Dreiss and Greenhill, *Chocolate*, 44; McAnany and Murata, "America's First Connoisseurs," 8; McNeil, "Introduction: The Biology, Antiquity, and Modern Uses of the Chocolate Tree," in McNeil, *Chocolate in Mesoamerica*, 9; Terry G. Powis et al., "Spouted Vessels and Cacao Use among the Preclassic Maya," *Latin American Antiquity* 13, no. 1 (March 2002): 91–94, 100.

CHAPTER 8: FAITH DIFFUSED CHOCOLATE AROUND THE WORLD

1. Cynthia Elyce Rubin, ed., *Bread and Chocolate: Culinary Traditions of Switzerland* (New York: New York Writer's House, 1993), 20, 57.

2. Ann Ball, "When the Church Said No to Chocolate," 3–4, accessed July 7, 2010, www.mexconnect.com/articles/1469-when-the-church-said-no-to-chocolate; Elisabeth Lambert Ortiz, "Mole Poblano and Turkey," in *The Wilder Shores of Gastronomy: Twenty Years of the Best Food Writing from the Journal Petits Propos Culinaires*, ed. Alan Davidson (Berkeley, CA: Ten Speed Press, 2002), 440–44. Rosenblum, *Chocolate*, 67ff.

3. A. J. R. Russell-Wood, *A World on the Move: The Portuguese in Africa, Asia, and America 1415–1808* (Manchester, UK: Carcanet Press, 1992), 92.

4. Liebman, *New Spain*, 124.

5. Forrest and Naijaj, "Sipping Sin," 42.

6. Norton, *Sacred Gifts*, 54.

7. Marcia Zoladz, "Cacao in Brazil or the History of a Crime," in *Food and Morality: Proceedings of the Oxford Symposium on Food and Cookery 2007*, ed. Susan Friedland (Devon, England: Prospect Books, 2008), 314.

8. Norton, *Sacred Gifts*, 55.

9. Maguelonne Toussaint-Samat, *History of Food*, trans. Anthea Bell (Oxford, UK: Blackwell Press, 1996), 576.

10. He compiled the *Historia general de las cosas de Nueva España* (*General History of the Things of New Spain, or the Florentine Codex*) in 1569.

11. Dreiss and Greenhill, *Chocolate*, 67.

12. *The History of the Indies of New Spain*, also known as the *Durán Codex* (c. 1581), *Book of the Gods and Rites* (1574–76), and *Ancient Calendar* (c. 1579). Fray Diego Durán, *Book of the Gods and Rites and the Ancient Calendar*, trans. and ed. Fernanco Horcasitas and Doris Heyden (Norman, OK: Oklahoma University Press, 1970).

13. Nathalie Bailleux et al., *The Book of Chocolate* (Paris: Flammarion, 1995), 71ff.

14. Forrest and Naijaj, "Sipping Sin," 44.

15. Norton, *Sacred Gifts*, 132.

16. Forrest and Naijaj, "Sipping Sin," 34.

17. Jean McClure Mudge, *Chinese Export Porcelain in North America* (New York: Clarkson N. Potter, Inc., 1986), 44.

18. McNeil, "Introduction," in McNeil, *Chocolate in Mesoamerica*, 22.

19. Brandon Head, *Food of the Gods: A Popular Account of Cocoa* (New York: Dutton, 1903), e-book from Project Gutenberg, 83.

20. Norton, *Sacred Gifts*, 77–78.

21. Ibid.

22. William G. Clarence-Smith, *Cocoa and Chocolate, 1765–1914* (London: Routledge, 2000), 17.

23. Norton, *Sacred Gifts*, 80–82. Valadés, the son of an Indian noble-woman and a Spanish conquistador who passed as pure Spanish, wrote *Rhetorica Christiana*.

24. Manuel Aguilar-Moreno, "The Good and Evil of Chocolate in Colonial Mexico," in McNeil, *Chocolate in Mesoamerica*, 278.

25. Norton, *Sacred Gifts*, 250.

26. Ibid., 251.

27. Ibid., 197.

28. Bailleux et al., *Book of Chocolate*, 75; Robert Ferry, "Trading Cacao," See Simon Martin, "Cacao in Ancient Maya Religion," in McNeil, *Chocolate in Mesoamerica*, 274–5; Norton, *Sacred Gifts*, 140, 196–97, 251; Toussaint-Samat, *History of Food*, 576.

29. Martin, "Cacao," in McNeil, *Chocolate in Mesoamerica*, 164.

30. McNeil, "Introduction," in McNeil, *Chocolate in Mesoamerica*, 22; Aguilar-Moreno, "Good and Evil," in McNeil, *Chocolate in Mesoamerica*, 278; Norton, *Sacred Gifts*, 65–66.

31. Norton, *Sacred Gifts*, 249.

32. Ibid., 69–75.

33. Ibid.

34. Ibid., 74–76.

35. Ibid., 67.

36. Ibid., 68.

37. Ibid., 68–69.

38. Ibid., 231, 234.

39. Forrest, "Sipping Sin," 33, 41.

40. Norton, *Sacred Gifts*, 131, 242, 244; Toussaint-Samat, *History of Food*, 576; Forrest, "Sipping Sin," 34.

41. Norton, *Sacred Gifts*, 243, 245.

42. Aguilar-Moreno, "Good and Evil" in McNeil, *Chocolate in Mesoamerica*, 283. Hurtado supported this opinion by quoting popes such as Gregory XIII, Paulus V, and Pius V, who shared his view. See also Forest, "Sipping Sin," 42.

43. Aguilar-Moreno, "Good and Evil," in McNeil, *Chocolate in Mesoamerica*, 283; Bailleux et al., *Book of Chocolate*, 83.

44. Bailleux et al., *Book of Chocolate*, 80; J. Piero Camporesi, *Exotic Brew: The Art of Living in the Age of Enlightenment*, trans. Christopher Woodall (Cambridge, MA: Polity Press, 1994), 55; Janine Gasco, "The Social and Economic History of Cacao Cultivation in Colonial Soconusco, New Spain," in *Chocolate: Food of the Gods*, ed. A. Szogyi (Westport, CT: Greenwood Press, 1997), 200; Norton, *Sacred Gifts*, 169, 173–74, 259.

45. Camporesi, *Exotic Brew*, 42.

46. Ibid., 72.

47. Ibid., 111.

48. Ibid., 110.

49. Jean Anthelme Brillat Savarin, *A Handbook of Gastronomy*, trans. Adolphe Lalauze (London: J. C. Nimmo and Bain), 161.

50. Camporesi, *Exotic Brew*, 117, 140.

51. Ibid.

52. Ibid., 141–42.

53. Ibid., 145–47, 163–64.

54. Ibid., 64; Zoladz, "Cacao in Brazil," in Friedland, *Food and Morality*, 310–12.

55. Timothy Walker, "Slave Labor and Chocolate in Brazil: The Culture of Cacao Plantations in Amazonia and Bahia (17th–19th Centuries)," *Food and Foodways* 15 (January 2007): 75, 85, 155, 164.

56. Willem Klooster and Alfred Padula, *The Atlantic World: Essays on Slavery, Migration and Imagination* (Upper Saddle River, NJ: Pearson/ Prentice Hall, 2005), 21.

57. Zoladz, "Cacao in Brazil," in Friedland, *Food and Morality*, 312.

58. Klooster and Padula, *Atlantic World,* 20; Zoladz, "Cacao in Brazil," in Friedland, *Food and Morality*, 311; Forrest, "Sipping Sin," 7.

59. Beatriz Cabezon, "Cacao, Haciendas and the Jesuits: Letters from New Spain 1693–1751," in Grivetti and Shapiro, *Chocolate*, 607–9.

60. Patricia Barriga and Beatriz Cabezon, "Sailors, Soldiers and Padres: California Chocolate 1542?–1840," in Grivetti and Shapiro, *Chocolate*, 440.

61. Ibid., 443.

62. Ibid.

63. Ibid., 445.

64. Ibid., 446.

65. Ibid.

66. Ibid., 441–42, 444, 447–48, 450–51.

CHAPTER 9: UTOPIAN CHOCOLATE SAVED SOULS: FROM CADBURY TO HERSHEY

1. See Bailleux et al., *Book of Chocolate*, 102.

2. Fry built upon the company of chocolate maker Churchman, who had advertised, "Mr Churchman's Chocolate Mills and works there which being a secret cannot be exposed to view." James Walvin, *Fruits of Empire: Exotic Produce and British Taste 1660–1800* (New York: New York University Press, 1997), 98–99; Bailleux, *Book of Chocolate*, 102.

3. Carol Off, *Bitter Chocolate: Investigating the Dark Side of the World's Most Seductive Sweet* (New York: Random House, 2006), 50.

4. Bertram Gordon, "Chocolate in England from Introduction to Industrialization," in Grivetti and Shapiro, *Chocolate*, 588.

5. Ibid., 589.

6. Emma Robertson, Marek Korczynski, and Michael Pickering, "Harmonious Relations? Music at Work in the Rowntree and Cadbury Factories," *Business History* 49, no. 2 (March 2007): 211–34.

7. Mark K. Smith, "Adult Schools and the Making of Adult Education," Encyclopedia of Information Education, 2004, accessed August 2010, www.infed.org/lifelonglearning/adult_schools.htm.

8. J. B. Priestley, *English Journey: Being a Rambling but Truthful Account of What One Man Saw and Heard and Felt and Thought During a Journey through England during the Autumn of the Year 1933* (London: William Heinemann, 1934), 95.

9. A. G. Gardiner, *Life of George Cadbury* (New York: Cassell and Company, 1923), 133, 281.

10. Deborah Cadbury, *The Chocolate Wars: The 150-Year Rivalry Between the World's Greatest Chocolate Makers* (New York: Public Affairs, 2010), 164.

11. Anne Vernon, *A Quaker Business Man: The Life of Joseph Rowntree 1836–1925* (Sydney, Australia: Allen and Unwin, 1958), 23, 27, 31, 60.

12. Ibid., 147.

13. Tammy L. Hamilton, archivist, Hershey Community Archives, e-mail message to author, July 14, 2010.

14. Joël Glenn Brenner, *The Emperors of Chocolate: Inside the Secret World of Hershey and Mars* (New York: Random House, 1999), 85.

15. Michael D'Antonio, *Hershey* (New York: Simon and Schuster, 2006), 86, 89, 91, 95, 102; Nicholas Westbrook, "Chocolate at the World's Fairs," in Grivetti and Shapiro, *Chocolate*, 185–205.

16. D'Antonio, *Hershey*, 114–5.

17. Brenner, *Emperors*, 114–16.

18. D'Antonio, *Hershey*, 130.

19. Brenner, *Emperors*, 133; D'Antonio, *Hershey*, 203; "Hershey Trust Company," Hershey Community Archives, accessed July 14, 2010, www.hersheyarchives.org/essay/details.aspx?EssayId=23&Rurl=%2fresources%2fsearch-results.aspx%3fType%3dBrowseEssay.

20. "Britain Wins EU Chocolate Battle," CNN World, accessed November 2011, www.cnn.com/2003/WORLD/europe/01/16/chocolate.war.

21. D'Antonio, *Hershey*, 91–92, 95, 119.

22. See more about this at: "Kissing Cousins: The Hershey's Kiss and the Wilbur Bud," accessed May 1, 2010, http://candyprofessor.com; on the naming of the Kiss, see "Hershey's: Why a Kiss Is Just a Kiss," accessed May 1, 2010, http://candyprofessor.com. See Zoe's Online Hershey Kisses Collection of more than fifty-five Kisses flavors, accessed June 2010, www.lauracarey.com/kisses.

23. Off, *Bitter Chocolate*, 61.

24. Lowell J. Satre, *Chocolate on Trial: Slavery, Politics and the Ethics of Business* (Athens, OH: Ohio State University Press, 2005), 8.

25. August Chevalier, "The Island of São Thomé," *Bulletin of the American Geographical Society* 42, no. 9 (1910): 665.

26. The Portuguese first populated São Tomé with Jewish children kidnapped from their parents in 1493. Also, Jews and New Christians were deported as undesirables to São Tomé, Cape Verde, and Angola with the expectation that they would not survive there. Russell Wood, *A World on the Move: The Portuguese in Africa, Asia, and America 1415–1808* (Manchester, UK: Carcanet Press, 1992), 107–8; Dagmar Schaffer, *Portuguese Exploration to the West and the Formation of Brazil 1450–1800: Catalogue of an Exhibition* (Providence, RI: John Carter Brown Library, 1988), 17.

27. Satre, *Chocolate on Trial*, 10.

28. Gillian Wagner, *The Chocolate Conscience* (London: Chatto and Windus, 1987), 93.

CHAPTER 10: GODS IN MY CHOCOLATE

1. Juliette Binoche, Johnny Depp, Judi Dench, and Alfred Molina, *Chocolat*, directed by Lasse Hallstrom (Santa Monica, CA: Miramax Films, 2000); Joanne Harris, *Chocolat* (New York: Doubleday Books, 1999).

2. Tom Waits, "Chocolate Jesus," *Mule Variations*, ANTI-, 1999, accessed September 8, 2015, www.azlyrics.com/lyrics/tomwaits/chocolatejesus.html; "Tom Waits' Chocolate Jesus," accessed March 23, 2017, https://steveyoutubepicks.wordpress.com/2007/11/28/tom-waits-chocolate-jesus/.

3. Stephan Jaramillo, *Chocolate Jesus* (New York: Berkley Books, 1998), 15.

4. Thomas Quinn, *What Do You Do with a Chocolate Jesus? An Irreverent History* (Charleston, SC: BookSurge, 2010), ix.

5. Victoria Emily Jones, "A Brief History of Chocolate Jesus," *The Jesus Question* (blog), accessed May 26, 2017, 2017, https://thejesusquestion.org/2014/03/24/a-brief-history-of-chocolate-jesus/.

6. Jesse Leavenworth, "Sacrilegious Sculptures? Messiah Depictions Highlight Longstanding Religion, Art, Tensions," *Hartford Courant*, April 5, 2007; "Confectionary Christ Raises Controversy," *Anderson Cooper 360 Degrees*, March 30, 2007, accessed August 10, 2015, http://transcripts.cnn.com/TRANSCRIPTS/0703/30/acd.01.html.

7. David Kuo, "That Chocolate Jesus," *Huffington Post*, March 30, 2007, accessed May 26, 2017, www.huffingtonpost.com/david-kuo/that-chocolate-jesus_b_44649.html.

8. Andy Newman, "A Deity Made of Chocolate Spurs a Religious Debate," *New York Times*, February 8, 2105, accessed May 26, 2017, www.nytimes.com/2015/02/09/nyregion/a-deity-made-of-chocolate-spurs-a-religious-debate.html?_r=0.

9. Cosimo Cavallaro, interview with author, August 11, 2015.

10. Ibid.

11. Ibid.

12. Ibid.

13. Jones, "A Brief History of Chocolate Jesus."

14. "Sculptor Defends Chocolate Crucifix," The Free Library, accessed September 20, 2015, www.thefreelibrary.com/Sculptor+defends+chocolate+crucifix.-a0143990733.

15. "Chocolate Saints, Sweet Jesus," The Proposition, accessed September 8, 2015, www.theproposition.com/exhibition-archive/chocolate-saintssweet-jesus/; Cavallaro, interview, August 11, 2015.

16. Cavallaro, interview with author, August 11, 2015.

17. Newman, "A Deity Made of Chocolate Spurs a Religious Debate."

18. Ibid.

19. Lynda Stern, interview with the author, August 13, 2015.

20. Allegra Hobbs, "Bond Street Chocolate Lives On after Shop Closure," DNAInfo, May 4, 2016, accessed May 26, 2017, www.dnainfo.com/new-york/20160504/east-village/bond-street-chocolate-lives-on-after-shop-closure.

21. Lori Kessler, interview with the author, August 27, 2015.

22. "Your Own Personal Chocolate Jesus," Kickstarter, accessed September 8, 2015, www.kickstarter.com/projects/persia13/your-own-personal-chocolate-jesus.

23. Chocolate Deities, accessed May 26, 2017, http://chocolatedeities.com/deities.php.

24. Jeanne Fleming, interview with the author, August 10, 2015.

25. Chocolate Deities, accessed March 23, 2017, www.chocolatedeities.com.

26. "Goddess of Willendorf," Chocolate Deities, accessed May 26, 2017, http://chocolatedeities.com/about.php?deity=willendorf.

27. Fleming, interview with author. Earlier versions appeared as: "The Chocolate Gods Unite," *Huffington Post*, March 15, 2017, accessed June 5, 2017, www.huffingtonpost.com/entry/the-chocolate-gods-unite_us_58c81e38e4b022817b29177e; "Would Pope Francis Eat a Chocolate Jesus?" *Huffington Post,* September 15, 2015, accessed June 5, 2017, www.huffingtonpost.com/rabbi-deborah-r-prinz/would-pope-francis-eat-a-_b_8130786.html.

28. Cindy Carcamo, "Chocolate Virgin Mary Still Stands at Fountain Valley Shop," *Orange County Register*, April 15, 2007, accessed May 26, 2017, www.ocregister.com/articles/chocolate-121668-mary-year.html.

29. "Candy Making Video," Trappistine Quality Candy, accessed February 15, 2017, https://www.trappistinecandy.com/candy-making-video/.

30. "Trappistine Candy," accessed February 15, 2017, www.trappistinecandy.com/candy-information/frequently-asked-questions/.

31. "Sister Christa-Maria," YouTube, posted June 5, 2014, accessed February 15, 2017, www.youtube.com/watch?time_continue=11&v=moLpSMXSC30.

32. Mother Maureen McCabe, e-mail message to author, July 15, 2015.

33. Sister Christa-Maria, e-mail message to author, July 6, 2015.

34. An earlier version appeared as: "Chocolate Devotions: Nuns Adore Chocolate," *Huffington Post*, updated August 6, 2016, accessed June 5, 2017, www.huffingtonpost.com/rabbi-deborah-r-prinz/chocolate-devotions-nuns-_b_5531350.html.

35. Rabbi Mark Gross, comment to "Would You Eat a Chocolate Jesus?," Deborah Prinz's Facebook page, accessed May 28, 2017, https://www.facebook.com/photo.php?fbid=534109750076281&set=a.110435075777086.18584.100004317810584&type=3&theater.

36. Reverend Susan Sica comment to "Would You Eat a Chocolate Jesus?," Deborah Prinz's Facebook page, accessed May 28, 2017, https://www.facebook.com/photo.php?fbid=534109750076281&set=a.110435075777086.18584.100004317810584&type=3&theater.

Chocolate Art

a. Jenn Harris, "Academy Awards: Behind-the-Scenes Look at 6,500 Chocolate Oscars," *Los Angeles Times*, March 2, 2014, accessed May, 1, 2017, www.latimes.com/food/dailydish/la-dd-academy-awards-6500-chocolate-oscars-20140228-story.html.

b. Electa Draper, "Denver Rabbi Builds 6-Foot-Tall, Dark Chocolate Menorah," *Denver Post*, updated April 28, 2016, accessed May 26, 2017, www.denverpost.com/2013/11/27/denver-rabbi-builds-6-foot-tall-dark-chocolate-menorah-for-hanukkah/.

c. "Nikolya Chocolate Museum Opens in Baku," Report News Agency, May 16, 2015, http://report.az/en/art/nikolya-chocolate-museum-opens-in-baku/.

d. Eva Respini, "Vik Muniz: Painting with Chocolate," Inside/Out, November 12, 2009, accessed May 26, 2017, https://www.moma.org/explore/inside_out/2009/11/12/vik-muniz-painting-with-chocolate/.

e. Brian Ferguson, "Chocolart: Exhibit you can Eat Comes to Edinburgh," *Scotsman*, April 17, 2014, accessed May 26, 2017, www.scotsman.com/lifestyle/chocolart-exhibit-you-can-eat-comes-to-edinburgh-1-3379162.

f. Randy Kennedy, "Chocolate Sculpture, with a Bitter Taste of Colonialism," *New York Times*, February 2, 2017, www.nytimes.com /2017/02/02/arts/chocolate-sculpture-with-a-bitter-taste-of-colonialism. html?_r=0.

Chocolate Meditation

a. Rabbis discuss which blessing should be recited for chocolate. Some say the blessing for the fruit of the tree would be most appropriate; others argue that the chocolate has been processed so it should be this blessing, known as *shehakol*. See more at "Jewish Ritual Chocolate FAQ's," On the Chocolate Trail, accessed May 26, 2017, http://onthechocolatetrail.org /2012/09/jewish-ritual-chocolate-faqs/.

b. Michael Shefrin, e-mail message to author, February 23, 2012.

CHAPTER 11: THE ETHICS OF CHOCOLATE: SELECTING THE BEST

1. Brian Woods and Kate Blewett, *Slavery: A Global Investigation* (London: True Vision, BBC, 2001), accessed April 16, 2017, https://freedocumentaries.org/documentary/slavery-a-global-investigation; "The Chocolate Industry Has a Century-Long History of Forced and Child Labor in the Production of Cocoa," International Labor Rights Forum, accessed April 16, 2017, www.laborrights.org/industries/cocoa.

2. "The C Spot," accessed April 17, 2017, www.c-spot.com/about /philosophy/. C Spot's Mark Christian argues that taste ultimately reflects ethics, regardless of certifications. A good-tasting chocolate will always, in his view, match the ethical commitments of the producer.

3. "First Taste of Chocolate in Ivory Coast," VPRO Metropolis, February 21, 2014, accessed May 28, 2017, https://www.youtube.com /watch?v=zEN4hcZutO0.

4. Carla D. Martin and Kathryn E. Sampeck, "The Bitter and Sweet of Chocolate in Europe," presented at The Social Meaning of Food Workshop, Institute for Sociology, Centre for Social Sciences, Hungarian Academy of Sciences, June 16–17, 2015, Budapest, Hungary; William R. Fowler, "Cacao Production, Tribute, and Wealth in Sixteenth-Century Izalcos, El Salvador," in McNeil, *Chocolate in Mesoamerica*, 308–9.

5. Walker, "Slave Labor and Chocolate in Brazil," 79.

6. Jorge Amado, *The Violent Land*, trans. Samuel Putnam (New York: Alfred Knopf, 1965), 273.

7. Satre, *Chocolate on Trial*; Off, *Bitter Chocolate*, 96; Sudarsan Raghavan, "Two Boys Tell of Descent into Slavery," *JSOnline: Milwaukee Journal Sentinel*, June 25, 2001, http://jsonline.com; Christian Parenti, "Chocolate's Bittersweet Economy," *CNN Money*,

February 15, 2008, http://archive.fortune.com/2008/01/24/news/
international/chocolate_bittersweet.fortune/index.htm.

8. Sarah Moss and Alexander Badenoch, *Chocolate: A Global History*
(Chicago: University of Chicago Press, 2009), 80ff.

9. *2013/14 Survey Research on Child Labor in the West African Cocoa
Sector*, Payson Program, Tulane University, July 30, 2015, accessed
April 7, 2017, www.childlaborcocoa.org/index.php/2013-14-final-
report; Brian O'Keefe, "Inside Big Chocolate's Child Labor Problem,"
Fortune, March 1, 2016, accessed April 7, 2017, http://fortune.com
/big-chocolate-child-labor/.

10. "Our Corporate Social Responsibility," Ghana Cocoa Board, accessed
April 16, 2017, https://cocobod.gh/social_esponsibility.php.

11. Carla Martin, interview with author, April 6, 2017.

12. Amanda Berlan, "Child Labour and Cocoa: Whose Voices Prevail?,"
International Journal of Sociology and Social Policy 29, no. 3/4 (April
2009):141–51, http://www.emeraldinsight.com/doi/full
/10.1108/01443330910947516.

13. Clay Gordon, e-mail and interview with the author, April 19–May 4,
2017.

14. "Protocol for the Growing and Processing of Cocoa Beans and Their
Derivative Products in a Manner That Complies with ILO Convention
182 Concerning the Prohibition and Immediate Action for the Elimination
of the Worst Forms of Child Labor" (Harkin-Engel Protocol), Chocolate
Manufacturers Association, accessed April 16, 2017, www.globalexchange.
org/sites/default/files/HarkinEngelProtocol.pdf.; "Africa: Child Labor in
Cocoa Fields/ Harkin-Engel Protocol," International Labor Organization,
accessed April 16, 2017, www.ilo.org/washington/areas/elimination-of-
the-worst-forms-of-child-labor/WCMS_159486/lang--en/index.htm; Brian
Campbell, "The Cocoa Protocol: Success or Failure?," International Labor
Rights Forum, June 30, 2008, accessed May 26, 2017, www.laborrights.org
/sites/default/files/publications-and-resources/Cocoa%20Protocol%20
Success%20or%20Failure%20June%202008.pdf. I reached out several
times to Representative Harkin's office for an update. My calls and e-mails
were not returned.

15. "Our Impact," World Cocoa Foundation, accessed April 16, 2017,
www.worldcocoafoundation.org/our-work/our-impact/; "Our
Approach," World Cocoa Foundation, accessed May 23, 2017,
www.worldcocoafoundation.org/our-work/our-approach/.

16. "Child Labor in Cocoa," International Cocoa Initiative, accessed April 3,
2017, www.cocoainitiative.org/our-work/child-labour-in-cocoa/.

17. "2008 Cadbury Cocoa Partnership Launched," Cadbury, accessed May
23, 2017, www.cadbury.co.uk/the-story/cadbury-cocoa-partnership-
launched; "Cocoa Life Sustainability Programme Expands to Cover

Cadbury Chocolate through New Partnership with Fairtrade," Fairtrade International, November 17, 2016, www.fairtrade.net/new/latest-news/single-view/article/cocoa-life-sustainability-programme-expands-to-cover-cadbury-chocolate-through-new-partnership-with.html.

18. "The Cocoa Life Challenge," Mondelēz International, accessed May 28, 2017, www.mondelezinternational.com/well-being/sustainable-resources-and-agriculture/agricultural-supply-chain/cocoa.

19. "Cocoa: Caring for the Future of Cocoa," Mars, accessed April 17, 2017, www.mars.com/global/sustainability/raw-materials/cocoa.

20. "Sustainability," Barry Callebaut, accessed May 26, 2017, www.barry-callebaut.com/new-sustainability-strategy; www.cocoahorizons.org/our-activities.

21. "Using Mobile Phones to Assist Farmers in West Africa," Hershey Company, accessed April 17, 2017, www.thehersheycompany.com/en_us/responsibility/good-business/creating-goodness/cocoa-sustainability/cocoa-link.html.

22. "Commitment to Ethical Cocoa Sourcing," International Labor Rights Forum, accessed April 16, 2017, www.laborrights.org/sites/default/files/publications-and-resources/Joint%20Cocoa%20Statement%2012%2007.pdf.

23. "The Climate Change Connection: Cashing In on Cacao and Chocolate," Catholic Relief Services, accessed April 17, 2017, www.crs.org/stories/climate-change-connection-cashing-cacao-chocolate.

24. "UCC Fair Trade Project," United Church of Christ, accessed May 26, 2017, www.ucc.org/fair-trade-project.

25. "Fair Trade," United Methodist Committee on Relief, accessed May 26, 2017, www.umcor.org/UMCOR/Programs/Global-Development/Fair-Trade.

26. "Mission and Strategy," Fair Trade Judaica, accessed May 26, 2017, http://fairtradejudaica.org/our-story/mission-and-strategy/.

27. "Cocoa," Fairtrade International, accessed May 26, 2017, www.fairtrade.net/products/cocoa.html; Fair Trade USA, accessed May 26, 2017, http://fairtradeusa.org/products-partners/cocoa.

28. "About Us," Divine, accessed May 26, 2017, www.divinechocolate.com/us/about-us.

29. "What Makes Fair Trade Cocoa and Chocolate Products Different?," Equal Exchange, accessed May 26, 2017, http://equalexchange.coop/products/chocolate/faqs/what-makes-fair-trade-cocoa-and-chocolate-products-different; Dary Goodrich, e-mail message to author, May 1, 2017.

30. Shawn Askinosie, interview with the author, July 15, 2008.

31. "Chocolate University," "A Stake in the Outcome," "Direct Trade," Askinosie Chocolate, accessed May 26, 2017, www.askinosie.com/; "America's Best Small Companies: Askinosie Chocolate," Forbes, accessed April 14, 2017, www.forbes.com/companies/askinosie-chocolate/.

32. Kallari Chocolate's Facebook page, www.facebook.com /Kallari-Chocolate-68963262649/; Judy Logback, e-mail message to author, May 22, 2010; Judy Logback, interview with author, April 8, 2010; Jill Santopietro, "When Chocolate Is a Way of Life," *New York Times*, November 5, 2008.

33. "Taza Direct Trade," Taza Chocolate, accessed May 26, 2017, www.tazachocolate.com/pages/taza-direct-trade.

34. Kristy Leissle, "'Artisan' as Brand: Adding Value in a Craft Chocolate Community," *Food, Culture & Society: An International Journal of Multidisciplinary Research* 20, 2017, 35–57, accessed April 5, 2017, www.tandfonline.com/eprint/6qZ6dRJ4fH74BiBCqdUB/full.

35. Dr. Carla Martin, e-mail to author, April 12, 2017.

36. Dr. Carla Martin, interview with author, April 6, 2017.

37. Rabbi Menachem Genack and Rabbi Moshe Elefant, interview with author, November 16, 2016.

38. Humaira Batool, e-mail to author, April 5, 2017.

39. "Category Selected: Chocolate Bars," Muslim Consumer Group, accessed April 5, 2017, www.muslimconsumergroup.com/category_ search_result.php?t=C&p=43.

40. "Halal Products," Cadbury, accessed May 26, 2017, https://www.cad-bury.com.au/products/halal-products.aspx; Zlata Rodionova, "Cadbury Forced to Explain Why Its Chocolate Is Halal after Being Accused of 'Muslim Appeasement,'" *Independent*, March 22, 2017, accessed April 5, 2017, www.independent.co.uk/news/business/news/cadbury-halal-chocolate-angry-customers-muslim-boycott-threat-a7642991.html.

41. "Halal Chocolate Takes Off as Sweet-Tooth Muslims Want Their Fix," *The Star*, accessed July 18, 2017, http:// www.thestar.com.my/business/business-news/2017/06/16/ halal-chocolate-takes-off-as-sweet-tooth-muslims-want-their-fix/

42. "About Us," Rescue Chocolate, accessed April 16, 2017, www.rescuechocolate.com/pages/about-us.

43. "Impact Report," Endangered Species Chocolate, www.chocolatebar.com /docs/doc_2016_Impact_Report.pdf.

44. "Chocolates with a Cause," Shaman Chocolate, accessed April 16, 2017, www.shamanchocolates.com/our-chocolate.

45. "Empowering Women with Cacao," Original Beans, accessed April 16, 2017, http://originalbeans.com/projects/femmes-de-virunga-dr-congo/.

46. "Benefit Corporation," Wikipedia, accessed April 16, 2017, https://en.wikipedia.org/wiki/Benefit_corporation; https://www. bcorporation.net/become-a-b-corp; "What are B Corps?," B Corp, accessed May 26, 2017, www.bcorporation.net/what-are-b-corps.

47. "Our Approach," Rainforest Alliance, accessed April 2010, www.rainforest-alliance.org/approach.

48. "Cocoa," Utz, accessed May 26, 2017, https://utz.org/what-we-offer /certification/products-we-certify/cocoa/.

49. The Protective Powers of Chocolate," DW Akademie, March 28, 2017, accessed May 26, 2017, www.dw.com/en/the-protective-powers-of-chocolate/a-38153178.

50. "FAQ," Original Beans, accessed April 16, 2017, http://originalbeans.com/about/faq/.

51. Jane Brody, "Rules Worth Following, For Everyone's Sake," *New York Times*, February 1, 2010, www.nytimes.com/2010/02/02/health/02brod.html.

52. "USDA Organic," U.S. Department of Agriculture, accessed April 16, 2017, www.usda.gov/topics/organic; "Mission," Non GMO Project, accessed May 26, 2017, www.nongmoproject.org/about/mission/. Some might consider raw chocolate; for information: http://cleanfoodcertified.org/.

53. For FDA guidelines and definition of white chocolate, see "Guidance for Industry: Standard of Identity for White Chocolate," U.S. Food and Drug Administration, July 17, 2008, accessed July 2011, www.fda.gov /Food/GuidanceComplianceRegulatoryInformation/GuidanceDocuments /FoodLabelingNutrition/ucm059076.htm.

54. Andrew Osborn, "Chocolate War Over after 30 Years," *Guardian*, accessed May 28, 2017 https://www.theguardian.com/uk/2003/jan/17 /foodanddrink; Colin Blane, "EuroChocolate War Ends," BBC News, May 25, 2000, accessed May 28, 2017, http://news.bbc.co.uk/2/hi /europe/764305.stm.

55. Clay Gordon, e-mail and interview with the author, April 19–May 4, 2017.

56. Judy Logback, interview with author, April 8, 2010, New York; Jill Santopietro, "When Chocolate Is a Way of Life," *New York Times*, November 5, 2008.

57. There are several examples of this: Green & Black's Maya Gold organic, which became the first fair trade chocolate in the United Kingdom in 1994, is now owned by Cadbury/Mondelēz; Hershey bought Dagoba and Scharffen Berger.

58. Bachya ben Asher ben Hlava, *Shulchan Shel Arba*, 497, cited in Jonathan Brumberg-Kraus, "'Torah on the Table': A Sensual Morality," in *Food and Morality: Proceedings of the Oxford Symposium on Food and Cookery 2007*, ed. Susan R. Friedland (Totnes, UK: Prospect Books, 2008), 47. An earlier version appeared as "Every Day Is Labor Day," *Reform Judaism*, August 29, 2014, accessed June 5, 2017, www.reformjudaism.org/blog/2014/08/29/every-day-labor-day.

What, No More Chocolate?

a. Sarah Gray, "Stephen Colbert Is Fearful of a Potential Chocolate Shortage," *Salon*, November 21, 2014, accessed May 26, 2017, www.salon.com/2014/11/21/ stephen_colbert_is_fearful_of_a_potential_chocolate_shortage/.

b. Stacey Vanek Smith, "Ecuador's Answer to the Global Cocoa Shortage," National Public Radio, February 19, 2015, accessed May 26, 2017, www.npr.org/2015/02/19/387420709/ecuadors-answer-to-the-global-cocoa-shortage; Tamasin Ford, Jonathan Vit, Rupert Neate, Tania Branigan, and Emine Saner, "The Cocoa Crisis: Why the World's Stash of Chocolate Is Melting Away," *Guardian*, November 21, 2014, accessed May 26, 2017, www.theguardian.com/lifeandstyle/2014/nov/21/cocoa-crisis-world-chocolate-stash-melting-away.

c. Mike Verdin, "Chocolate Needs Promotion Drive, If Cocoa Prices Are to Recover," Agrimoney.com, April 12, 2017, accessed April 12, 2017, http://www.agrimoney.com/feature/chocolate-needs-promotion-drive-if-cocoa-prices-are-to-recover--512.html.

d. Dr. Carla Martin, interview with author, April 11, 2013.

Grenada's Green Chocolate

a. "Why Ship with Us?," Fairtransport, accessed April 3, 2017, http://fairtransport.eu/shipping/. Fairtransport also sells chocolate made from Dominican Republic beans in Amsterdam under the name Tres Hombres Chocolate.

b. A venture with Britain's Rococo Chocolate helped develop one of the founding farms of Grenada Chocolate; all of Rococo's organic bars include beans from Grenada Chocolate. "Grenada and Grococo," Rococo Chocolates, accessed April 3, 2017, www.rococochocolates.com/pages/grococo-1; Grenada Chocolate, accessed April 3, 2017, www.grenadachocolate.com/.

Mast Brothers Chocolate Mysteries

a. This definition: "Craft chocolate made from scratch, starting with the unroasted cacao bean in a company's own facilities using traditional methods of chocolate making.... Craft chocolate companies also typically produce at a small scale, processing significantly less than 200 metric tons of cacao beans per year." Martin and Sampeck, "The Bitter and Sweet of Chocolate in Europe."

b. Megan Giller, "Chocolate Experts Hate Mast Brothers," *Slate*, March 16, 2015, www.slate.com/articles/life/food/2015/03/against_mast_brothers_why_chocolate_experts_hate_the_best_known_craft_chocolate.html; Scott Craig, "Mast Brothers: What Lies behind the Beards," *DallasFood*, December 7, 2015, accessed April 17, 2017, http://dallasfood.org/2015/12/mast-brothers-what-lies-behind-the-beards-part-1-tastetexture/ (this link leads to the four-part series); Giller, "Why Chocolate Experts Think the Mast Brothers Are Frauds," *Slate*, December 18, 2015, accessed April 17, 2017, www.slate.com/articles/life/food/2015/12/why_chocolate_experts_think_the_mast_brothers_are_frauds.html; Sarah Maslin Nir, "Unmasking the Mythos of Mast Brothers Chocolate," *New York Times*, December 21, 2015, www.nytimes.com/2015/12/21/nyregion/unwrapping-mast-brothers-chocolatier-mythos.html?_r=0; Peter Wells, "Picking the Best in Bean-to-Bar Chocolate," *New York Times*, https://www.nytimes.com/2015/12/30/dining/mast-brothers-taste-test-bean-to-bar-chocolate.html?_r=0.

c. Craig, "Mast Brothers."

d. Rick Mast and Michael Mast, *Mast Brothers Chocolate: A Family Cookbook* (New York: Little, Brown, 2013).

e. Megan Giller, interview with author, April 12, 2017.

Truth in Maccabees

a. Lior Zaltzman, "The War on Hanukkah Is Real—Your Chocolate Maccabees Are Really Santas," *Forward*, November 12, 2015, http://forward.com/schmooze/324637/the-war-on-hannukah-is-real/. Earlier versions appeared as: "What Happened to My Kosher Secret Santa Maccabees?," *Forward*, December 22, 2016, accessed June 5, 2017, http://forward.com/food/357863/what-happened-to-my-kosher-secret-santa-chocolate-maccabees/; "What Happened to My Kosher Secret Santa Maccabees?," *Huffington Post*, December 23, 2016, accessed June 5, 2017, www.huffingtonpost.com/rabbi-deborah-r-prinz/what-happened-to-my-koshe_b_13789728.html.

b. Dr. Jonathan Sarna, e-mail message to author, December 9, 2015.

c. Rite Lite Claims Department, e-mail message to author, December 7, 2015.

d. Alfred Rubens, *History of Jewish Costume* (Worthing, UK: Littlehampton Book Services, 1973).

AFTERWORD

1. Dr. Howard Marcus, snail mail communication, February 16, 2010.

A CONSUMER'S GUIDE TO THE ETHICS OF CHOCOLATE: SELECTING THE BEST

1. For more information about small bean-to-bar companies that roast and process by hand see Giller, Megan. *Bean-to-Bar Chocolate: America's Craft Chocolate Revolution: The Origins, the Makers, and the Mind-Blowing Flavors.* New York: Storey Publishing, 2017.

Glossary

Ashkenazi (plural, Ashkenazim): A Jewish person of Central and Eastern European descent.

bain-marie: A cooking technique used for melting chocolate, by which one melts the chocolate in a bowl laid atop a pot of hot water.

bean to bar: Processing of the cocoa bean into chocolate, rather than using melted chocolate from slabs or from disks.

bicerin: An Italian layered drink of espresso, hot chocolate, and milk or cream, named for the glass in which it is served.

bloom on the chocolate: A whitish tinge that suggests improper temperatures in storage, perhaps too cold or too warm. It is still edible, however.

cacao: May refer to the bean, the pod, or the tree. Some use the terms cacao and cocoa interchangeably.

chocolate: Processed cacao beans in a liquid or solid form; before the end of the eighteenth century this often referred to the beverage.

cocoa butter: The yellowish fat derived from the cacao bean. Also known as cocoa fat.

cocoa liquor: Liquid form of chocolate that contains both cocoa butter and cocoa solids. Sometimes called cocoa mass or cocoa solids.

cocoa powder: A low-fat component of chocolate made from the roasted beans. May be mixed with milk solids or water for preparing hot cocoa.

cocoa solids: These give chocolate color, flavor, and a low melting point; cocoa butter aids its smoothness. Cocoa solids also contain the greatest concentration of the psychoactive chemicals caffeine and theobromine, which are mostly absent in the other part of chocolate, the cocoa butter or fat.

compound chocolate: Includes a cocoa butter equivalent. FDA requires labeling to indicate compound.

conching: Mixing, agitating, and aerating chocolate in a machine that early on looked like a conch shell.

conversos: Jews from the Iberian Peninsula who converted to Christianity to avoid persecution during the Spanish Inquisition, many of whom maintained secret Jewish practices at home.

couverture: Used for dipping, coating, molding, and garnishing, and contains a higher percentage of cocoa solids than compound chocolate.

dreidel: The children's game of Chanukah using a spinning top; the winner is sometimes paid in coins.

emulsifier: An additive such as soy lecithin that creates a smoother chocolate. Additives are used in place of longer conching.

gelt: The Yiddish word for money.

hechsher: A mark of rabbinic certification that a food or an item is kosher.

Inquisition: Established in 1478 by Catholic monarchs Ferdinand II of Aragon and Isabella of Castille to ensure orthodoxy of Catholic religion and elimination of heresies.

jicara (**Spanish**), *xicara* (**Portuguese**): A term for a gourd used as a vessel for drinking chocolate.

kashrut: Jewish dietary laws. When a food is permissible according to the laws of kashrut, it is kosher.

metate, *piedre, pierre,* **chocolate stone, or quern:** A stone for warming and crushing cacao beans to make chocolate.

molinillo, **mill, stirrer, or stick:** Used for mixing the chocolate beverage in a pot.

pareve: Containing neither dairy nor meat. According to Jewish dietary law, meat and dairy cannot be mixed, so a pareve food may be eaten at either a dairy or meat meal.

Seder: Ritual meal for Passover.

Sephardi (plural, Sephardim): A Jewish person of Iberian descent.

tecomate: A deep clay cup used for drinking chocolate in Mesoamerica.

torta di nocciole con cioccolata calda: Hot chocolate soup poured over a fresh hazelnut cake.

white chocolate: A confection comprised of cocoa butter, milk solids, and sugar without cocoa mass or cocoa liquor; some do not consider it chocolate.

Resources for Further Learning

ON THE CHOCOLATE TRAIL WEBSITE

For further learning and engagement around chocolate, additional resources may be found at the *On the Chocolate Trail* website, www.onthechocolatetrail.org/booksupplement/, including the following:

- Lesson plans for teaching about Jews and chocolate
- *A Socially Responsible Haggadah for a Chocolate Seder* for Passover
- Selected responsa and Jewish texts related to chocolate, cocoa, or cacao
- Detailed charts of citations and data for "Jews Dip into Chocolate in the American Colonial Period"

BIBLIOGRAPHY

Bailleux, Nathalie, et al. *The Book of Chocolate.* Paris: Flammarion, 1995.

Brenner, Joël Glenn. *The Emperors of Chocolate: Inside the Secret World of Hershey and Mars.* New York: Random House, 1999.

Coe, Sophie D., and Michael D. Coe. *The True History of Chocolate.* London: Thames and Hudson, 1996.

Dreiss, Meredith L., and Sharon Edgar Greenhill. *Chocolate: Pathway to the Gods.* Tucson: University of Arizona Press, 2008.

Giller, Megan. *Bean-to-Bar Chocolate: America's Craft Chocolate Revolution: The Origins, the Makers, and the Mind-Blowing Flavors.* New York: Storey Publishing, 2017.

Gordon, Clay. *Discover Chocolate: The Ultimate Guide to Buying, Tasting, and Enjoying Fine Chocolate*. New York: Gotham Press, 2007.

Grivetti, Louis Evan, and Howard-Yana Shapiro, eds. *Chocolate: History, Culture and Heritage*. Hoboken, NJ: John Wiley & Sons, 2009.

Lebovitz, David. *The Great Book of Chocolate*. Berkeley, CA: Ten Speed Press, 2004.

Lopez, Ruth. *Chocolate: The Nature of Indulgence*. New York: Harry N. Abrams, in association with the Field Museum, 2002.

McNeil, Cameron L., ed. *Chocolate in Mesoamerica: A Cultural History of Cacao*. Gainesville: University of Florida Press, 2009.

Norton, Marcy. *Sacred Gifts, Profane Pleasures: A History of Tobacco and Chocolate in the Atlantic World*. Ithaca, NY: Cornell University Press, 2008.

Presilla, Maricel E. *The New Taste of Chocolate: A Cultural and Natural History of Cacao with Recipes*. Berkeley, CA: Ten Speed Press, 2000.

Rosenblum, Mort. *Chocolate: A Bittersweet Saga of Dark and Light*. New York: North Point Press, 2005.

Terrio, Susan J. *Crafting the Culture of French Chocolate*. Berkeley: University of California Press, 2000.

DVDs

Chocolate: The Bitter Truth of Child Trafficking, five-part documentary report, www.youtube.com/watch?v=LD85fPzLUjo, 2010.

Chocolate Country, a film about farmers in Dominican Republic's Loma Guaconejo and their approach to cooperative chocolate production and shipping directly to the United States, accompanied by the music of local folk musicians, www.chocolatecountryfilm.com, 2010.

Cocoa Slave Tastes Sweet Freedom, a film about the rescue of a twelve-year-old slave on a cocoa farm and his reunion with his mother; http://news.bbc.co.uk/panorama/hi/front_page/newsid_8584000/8584847.stm, 2010.

The Dark Side of Chocolate, an investigation into trafficking of children in cacao plantations of West Africa, www.thedarksideofchocolate.org, 2010; also available inexpensively from www.greenamerica.org.

Credits

A version of "Christmas and Chanukah Chocolate Melt Together" was first published in *Petits Propos Culinaires* 89, January 2010. Used by permission.

A small section of the chapter "Israelis: *Meshuga* for Chocolate" originally appeared on, "The Jew and the Carrot," a *Jewish Daily Forward* and Hazon partnership blog. Used by permission.

A version of "Camel's Milk in My Chocolate?" was posted at porkmemoirs.com, a blog created by Jeff Yoskowitz, and also at www.jews-onthechocolatetrail.org. Used by permission.

"Our Dark Addictions: Chocolate, Coffee and Tea" by Deborah Prinz in the *Sacred Table: Creating a Jewish Food Ethic*, edited by Mary L. Zamore, © 2011 by Central Conference of American Rabbis. All rights reserved. Used by permission. A version of this piece originally appeared on, "The Jew and the Carrot," a *Jewish Daily Forward* and Hazon partnership blog.

Earlier versions of material appeared on the *Forward* (forward.com). Used by permission:

"Getting Good Chocolate Gelt," November 25, 2013.

"10 Very Best Babkas for Valentine's Day," February 11, 2014.

"What Happened to My Kosher Secret Santa Maccabees?" December 22, 2016.

"Chocolate at Passover? Not So Fast!" April 5, 2017.

An earlier version "From Prins to Prinz: The Mysteries of the Chocolate Trail," appeared in the *Jerusalem Post* (jpost.com) May 15, 2014. Used by permission.

An earlier version "Chocolatiers Raising the Bar When It Comes to Hanukkah Gelt," appeared in the *Jewish Telegraphic Agency*, December 11, 2014. Used by permission.

An earlier version "The Ethics of Hanukkah Gelt," appeared in *Lilith Magazine: independent, Jewish & frankly feminist* (Lilith.org), November 25, 2015. Used by permission.

Material has been adapted from blog posts that originally appeared on ReformJudaism.org.

"December Dilemmas Melt into Chocolate," December 18, 2014.

"How Fair Trade Gelt Embodies Hanukkah's Message," December 11, 2015.

"Escaping Danzig with Help from a Box of Chocolate," September 1, 2016.

"Finding the Afikoman May Be Easier: The Best Chocolate for Passover," n.d.

Chocolate Meditation by Rabbi Michael Shefrin. Used by permission.

Earlier versions appeared at my blog, "Jews on the Chocolate Trail," at the *Jewish Journal*. Used by permission:

"From Prins to Prinz: The Mysteries of the Chocolate Trail," September 21, 2013.

"Chocolate from Chanukah's Gelt," November 30, 2014.

"A Chocolate Escape from Danzig 1939, July 26, 2016.

"Chocolate Survival: Holocaust and Hurricane," November 28, 2016.

"Happy Babka-ka/Chocolate Babka for Chanukah," December 22, 2016.

"Rabbi Diaries: Chocolate Drinking in Eighteenth Century," March 1, 2017.

Earlier versions appeared on the *Jewish Week*. Used by permission:

"Chocolate Revives: Hurricane and the Holocaust," November 11, 2016.

"Babka Love is Blind, In This Taste Test," December 16, 2014.

Reproduction of Negro Cornelius Casey entry from the *Lopez Memorandum Book* 142c, Newport Historical Society. Used by permission.

Photo of the Chocolate Candy Bar Bomb, The National Archives of the U.K., Ref KV4/284. Used by permission.

Photo of cocoa tree and pods from Wikimedia Commons. Used by permission.

Photo of *A Man Scraping Chocolate*, anonymous artist, Spanish School, 1680–1780, oil on canvas, North Carolina Museum of Art, Raleigh, North Carolina, gift of Mr. and Mrs. Benjamin Cone, G69.20.1. Used by permission.

Photo of *mendiants* taken by Paola Paska. Used by permission.

Photo of the Santa Catalina Bakery in Valencia taken by Juan Costa, Sinagoga Conservador la Javurá. Used by permission.

Photo of St. Nicholas coins from the St. Nicholas Center. Used by permission.

Photo/s of *My Sweet Lord* sculpture and of *Chocolate Saints* sculptures by artist Cosimo Cavallaro, courtesy of Sarah and Cosimo Cavallaro. Used by permission.

Photo of chocolate deity, Hotei Buddha, from Jeanne Fleming. Used by permission.

Photo of Einstein chocolate cup, courtesy of the Leo Baeck Institute. Used by permission.

Index

Index of Recipes

About the Author

RABBI DEBORAH R. PRINZ lectures about chocolate and religions around the world. A regular contributor to the *Huffington Post*, the *Daily Forward*, and elsewhere on the topic of chocolate, she has presented in five countries at chocolate festivals, libraries, museums, culinary events, and congregations. She co-curates *Jews on the Chocolate Trail*, a traveling exhibit created for the Herbert and Eileen Bernard Museum of Temple Emanu-El, New York City, on display October 2017–February 2018. Also, she created the blog *On the Chocolate Trail* (visit www.onthechocolatetrail.org). Prinz received a Starkoff Fellowship and a Director's Fellowship from the American Jewish Archives as well as a Gilder Lehrman Fellowship from the Rockefeller Library to research *On the Chocolate Trail*. Rabbi Prinz is available to speak to your group or at your event. For more information, please contact her at onthechocolatetrail.org.

CPSIA information can be obtained
at www.ICGtesting.com
Printed in the USA
JSHW032259301222
35554JS00001B/1

9 781683 366768